PORTRAITS
IN AMERICAN
SANCTITY

PORTRAITS IN AMERICAN SANCTITY

Edited by
Joseph N. Tylenda, S.J.

FRANCISCAN HERALD PRESS
CHICAGO, ILLINOIS 60609

Portraits in American Sanctity, edited by Joseph N. Tylenda, S.J. Copyright © 1982, Franciscan Herald Press, 1434 West 51st Street, Chicago, Illinois 60609.

Library of Congress Cataloging in Publication Data:

Portraits in American sanctity.

    1. Catholics—United States—Biography. I. Tylenda, Joseph N.
BX4670.P67   282'.092'2 [B]   81-22098
ISBN 0-8199-0846-0   AACR2

Published with Ecclesiastical Permission

MADE IN THE UNITED STATES OF AMERICA

*To Our Parents
the first teachers in holiness*

Declaration of the Authors

In obedience to the decrees of Urban VIII, of March 3, 1625, and June 16, 1631, and to other similar Pontifical legislation, the authors declare that no other credence is to be given to the contents of this volume than that given to human authority, especially in relation to supernatural gifts and graces where the Church has not intervened in her judgment. They declare, moreover, that in no way is it intended to anticipate the decision of the supreme Ecclesiastical Authority.

INTRODUCTION

Marion A. Habig, O.F.M.

THE SAINTS ARE BACK! That is what Bishop Norbert F. Gaughan, auxiliary of the Greensburg diocese, tells us (*Visitor,* Sept. 13, 1981); and he offers as evidence the fact that during recent years an unusual number of important and scholarly books about the saints have been published and well received.

"The 1960s," wrote Bishop Gaughan "saw churches emptied of many statues. (What Reformation enthusiasts could not do, Catholics did.) Devotion to the saints went underground. Many blamed a Vatican spirit as interpreted to them; it betrayed 'true' Catholic belief."

At long last, many Catholics have discovered that it was an unfortunate misinterpretation. "Far from banishing the saints from the church buildings, the sacred liturgy, and the spiritual life of the People of God, both as individuals and as a community, Vatican II has not only restated the pronouncements of previous councils, but has also set forth in a masterful, concise, and lucid manner the role which the saints in heaven play in the Church on earth.

"The Council calls attention to the union and fellowship of the saints with their pilgrim brethren, the power of their

ix

intercession for us with God, the inspiring influence of their example upon us. It points out the correctness, appropriateness, and timeliness of the honor we bestow upon the saints by the observance of their feasts, the veneration of their images, and the study and imitation of their lives. Yes, the council exhorts us to have and cherish a deep love of the saints" (see especially the *Constitution on the Church,* nos. 49, 50, and 51).

The quotation is from the writer's *Saints of the Americas,* which he succeeded in having published in 1974, after a delay of several years during which some leading publishers would not even look at the manuscript because it was about saints. One of them replied: "You would not sell enough copies to pay for the printing." Another finally accepted it for publication and had it set in type; but then he changed his mind because somebody convinced him that the book did not have a chance. However, my friend Father Albert Nevins, M.M., thought otherwise and recommended it for publication by Our Sunday Visitor Press. It proved to be a successful venture. The edition of 10,000 copies has been exhausted except for about 200, which are still available from Franciscan Herald Press.

Saints of the Americas, a book of 384 pages, contains biographies of 45 men and women who spent at least a part of their lives in one of the Americas, North, Central, or South. Of this number 22 have been canonized and 23 have been beatified. The "Blessed" were added because they may not be declared to be "Saints" except after a long time or they may never be canonized. It was not possible to add biographies of other candidates for sainthood, because their number is too great. An appendix of ten pages (pp. 353- 364) lists some of these, for whom at least some initial steps have been taken to have their causes introduced. They are a suitable subject for another book or several.

Such a book is Father Tylenda's *Portraits in American Sanctity.* In one volume he has assembled carefully researched as well as very readable biographies of 29 American candidates for beatification and/or canonization, all of them belonging in a special way to what is now the 50 United States of America. Two blessed are included because they remain candidates for canonization.

These *Portraits* are an update of another book entitled *Sanctity in America,* published in 1939, "the Sesquicentennial Year of the Constitution of the American Hierarchy." It was written by the Most Reverend Amleto Giovanni Cicognani, who was then the apostolic delegate to the United States (1933-1958).

Recalling the many new saints and blessed proclaimed as such during the pontificate of Pope Pius XI (1922-1939), Archbishop Cicognani offered this comment:

"Saints, as great heroes and geniuses, eventually belong to all mankind, rather than to particular localities, but it is natural that a brighter ray of their glory should illuminate the land of their birth.

"In general the Servants of God honored by Pius XI belonged to European nations; and to some it seemed rather presumptuous that a young nation should seek to have its own processes of beatification and canonization. Yet holiness is of all times and places: among the new saints have been some who lived in our own age and were personally known to many among the living.

"Cannot the United States of America then have its saints also? In truth, on June 21, 1925, Pope Pius XI proclaimed blessed the eight Jesuit Martyrs [of North America, i.e. Canada and the United States], and only five years later (June 29, 1930) the same Pontiff pronounced them saints. These saints, of the period of exploration and colonization of America three centuries ago, were French by birth, but it was in this land that they practised sanctity, and here they terminated their mortal existence.

"Sanctity is one of the characteristic marks of the Church, serving to distinguish it throughout the world. Nor can it be otherwise in the United States of America, where Christianity in a relatively short time has attained singular success. . . .

"It seems timely and useful to undertake investigations for the purpose of bringing to general knowledge the names of the Servants of God whose sanctity has enriched this nation, and whose fame has aroused among our people a desire for canonical processes leading to the glory of the altar. . . .

"May it please Divine Providence to grant that America may soon venerate in its churches a goodly number of its own saints; and may the fervent prayers of the faithful hasten such a joyous event for the spiritual glory of this nation!"

Besides an opening chapter on the Jesuit Martyrs of North America (five of Canada and three of the United States), Archbishop (and later Cardinal) Cicognani's book contains biographical sketches of sixteen others whose cause of beatification and/or canonization was being promoted at that time in the United States. Since then, three have been canonized: in 1946, St. Frances Xavier Cabrini, foundress of the Missionary Sisters of the Sacred Heart; in 1975, St. Elizabeth Ann Seton, foundress of the Sisters of Charity in the United States; in 1977, St. John N. Neumann, C.SS.R., fourth bishop of Philadelphia. Two have been beatified: in 1940, Bl. Rose Philippine Duschesne, R.S.C.J., foundress of the Religious of the Sacred Heart in the United States; in 1980, Bl. Kateri Tekakwitha, "the Lily of the Mohawks."

Archbishop Cicognani wrote that the sketches in his book had "the sole purpose of blazing the way. The collection is not complete — it is merely a first attempt, that may be further developed by specialists." *Portraits in American Sanctity* is such a further development — a sequel and an update. In 25 chapters it presents profiles of 29 men and women who are being proposed in the United States, as candidates for canonization. Most of the specialists who wrote them are "vice-postulators" who are actively promoting causes which have been initiated in some way or formally introduced.

Two have already been proclaimed "blessed" and three "venerable," and the causes of the others are in various stages of the required preliminary investigations and so-called processes. All of them were either born in the United States, and/or lived and worked within the area of the present fifty United States, and/or died in that area. Eight were natives of the present United States and one was born in Canada; the other 20 came to what is today the United States of America from eight European countries: Austria (Slovenia), Belgium, France, Germany, Italy, Poland, Spain, Switzerland. The period of time covered by their earthly lives extends from before 1597 to 1961 — about four centuries.

Not included are those candidates for canonization who merely visited the United States. As far as we could ascertain they are the following:

(1) Bl. Mary Frances Schervier (1819-1876), foundress of the Sisters of the Poor of St. Francis (Germany and Belgium) and of the Franciscan Sisters of the Poor (United States). She also played an important role in the founding of the Brothers of the Poor of St. Francis. Twice, in 1863 and 1868, she visited the United States, where her Sisters had made foundations in New Jersey and New York in the East and in Ohio, Indiana, and Illinois in the Midwest. She was beatified on April 28, 1974.

(2) Bl. Louis (Aloysius) Guanella (1842-1915). He had St. John Bosco as his friend and teacher, and for a short time he was a Salesian. As a diocesan priest he was a member and promoter of the Third Order Secular of St. Francis. In 1885 he became the co-founder of the Daughters of St. Mary of Providence; and in 1908 he founded his own religious congregation of men, the Servants of Charity. The primary Pious Union in Honor of St. Joseph for the Dying

was also founded by him. His visit to the United States lasted from November, 1912, to February, 1913. He was beatified in 1964.

(3) The Servant of God Mother Mary Frances of the Cross Streitel (1844-1911), founder of the Franciscan Sisters of the Sorrowful Mother (1885). She visited the United States three times — in 1890, in 1891, and in 1895-1896. The episcopal process for her beatification was carried out in 1911 (in the diocese of Nepi and Sutri, Italy), and the apostolic process in 1947. After the cause had become dormant for a while, it was reopened in 1963. (A biography of Mother Mary Frances, *Walk in Love,* by Sister M. Carmeline Koller, will be published by Franciscan Herald Press.)

(4) The Servant of God Father Francis Mary of the Cross Jordan (1848-1918). He founded the Society of the Divine Savior, also called Salvatorians, in 1881; and in 1896, during a visit to the United States, he established their first foundation in this country at St. Nazianz, Wisconsin. With Mother Mary of the Apostles, in 1888, he also founded the Sisters of the Divine Savior. Previously he had asked Mother Mary Frances Streitel to assist him in this project, but she and her first companions were made a separate religious congregation. Father Jordan's cause of beatification has reached an advanced stage inasmuch as the *decretum super scripta* was issued in 1956.

Likewise not included in this book are most of the early missionary martyrs who lost their lives while engaged in announcing the Good News in the present fifty United States as well as the American missionaries who went to foreign lands and died there as martyrs. After the canonization of the Jesuit martyrs in 1930, Bishop John M. Gannon of Erie, at a meeting of the American Hierarchy held in November of the same year, proposed that a petition be sent to the Holy See requesting the beatification of the numerous other missionaries who died as martyrs within the present confines of the United States. The motion was passed, and a commission was appointed for the purpose of drawing up a list of such martyrs with a brief account of the principal historical facts and the sources of information. By the summer of 1941, a roster of 116 martyrs (including all who suffered a violent death, without determining to what extent it was *in odium fidei*) was ready. Two more martyrs were added shortly afterwards. The papers were signed by the president of the Conference of U.S. Bishops; and the Apostolic Delegate to the United States sent the petition and list to the Sacred Congregation of Rites.

Subsequently a group of five martyrs, for whom the historical evidence of true martyrdom was particularly convincing were selected for special investigation as likely candidates for beatification. They are Father Peter de Corpa and four companions who were put to death *in odium fidei* in the present State of Georgia, 1597. Their story is told in one of the chapters of this book. (Father Albert J. Nevins, M.M., is engaged in writing a book on American Martyrs which will include those who went as missionaries to foreign lands and died there as martyrs as well as those missionaries who suffered a violent death in the territories which now comprise the United States of America.)

The "portraits of sanctity," presented in this book, are the fruit of the most meticulous research. No "cause" or "case" is subjected to such a minute and thorough investigation as that of the life and writings of a person who enjoyed the reputation of sanctity at the time of his death and is proposed for eventual canonization.

Formerly the bishop of the place where the person (or servant of God) died could launch the cause for beatification by appointing a tribunal and beginning the three-fold episcopal process (concerning writings, reputed holiness and miracles, and non-cult). But now, because of recent decrees (especially the "motu proprio" *Sanctitas Clarior* of March 19, 1969), the bishop must first obtain a "nihil obstat" or permission from the Sacred Congregation for the Causes of

Saints. To obtain this permission he must submit the following documents: (1) a documented and scientifically prepared biography of the servant of God with indication of archives; (2) some postulatory letters, i.e. requests for the official introduction of the cause; (3) a statement of the bishop concerning the timeliness of the cause, indicating the spiritual advantages expected for the faithful. In other words a preliminary "process" must now precede the official episcopal or ordinary process.

After the Sacred Congregation accepts the findings of the episcopal process, the apostolic process is held, first outside Rome and then in Rome. The first phase is fact-finding, and the second appraises the findings. If it is established that the servant of God practised the virtues in a heroic or extraordinary degree, the Supreme Pontiff bestows on him or her the title of "venerable." The discussion concerning the heroic virtues may not begin until fifty years after the death of the servant of God, unless the pope grants a dispensation.

In the apostolic process also alleged miraculous answers to prayer which are attributed to the servant of God's intercession are examined, and at least two must be adjudged to be genuine miracles. The venerable servant of God may then be beatified or declared blessed by the Holy Father. Beatification permits public religious honors to be paid to the blessed servant of God in a certain locality or by some religious organization.

If new miracles are reported after beatification, the cause of canonization may be opened and there is another double apostolic process, first outside Rome and then in Rome. If two additional miracles are proved to be genuine, the date for the canonization may be set. Canonization is an infallible declaration of the pope and carries with it the command that the new saint be venerated in the universal Church, though his or her feast may not be observed everywhere. There are not enough days in the year or in many years for the observance of the feasts of even a small percentage of outstanding saints.

One of the main reasons for the revision of the Roman Liturgical Calendar by Pope Paul VI in 1969 was the fact that, as the Holy Father said, "over the course of the centuries more feasts of the saints were introduced than necessary." Pope Paul, therefore, carried out the recommendation of Vatican II expressed in the *Constitution on the Sacred Liturgy* (no. 111): "Lest the feasts of the saints should take precedence over the feasts which commemorate the various mysteries of salvation, many of them should be left to be celebrated by a particular Church, or nation, or family of religious. Only those should be extended to the universal Church which commemorate saints who are truly of universal importance."

That the revision of the calendar was not what the news media made it out to be at that time is evident from the statement made by Pope Paul in the very decree of approval: "We do not feel that it is incongruous to emphasize also the feasts of the Blessed Virgin Mary, 'who is joined by an inseparable bond to the saving work of her Son' (*Const. on the Liturgy,* no. 103), and the memorials of the saints, which are rightly considered as 'the feasts of our leaders, confessors, and victors' (*Syriac Breviary*, of the fifth century). 'The feasts of the saints proclaim the wonderful work of Christ in his servants, and offer fitting example for the faithful to follow' (*Const. on the Liturgy,* no. 111). The Catholic Church has always believed that the feasts of the saints proclaim and renew the paschal mystery of Christ" (*The Roman Calendar: Text and Commentary,* United States Catholic Conference, Washington, D.C., 1976, p. 2).

True Catholic doctrine is nowhere expressed in a more lucid and admirable manner than in the liturgical books of the Church. This is strikingly true of what the Church has always taught concerning the veneration of the saints. To be convinced that neither Vatican II nor the revision of the liturgical calendar and of the liturgical books has made any alteration in that doctrine, one need but examine a little more carefully the new *Sacramentary,* which is the revised Missal minus the Readings (now in a separate Lectionary).

Can the glory of the saints and their relation to us be expressed more beautifully and clearly than is done in Preface no. 69, the first of two for the feasts or memorials of "Holy Men and Women":

"Father . . . you are glorified in your saints, for their glory is the crowning of your gifts. In their lives on earth, you give us an example. In our communion with them, you give us their friendship. In their prayer for the Church, you give us strength and protection. This great company of witnesses spurs us on to victory, to share their prize of everlasting glory, through Jesus Christ our Lord. With angels and archangels and the whole company of saints we sing our unending hymn of praise."

In the second Preface for Holy Men and Women (no. 70) we pray: "Father . . . you renew the Church in every age by raising up men and women outstanding in holiness, living witnesses of your unchanging love. They inspire us by their heroic lives, and help us by their constant prayers, to be the living sign of your saving power."

The saints are mentioned in all four forms of the Eucharistic Prayer, the very heart of the holy sacrifice of the Mass; but it is especially in the first, the ancient Roman Canon slightly revised, that the role of the saints in the Church and in our lives is emphasized both before and after the Consecration.

Before: "In union with the whole Church, we honor Mary, the ever-virgin mother of Jesus Christ our Lord and God. We honor Joseph, her husband, the apostles and martyrs, Peter and Paul, Andrew." The list of 21 saints which follows may be omitted, but we can appropriately add it at least when we celebrate the feast or memorial of any of them. It contains the names of nine apostles, five early successors of St. Peter as bishops of Rome, and five other early martyrs, to which is added "and all the saints. May their merits and prayers gain us your constant help and protection."

After the Consecration; after praying for "those who have died and gone before us marked with the sign of faith": "For ourselves, too, we ask some share in the fellowship of your apostles and martyrs, with John the Baptist, Stephen, Matthias, Barnabas." An optional list of eleven more early martyrs, seven of them women, follows and then the words: "And all the saints."

The Roman Canon is without doubt the best refutation we can offer to those who may still question the correctness, propriety, and need of the commemoration and veneration of the saints. This Eucharistic Prayer confirms most convincingly what Vatican II and Pope Paul said about the observance of the feasts of the saints: "they (the feasts) proclaim and renew the paschal mystery of Christ."

When the Roman Canon mentions "all the saints" (twice), we can well include also those who have been only beatified, those whose causes for beatification have been introduced merely in a preliminary way, and all the saints who have not been canonized and never will be. Though it is not permitted to bestow public religious honors on those who are still candidates for beatification and canonization, even those whose causes have been officially introduced, there is no objection to a private cult. We are allowed to pray to them privately and ask them to intercede for us at the throne of God or to ask God to grant us special favors and even extraordinary ones through their intercession for us. That is the way in which their causes are promoted and make progress. Whether or not these servants of God will be beatified and/or canonized will depend on our interest in their causes and the will of God. Even if their causes are never completed and they are never declared blessed or enrolled among the saints of the Church, much spiritual good will certainly come to us if we read and study their lives, seek to emulate their inspiring example, and make them our friends and intercessors in heaven.

By way of a word of encouragement to do just that, I would like to quote a few lines from an All Saints Day sermon preached by the saintly and gifted Monsignor Ronald A. Knox: "Let us always remember that the curtains of heaven are transparent curtains. Not in the sense that you and I can look in; ah, if only we could! What a world of good it would do us! No, but the saints can look out; they can see you and me still ploughing our way through the mud and the darkness of this earthly existence, feeling our way with difficulty and falling, every now and then, into the ditch. And they can help us; not only because the light of their example shines down on us, and makes it easier, sometimes, to see what we ought to do. They can help us with their prayers, strong prayers, wise prayers, when ours are so feeble and so blind." (*The Pastoral Sermons of Ronald A. Knox,* edited, with an introduction, by Philip Caraman, S.J., new printing, 1981, Franciscan Herald Press, Chicago.)

Note: Pope John Paul II, on January 25 and February 7, 1983, approved a new set of rules for new causes as well as those in progress, which will make it possible to complete the causes in ten years. The approval is for a trial period of three years, after which revisions may be made. The faculty of local bishops to initiate a cause, which was taken away from them in 1969, has now been restored. The strictly scientific and historical investigation of the causes is overseen by a new office called College of Prelates Relators and a layman may serve as postulator or main promoter of a cause.

TABLE OF CONTENTS

xxi

LIST OF ILLUSTRATIONS

CHAPTER 1

BLESSED KATERI TEKAKWITHA
The Lily of the Mohawks
A painting by Sr. M. Felicitas, R.S.M.

1

America's Fairest Flower

BLESSED KATERI TEKAKWITHA (1656-1680)

Leonard Mahoney, S.J.

THE MOHAWK VILLAGE of Ossernenon stood on an elevation overlooking open fields as they softly rolled towards the banks of the clear and meandering river. It was so advantageously placed that no one, neither friend nor enemy, could escape the Mohawks' purview. Because of nature's lavish beauty Ossernenon had the appearance of peace and calm, but, in truth, it was the home of the most ferocious of the five Indian tribes that formed the Iroquois confederation. Their fierceness in battle matched their cruel hatred for the gentle blackrobed missionaries and the God whom they faithfully preached, for it was at Ossernenon (today's Auriesville, New York) that America's first canonized martyrs had shed their blood. On September 29, 1642, a Mohawk mercilessly slew René Goupil for making the sign of the

3

cross over a child's head, and on October 18, 1646, they
tomahawked Fr. Isaac Jogues and, on the following day,
his companion Jean Lalande. These martyrs were canonized
in 1930 together with five others who had given their lives
for the faith in Canada. Martyrs' blood had soaked into
Ossernenon's soil and ten years later the village bore its
choicest fruit when the most beautiful flower that ever
blossomed among the American Indians was born.

In April, 1656, a daughter was born to Tsaniton-gowa
(Great Beaver), the young chief of the Mohawks at Ossernenon, and his wife Kahontake (Meadow). Because the
child was born at sunrise Meadow fittingly called her Iora-
gade (Sunshine). Meadow was an Algonquin, a tribe known
for its peaceful nature, and had been baptized a Catholic
at Three Rivers in Canada where her family and tribe lived.
When her village had been attacked by a raiding Mohawk
party she and her mother were captured and made to serve
as slaves to the Mohawks. For several years Meadow endured the shame and burdens of slavery until the young
warrior Great Beaver took notice of her and asked her to
be his wife.

Meadow's marriage redeemed her from slavery but her
newly found freedom did not mean that she had the opportunity to practice her Catholic faith openly. Ossernenon was
without missionary and chapel, hence she was without the
consolation of Mass and Communion; furthermore, it was
unthinkable that a pagan chief's wife could exercise a religion other than that of her husband. It was only in silence
and in secret that she could say her prayers and be faithful
to her faith. Moreover, she was fortunate in not being the
only Catholic at Ossernenon for she had found a remarkable friend in Anastasia Tegonhadshongo, the widow of an
Onondaga warrior, who returned to her native village when
her husband died. Their companionship strengthened each
other and their conversation encouraged each other to live
the faith they had in their hearts. When Sunshine was born,

Meadow took joy in being able to teach her young daughter the rudiments of her faith, and even though the child could not be baptized, nevertheless, it was possible for her to be raised a Catholic.

During the spring of 1657, the Jesuit blackrobe, Fr. Simon Le Moyne, famous among the Huron Indians as Ondessonk (Bird of Prey), made a visit to Ossernenon. He came as an official messenger of peace representing the government of New France and as a missionary to the needs of the Catholic Hurons who had been captured during the Huron-Iroquois war of 1648-1649, and who now resided among the Mohawks as slaves. The Mohawks deeply resented the blackrobe's visit, but since he came with the authorization of the Great Council of the Iroquois Confederation they could neither refuse him welcome nor dare injure his person. Le Moyne remained among them for two weeks but he confined his religious activities to the enslaved Christian Hurons who had not seen a priest for eight years. Meadow would have so loved to have spoken with him and receive his blessing for her child, but she dared not enflame her husband's ire.

Towards the end of 1659, suddenly and without warning, the dread scourge of smallpox struck the village. The Indians were helpless against its attack and many, unfortunately, became its victim. Great Beaver succumbed after a week of intense pain, and two days later his wife, Meadow, followed him as did their son born a year after Sunshine's birth. Sunshine too had fallen to the disease but thanks to constant ministrations of the faithful Anastasia, she recovered. Sunshine's health returned but the telltale marks of smallpox remained on her cheeks and her eyes were greatly weakened so that the sun's brightness caused her pain. Because she was now alone, her father's brother, Iowerano (Cold Wind), together with his wife, Karitha (Cook), and his sister, Arosen (Squirrel), moved into the deceased chief's long house, and when Cold Wind was elected to succeed Great Beaver as chief, he and his wife, being childless, adopted Sunshine as their daughter.

The Indians erroneously believed that the evil demons of the smallpox epidemic continued to reside within the enclosed village of Ossernenon and in order to escape them it was necessary for everyone to move to another site. In late 1660 they left Ossernenon for another hill about a mile to the west, and from their new location, which they called Ganawage (Whirling Water), they watched Ossernenon's buildings and fields go up in flames. It was in Ganawage that Sunshine learned how to carry out her daily duties: grind corn for the daily meals, collect firewood, and draw water. Because of the pain that the bright light caused her, she preferred to remain within the lodge and perform her duties there. As Sunshine approached adolescence it was time for her to surrender her childhood name and take on, according to Indian custom, her true name. Due to her feeble sight Sunshine used to walk about home and village with her hands outstretched, an obvious precaution to avoid collision and injury to herself. Seeing her walking with arms extended in front of her, her uncle one day dubbed her Tekakwitha ("who stretches out her hands") which, in time, became the name by which she was known.

In the fall of 1666, the French in Quebec decided it was time to teach the Mohawks a lasting lesson and sent a force of some 1200 men to negotiate a permanent peace. When the Mohawks at Ganawage learned of the Frenchmen's approach, they abandoned their village and sought safety in the forest. Discovering the village deserted, the French set fire to its long houses and its fields. This scene was repeated in village after village so that the Mohawks had no alternative but to hold a council and seek peace with the French. To prove their good faith and their intention to keep the peace the Mohawks requested the French to send blackrobes to live among them.

In September, 1667, three Jesuit blackrobes came to the

rebuilt village of Ganawage, now on the northern side of the Mohawk river near today's Fonda. Since Cold Wind was village chief it was his duty to welcome the three priests and offer them the hospitality of his lodge. The missionaries spent four days among them and Tekakwitha was assigned by her uncle to minister to their needs. She felt a closeness to these missionaries remembering that her mother and Anastasia had told her that it was blackrobes such as these that had given them their new faith. Tekakwitha, now eleven years old, longed to learn about the God whom her mother worshiped but she either had no chance to approach the missionaries, or refrained from doing so out of fear. After four days the missionaries advanced to Tionnontoge, the largest of the Mohawk villages.

After these preliminary visits each missionary was assigned to a definite area. Fr. Pierron was given Andagoron and Ganawage, but he resided at Andagoron, the larger of the two villages. He initiated his missionary work by ministering to the enslaved Christian Hurons but eventually his natural goodness and kindness attracted some Mohawks to come and listen to his preaching. In time he had a class of catechumens awaiting baptism.

In 1670 Fr. Francis Boniface came to Ganawage as its first resident missionary and set about building a chapel in the style of an Iroquois long house. With the erection of the "prayer wigwam" Mass was daily celebrated for the Christians and the chapel likewise served as the meeting place for instructing the catechumens. Fr. Boniface started a children's choir and conversions began to multiply, but Tekakwitha was not among them.

The following summer, 1671, when Chief Ganeagowa (Great Mohawk), who two years before successfully led his nation against the Mohicans, returned to his village after a prolonged hunting expedition, he startled everyone in revealing that while in the forests on the shores of the Saint Lawrence near Montreal, he came upon a settlement of Catholic Iroquois who had formed a "prayer village" where everyone lived in peace with one another. There he met some of his former acquaintances and after having lived with them for a time became so attracted to this new way of life — so different from the warring life he had lived in the past — that he became a Christian receiving the name Joseph. His return to the Mohawk village was only to get his wife, who was already a Christian, and family and take them to this new village. So enthusiastically did he speak of this settlement, which was founded only a few years before, that many Christian Mohawks desired to go with him. Among the thirty who chose to go was Anastasia. Great Mohawk's conversion and his plan to leave the village was not acceptable to the other chiefs. Cold Wind denounced him as being a traitor to his people, of weakening the nation and dividing the tribe. But Great Mohawk's reply was that he was and would always be a Mohawk and would gladly return to the village when it gives up its war-loving manner of life and savage customs. Before the year came to an end eight large canoes, carrying the chief's family and thirty others, slipped from the shores near Ganawage and began their journey to a new life in a new village.

During these years when Tekakwitha was growing into a young woman, she voluntarily refrained from all association and familiarity with the young braves of the village, and when her family attempted to trick her into a marriage she was clever enough to recognize that a net was being prepared for her. She left the house and refused to return until the young warrior had left. In all things Tekakwitha was docile and obedient to her uncle and aunt except in the question of marriage. Eventually the family had to admit defeat and gave up trying to get Tekakwitha married.

Fr. Boniface remained at Ganawage for three years and during that time the number of Christians increased but Tekakwitha was still not among them. The rigors of missionary life began to have its effect on the blackrobe and in the summer of 1673 he had to relinquish his post and return to Quebec where he died shortly thereafter. The new missionary did not come until 1675 and he was Fr. James de Lamberville.

Tekakwitha had never met the new missionary though she had seen him many times in the village. One day when she was forced to remain at home and nurse an injured leg, and as Fr. de Lamberville made his usual rounds of visiting the sick he unexpectedly entered Cold Wind's long house. The priest had never visited here before because he knew of the chief's hatred towards him, but on this particular occasion, he knew not what inspired him to enter it. He was surprised to find it empty except for Tekakwitha resting on her mat. When the priest began to speak to her Tekakwitha found that she could no longer keep her heart closed but had to speak out. She told him that her mother had been a Christian, that she was Anastasia's friend, and that she wanted to be a Christian like them. The missionary was especially impressed by her sincerity and sensed that she had great strength of character; nevertheless, he told her of the difficulties she was sure to encounter with her family, but these she confidently felt she could handle. The black-robe then accepted her among the catechumens and invited her to attend instructions in preparation for her baptism. Up to this point in her life Tekakwitha never had any religious training except what her mother had taught her when she was a child. But what her mother had given her was carefully nurtured through the years. When Tekakwitha finally made her intentions known to her uncle, Cold Wind granted his permission knowing well that he would never succeed in changing the young girl's mind.

After eight months of instruction, Tekakwitha was baptized on Easter Sunday, April 18, 1676, and chose Kateri as her Christian name, the Iroquois form of Catherine. Having been baptized she now attended Mass for the first time but her First Communion was postponed until she had more instruction. Because she found joy in her freedom to live her Christian religion Kateri's aunts became jealous of her happiness. They would never call her by her Christian name, and when she tried to observe the Lord's day by not doing any servile work, the aunts refused to share their food with her. Kateri remained firm in her resolve though each succeeding Sunday meant a fast day. Since the aunts did not achieve their aim in breaking Kateri's determination they resorted to new forms of persecution — scolding her and finding fault with all that she did, criticizing and insulting her, as well as making her do all the household chores. In all this Kateri never complained. The non-Christian villagers soon began to imitate the aunts in ridiculing her and spitting upon her, and even young braves were told to lie in wait and threaten to kill her if she did not abandon her Christian faith. Kateri realized the purpose of this harassment and bravely bore the humiliations.

Eventually this harsh treatment towards Kateri was brought to Fr. de Lamberville's attention and since he could not see how the situation would ever get better he suggested that Kateri might think of moving to the Christian settlement near Montreal where Anastasia and other Christian Mohawks had gone over the past few years. Since the move would bring her peace and freedom to practice her faith, Kateri said she would consider it.

In August, 1677, three Christian Iroquois from Caughnawaga, the "prayer village" near Montreal, came to Ganawage in central New York. One of the Indians was a relative of Kateri, and having heard of her conversion and subsequent persecution he hoped to convince her to join the Christians in Canada. Fr. de Lamberville acted as go-between for the visiting Indians and informed Kateri that the time had come to leave — a canoe was waiting and her uncle was away on a fur-selling expedition. Before Kateri left the village the missionary gave her a letter for Fr. Cholenec, who was in charge of the Canadian mission, and which was intended to introduce Kateri to her new spiritual director. Unknown to her, Fr. de Lamberville wrote: "Kateri Tekakwitha now comes to join your community. Granting her your spiritual guidance and direction, you will soon realize what a jewel we have sent you. Her soul is very close to the Lord. May she progress from day to day in virtue and holiness of life, to the honor and glory of God."

That evening when everyone was asleep, Kateri anxiously awaited the prearranged signal. The owl hoots told her it was time; she quietly rose and wrapped herself in a blanket, passed her sleeping aunts and advanced into the dark night to meet her guardians on the edge of the forest. The Christian Indians were awaiting her and like shadows they silently made their careful way to the water's edge where the canoe was ready for departure. They began their journey seeking God's protection upon them. Two hours later, as dawn was approaching, they took to land, concealed the canoe and took a much needed rest.

Cold Wind was at the Dutch trading post at Skenadada and was startled when a messenger broke the news that Kateri had fled the village and that she was probably on her way to Caughnawaga with the Christian Indian who had been seen in the village the day before. Of the three who had come for Kateri, only one visited the village while the other two wisely remained in the forest, hence it was presumed that Kateri was traveling with only one brave. Cold Wind immediately started in pursuit thinking he could easily overtake them, but the braves were more clever than the chief. The two who were unknown to Cold Wind leisurely paddled their canoe along the Mohawk River waiting to be spotted by Cold Wind, while Kateri and the other brave carefully walked the hidden forest path that followed the river's bank. Unable to find his niece Cold Wind gave up the search and returned home. The ruse was successful and Kateri again entered the canoe and for the next few weeks they made their way to Canada — into the Hudson River and then they followed the water way, passing Lake George into Lake Champlain down the Richelieu River and into the Saint Lawrence. The weary group finally arrived in Caughnawaga's Mission St. Francis Xavier in October.

Happily, the first person Kateri met in the new village was the elderly Anastasia; their reunion was most joyous and Kateri was invited to reside with her and her family. From the moment that Kateri arrived at Caughnawaga she relished the place — she felt like a bird that had finally found its nest. She met the three missionaries and visited her old friends and acquaintances who once lived at Ganawage. Kateri rejoiced in her new life. She now attended Mass every day and at noon took part in the instructions in preparation for her First Communion, and whatever time she may have had free after her regular house duties she spent in private prayer before the Blessed Sacrament.

It was the custom among the missionaries not to allow Indian converts to receive their First Communion until they had given sufficient proof of their sincerity in living the Christian life. Kateri had been baptized eighteen months previously and because her spiritual director recognized how greatly she advanced in the faith and felt that she was truly being guided by the Holy Spirit, he shortened her period of probation and permitted her to receive her First Communion at the Christmas Midnight Mass of 1677.

Shortly after Christmas the village went on its annual three-month winter hunt and Kateri went with them. They returned in time for Holy Week and it was during these prayerful days that Kateri decided to increase her penances for the conversion of her Mohawk nation. She now made Wednesdays and Fridays days of complete fast, spent long hours in prayer, mortified herself by sleepless nights, endured freezing cold, and even scourged herself to the point of drawing blood.

During the summer of 1678 Kateri and several other women crossed the river to Ville-Marie, which was Montreal's original name, to sell their handiwork to the French. Kateri had heard about the white women who had no husbands and who lived together in one house, who dressed in the same manner and cared for the sick. Since Kateri and her friend, Theresa Tegaiagonta, were visiting the city, they decided to pay these women a visit. Kateri had never heard of nuns or religious orders of women, so what she saw and learned was totally new to her. When Kateri and Theresa returned to their mission they seriously thought of imitating the manner of life lived by the French nuns. They added Marie Skarishion to their number, and dreamed of building a convent on an island in the river where they would spend their time caring for the sick. Theresa was deputed to bring this project before Fr. Cholenec, but he sadly informed them that they were without the training and experience necessary to start such a convent at the mission, and obediently they gave up their plans. But Kateri's desire for such a regulated religious life always remained with her.

When it was time for the winter hunt of early 1679, Kateri requested to remain at the mission and care for the sick and elderly. Thus she would not miss her daily Mass and weekly Communion, and at the same time she could devote herself to caring for the sick just as if she were a French nun. She made them their meals and their beds, collected firewood and cared for the fires, and all that was needed to make them more comfortable. When the villagers returned in March they noticed how thin Kateri had become. Her excessive penances were beginning to take their toll, and towards the end of summer she became seriously ill. Kateri recovered for a time but she never fully regained her strength; she was always tired and exhausted but somehow she managed to conceal this from others.

The following year, when it was time for the winter hunt, Kateri had to remain at home and most of that time was spent on her cot. When the Indians returned and saw her it was obvious that she did not have long to live. On Tuesday of Holy Week, Fr. Cholenec brought her Holy Communion and on Wednesday anointed her. That afternoon, April 17, 1680, Kateri returned her soul to God. She was twenty-four years old and had been a Catholic for only four years.

Those who attended her at her death witnessed the remarkable transformation that took place on the dead Kateri's face. The ravages of sickness and the lines of suffering gradually disappeared and her countenance was once again fresh and incredibly beautiful. Kateri was buried on Holy Thursday at the foot of the great cross in the cemetery. Later on her body was transferred to the transept of St. Francis Xavier church at the mission. In 1890 a monument was erected on the site of her original tomb. It bears the inscription that aptly describes this outstanding Indian maid: "Kateri Tekakwitha, April 17, 1680, the most beautiful flower that blossomed among true men."

Favors and miracles obtained through her intercession began almost immediately. In 1715, only twenty-five years after her death, her former spiritual director, Fr. Cholenec, wrote: "All the French living in these colonies as well as the Indians have a singular veneration for her. They come from far off to pray at her tomb and several through her mediation have been cured of their illnesses, and have received from heaven other wonderful favors." In 1884 the American Bishops petitioned Rome to consider Kateri's cause, and the petition was renewed in 1922 by the Bishop of Albany. In 1943 Pope Pius XII approved the decree declaring Kateri, "Venerable" and on June 22, 1980, the tercentenary of her death, Pope John Paul II declared that Kateri now ranks among the "Blessed" in heaven.

The Vice Postulator of Blessed Kateri's cause is Rev. Joseph S. McBride, S.J., National Kateri Center, Auriesville, New York, 12016.

PRAYER

O God, who, among the many marvels of Your Grace

in the New World, did cause to blossom on the banks of the Mohawk and of the St. Lawrence, the pure and tender lily, Kateri Tekakwitha, grant we beseech You, the favor we beg through her intercession, that this Young Lover of Jesus and of His Cross may soon be counted among the Saints of Holy Mother Church, and that our hearts may be enkindled with a stronger desire to imitate her innocence and faith. Through the same Christ our Lord. Amen.

FOR FURTHER READING

Francis X. Weiser, S.J., *Kateri Tekakwitha* (Caughnawaga, Canada: Kateri Center, 1972).

CHAPTER 2

BLESSED ROSE PHILIPPINE DUCHESNE, R.S.C.J.
Foundress of the Religious of the Sacred Heart in the United States.

2

Pioneer Missionary of the New World

BLESSED ROSE PHILIPPINE DUCHESNE, R.S.C.J. (1769-1852)

Sr. Marion Bascom, R.S.C.J.

THIS IS THE STORY of a frontier missionary. Like other pioneer women of equal intrepidity she took in her stride hardships whose mere enumeration makes our softer age recoil. "Some names must not wither," says the bronze tablet bearing the Pioneer Roll of Fame in the Jefferson Memorial in St. Louis. Philippine Duchesne heads this list of women. She had as her single and unswerving purpose to bring Christ to souls and souls to Christ.

What does it take to forge an apostle? Fire, hammer and steel. Love of the Sacred Heart took flame early in the soul of Rose Philippine. The shaping hammer strokes came with steady persistency from sufferings of every kind. The metal she supplied herself from the invincible *caractère Duchesne*.

This meant an indomitable devotion to a cause at whatever cost to self.

Philippine was born in an austere house in Grenoble, France, on August 29, 1769. But the warmth and love of a Christian home life made the childhood of Philippine and her three sisters and brother very happy. With their nine Perier cousins who lived next door they studied and played or trooped through the picturesque streets of Grenoble to visit some medieval or ancient ruin.

As a little girl Philippine was ardent, impetuous, vehement and singularly free from pettiness and jealousy. But she had her full share of the family stubborness of iron inflexibility. Madame Duchesne, intelligent, practical and deeply Catholic, led her daughter by motives of faith and directed her virile energy and natural generosity to the love and service of the sick and poor. To the children of the families she visited with her mother Philippine gave her small possessions. To the beggars who came to the house she gave her spending money.

When Philippine was sent to boarding school at Ste. Marie-d'en-Haut the controlling love of her life flamed into being — devotion to the Sacred Heart of Jesus. Now there was fire intense enough to make that iron will malleable. A tormenting need to bring others to that open Heart of love took extraordinary hold of the child, whose eyes were already on the Indians in their Christless forest and on Chinese babies abandoned by the roadside. Philippine made up her mind to follow the heroic Jesuits in the French province of Louisiana, but first she would have to become a nun.

Her somewhat anticlerical father, suspecting that Philippine was headed for the cloister, withdrew her from Ste. Marie, sent her to dancing school, and put her to the study of Latin and mathematics with the Perier boys. She studied drawing with some success and music with none. After five years of this her father proposed a husband. Oak fronted oak. But though Monsieur Duchesne would not listen to his daughter's intention of entering the noviceship, he showed remarkable forbearance when she refused to attend any more parties or to wear any but the severest clothes. Then one day Philippine persuaded her aunt to accompany her on a visit to Ste. Marie. Once there she had an overwhelming inspiration to stay. Her aunt went down the mountainside alone to face the family. A day or so later Philippine had it out with them from behind the grille. This was in 1787. She was eighteen years old.

Her goal now seemed attained and the novice gave herself with all the ardor of her nature to her religious formation. She was jubilant in her preparation for the vows, that would make her a Visitation nun forever. The French Revolution broke, Monsieur Duchesne forbade his daughter to make her vows and took her from stormy Grenoble to safety in their country home at Grannes. Philippine did not complain. More than ever she made herself indispensable to her family; she reserved the hardest household drudgery for herself. She sought out the poorest of the poor, sick and dying in their wretched hovels. Scorning danger, she would go alone at any hour of the night to answer a summons, or to lead a proscribed priest to administer the Last Sacraments. Unable to resist the call of Grenoble, she returned and joined a band of courageous women who risked imprisonment themselves by their ministrations to the victims of the terror. Driven by her imperative need of spreading the Kingdom of Christ, she prevailed upon a handful of street urchins to come to her lodgings for catechism lessons.

When last the Revolution was over, Philippine bought Ste. Marie from the government. She moved in one rainy December day with a single companion, helped only by her urchin scholars who staggered up the mountain with dripping bundles. During the long years of waiting and desire she had never wavered from her first ideal. Nothing had been wasted. Deprivation, danger, abnegation to the point of heroism, above all the growing habit of alertness to God's lead even when it meant the relinquishing of cherished plans for His glory, had only stimulated her sense of consecration. Intimate association with pain and death had brought the needed insight and keen sensitiveness to the sufferings of others. The former nuns were old and could not return to live at Ste. Marie. Philippine was alone in her great and empty house on the mountain.

In August, 1802, the Abbé Rivet told her of St. Madeleine Sophie Barat and her newly founded Society of the Sacred Heart at Amiens, with its work of educating youth and its spirit of love, zeal, generosity, and prayer. His proposal that Philippine should offer the monastery and herself to the young foundress revived her hope, and negotiations were begun. After two years Mother Barat came and gave a new direction to Blessed Philippine. The young superior, only twenty-five, and the novice, ten years older, understood each other at once. Though so different in character, they were united in vision and aim. In the warmth of peace and happiness of the noviceship Philippine expanded and mellowed. At the end of the year when the novices had made their vows M. Barat returned to Amiens.

Philippine's missionary desires grew stronger, but they would not be realized for twelve years. Meanwhile M. Duchesne was treasurer, secretary, infirmarian, teacher of the higher classes, and accumulator of odd jobs at Ste. Marie. In 1815 M. Barat invited her to attend the Second General Council of the Society. Here she was made Secretary General and remained at the motherhouse in Paris. Two years later M. Barat gave permission for M. Duchesne to answer Bishop Dubourg's request for missionaries. On March 21, 1818, M. Duchesne and four companions sailed for America.

The voyage of the *Rebecca* lasted eleven eventful weeks. Landing south of New Orleans on May 29, M. Duchesne remained with the Ursulines for six weeks before boarding the *Franklin*. A trip of forty days took her to St. Louis where Bishop Dubourg greeted her warmly and took the nuns to

St. Charles. The "Duquette Mansion" with its large central room and six small ones which the bishop had leased for a year stood on a bluff overlooking the tawny Missouri river. On the banks of the river below could be seen the daily passage of Indians and immigrants — hunters, trappers, adventurers, pioneer families — on their way to the Far West.

In September the first free school west of the Mississippi opened with twenty-one pupils. In October, Emilie and Celeste Pratte and Pélagie Chouteau became the pensionnat. Each day the children helped to put up their beds so that their dormitory might become the classroom for the poor school. The little girls arrived — hungry as usual, and barefoot, though the roads were ice covered. The children were of all ages. Some understood only English, some only French, while a few spoke both. Five little Protestant sisters wanted to learn catechism, but there was only one book among them — also only one reader, which they passed up and down the line. Many could not read and had to be taught their lessons word by word. M. Duchesne, despairing of mastering English, wrote M. Barat, "God has not bestowed on us the gift of tongues. Perhaps He wants His missionary nuns to sanctify themselves by failure."

Bishop Dubourg was pleased with their work but was convinced there was no future for the school in St. Charles. He arranged for the move to Florissant in September. While the three-story brick convent was being built, the nuns and their five pupils lived in a small log cabin on the bishop's farm. They moved to their new convent on Christmas eve. By May, 1920, they had twenty-two pupils. M. Duchesne insisted on strong studies and paid an outside examiner to test the progress of the English speaking pupils.

It was not long before vocations developed in the school and M. Duchesne opened a novitiate. She transmitted her own spirit to them and all showed the same abnegation, the same ardent seeking of privations, the same strong interior life. Through these American religious the Society of the Sacred Heart became a potent factor in the religious and educational life of the Mississippi Valley and was enabled to carry into many parts of North America the knowledge and love of the Sacred Heart and the cultural influence of a truly Catholic training.

In 1821 M. Barat gave permission to accept the generous offer of a house and extensive property for a convent in Grand Coteau, Louisiana. Another house was established in Louisiana at St. Michael's in 1825. Then in 1827 Mr. John Mullanphy, of St. Louis, leased to M. Duchesne for 999 years a house on Broadway on condition that twenty orphans should be educated there in perpetuity. In the following year the convent at St. Charles was reopened. After a four months' absence from Florissant in 1823, M. Duchesne found a dwindling boarding school upon her return. Illness, cyclone, flood, and financial depression had all contributed to this state of affairs. This time of trial was lightened for the nuns by the Belgian novitiate of the Jesuits under Father Van Quickenborne in Florissant. Among these novices was Father De Smet, the apostle of Kansas, Oregon, and the Rocky Mountains, who called himself the son of M. Duchesne and kept up a correspondence with her till her death.

M. Duchesne eagerly helped the novices with the first Catholic Indian school on territory under the control of the United States. For a brief time she opened a companion school for girls. Then in 1827 she added a private school and a free school to the school for orphans in St. Louis. Again M. Duchesne was pioneering and opening the way for the parochial school system. The first years in St. Louis followed the familiar pattern of stark poverty, failure, illness, moral and physical suffering. Six years at Florissant were followed by a return to St. Louis in 1840 without the title of superior.

And then at last, in her seventy-second year, came the great opportunity toward which the desires of her life had been converging. She was sent to the Indians with three other religious in June, 1841. With $500 collected by Father De Smet she went to the Potawatomi at Sugar Creek, Kansas, to establish a school for girls. A unique reception awaited the missioners. A cavalcade of Indians in festive dress escorted them the last mile, circling around them on plumed horses. The chief made a formal speech of welcome, and seven hundred braves and squaws filed past to shake hands. While a house was being built for them the nuns occupied the vermin-infested cabin of an Indian. M. Duchesne learned not to mind the gifts of scalps as a testimony of affection, the complete lack of privacy — the cabin was always full of unbidden guests squatting stolidly but observantly on the floor — and the theft of the morning meal by the prairie dogs that burrowed silently through the floor. The solid piety of the Indians and their responsiveness made up for all this. Her remaining desire was to end her life among them. But God asked the sacrifice of this, too. Her failing health made it impossible for her to work; she could not learn the different language with its ten-syllable words, so she could not instruct the Indians. But Indians venerated her as a saint and called her the "Woman Who Prays Always." No wonder — for she spent four hours in the morning and four hours in the afternoon before the Blessed Sacrament.

After just one year she was recalled to St. Charles. The renunciation was simply made, but a letter to her sister revealed what was in her heart: "It seems to me that in leaving the savages I have left my element, and that henceforth, I can do nothing but languish for the heavenly court from which happily, there will be no more departures."

The last decade of her life was spent at St. Charles, which she sanctified by her presence, making it the shrine of the Society of the Sacred Heart in the New World, where her spirit is marked today. From her continual place before the tabernacle her strong prayer went out to the Church, to the missions and to the Society. Often after Holy Communion her face was illumined with light not of this earth. On days when the Blessed Sacrament was exposed it was almost impossible to get her attention and to draw her from the chapel for her meals. "She saw nothing, heard nothing, knew nothing except that Jesus was there," said one of her companions. The generous heart had still more redemptive sacrifices to make before the holocaust should be perfect. St. Charles was under constant threat of suppression, and in 1846 Florissant, in spite of her pleading, was suppressed. "I shall submit, but I shall never be consoled," she wrote. "The wound is too deep."

St. Madeleine Sophie characteristically took action. She sent M. Duchesne's niece, Amelie Jouve, destined for the new convent in Canada, hundreds of miles out of her way to visit her aunt and to bring her the assurance of the love, veneration and anxious concern of her Mother and of the whole Society. Five years later she sent another great missionary to see her. M. Anna du Rousiers' apostolic desires had first been awakened when as a child at Poitiers her heart had responded to the grace-bearing words of M. Duchesne as she spoke to the school before sailing for America. Now, just before the death of the Society's first missionary she brought her St. Madeleine Sophie's blessing and reverently knelt to receive hers in return. Two days later on November 18, 1852, the heroic heart of Philippine Duchesne ceased to beat. She was eighty-three years old and had spent thirty-four years in America. Long before she and Father De Smet had made a compact that the first to die should obtain for the other a particular favor. Immediately after her death Father De Smet received the favor.

M. Duchesne's work, like that of the Master she served so well, brought no harvest of success within her lifetime. "We have desired the cross and not honor, poverty and not ease, the Will of God and not success," she had written when she realized her uselessness at Sugar Creek. This, she had received and with this she was content. But how abundantly productive her work has been since her death! "You will see that when I am dead everything will prosper," she had said. The prophecy was at once fulfilled; but the beginning of the rapid expansion of the Society in North America dates from the opening of the Indian mission.

What do we owe to her? The Society of the Sacred Heart in North and South America, in New Zealand and Australia; a share in the spread of devotion to the Sacred Heart on three continents; the ever growing missionary movement in the Society; the survival of the Jesuit mission in Missouri; pioneer work in education for girls in the Mississippi Valley and through native vocations in other parts of the United States. These are the reasons why the name of Philippine Duchesne is on the Pioneer Roll of Fame.

Mother Rose Philippine Duchesne was beatified by Pope Pius XII on May 12, 1940, and her sacred relics are at the Academy of the Sacred Heart, Saint Charles, Missouri.

PRAYER

O God, our refuge and our strength, who are Yourself the author of mercy, hearken to our prayer, and grant that what we ask with all confidence we may speedily obtain and thus increase the glory of Your faithful Servant, Blessed Philippine Duchesne. Amen.

FOR FURTHER READING

Louise Callan, R.S.C.J., *Philippine Duchesne: Frontier Missionary of the Sacred Heart 1769-1852.* (Westminster, Md.: Newman, 1957).

CHAPTER 3

Verdadero Retrato del V:P:Fr. Antonio Margil de Iesus natural de la Ciudad de [...]
[...]encia Missionero Apostolico Fundador de los tres Collegios de Querétaro [...]
[...] y Zacatecas: P[...] de la Prov[...] de Zacatecas: murió en este Conv[...] de N.P.S.F[...]
Mexico el dia 6 de Ag[...] de 1726 años d edad de 7[...]

VENERABLE ANTONIO MARGIL DE JESÚS, O.F.M.
An Apostle of North and Central America
A painting described as a "Verdadero Retrato" (true likeness), at the
Friary of Santa Cruz (former Missionary College) in Querétaro, Mexico.

3

Nothingness Itself

VENERABLE ANTONIO MARGIL DE JESUS, O.F.M. (1657-1726)

Benedict Leutenegger, O.F.M.

ANTONIO MARGIL, the future Apostle of Texas, was born of poor parents in Valencia, Spain, on August 18, 1657, and baptized in the parish church of San Juan del Mercado, also called Santos Juanes (the two Saints John). Antonio was a good-natured lad and had a sense of humor, qualities he kept all through his life. At age fifteen, in April, 1673, he entered the Franciscan novitiate at La Corona de Cristo in Valencia and received the name Fray Antonio de Jesús. As a novice he was somewhat over-zealous and at times had to be restrained in his practice of penance. A year later (1674), he pronounced his vows as a Friar Minor and began his course in philosophy in the friary of San Antonio de Denia in Alicante, south of Valencia.

In 1677, Fray Antonio began his study of theology in Valencia and pursued this course for five years. He was ordained to the priesthood late in 1682, at age twenty-five, and was assigned to the friary of Santa Catarina de Onda, north of Valencia. The following year (1683), under the leadership of Fr. Antonio Llinas, he and twenty-two other Franciscans set sail for the New World on March 4, to open the first *Colegio de Propaganda Fide* (College for the Propagation of the Faith) at Querétaro, Mexico. After a three-month voyage, the missionaries landed at Vera Cruz, fortunately just shortly after pirates had attacked and plundered the city. Two by two the friars set out on foot for Mexico City and on their way they preached in the towns through which they passed. It was June when they arrived — a century and a half after the first group of Franciscans, known as the twelve apostles, had entered Mexico City and been received by Cortés.

In August, Fr. Margil was in Querétaro, northwest of Mexico City, founding the Apostolic College of Santa Cruz in what had previously been a Franciscan friary. The college, not an educational institution but an apostolic center, had a two-fold purpose: to preach parish missions in Christian cities and towns, and to establish and staff missions among Indians who had not as yet been converted to the Catholic faith. By October, together with other friars, Fr. Margil was active in Mexico City and in March, 1684, he began a missionary journey that was to last thirteen years, traveling through the Yucatan Peninsula and all of Central America. He and his companion, Fr. Melchor López, visited town after town, preached missions and heard confessions of Indians and Spaniards in the present southern Mexican states of Tabasco and Chiapas. As traveling missionaries they learned to be satisfied with whatever food they found on their way — beans, bananas, herbs, chocolate. They slept beneath the open skies and kept themselves safe from animals and savage Indians by taking turns praying and sleeping during the night. As they journeyed they sang a hymn of praise, an Alabado, composed by Fr. Margil. A sample portion of one is:

> Whoever seeks to follow God
> And strives to enter in His glory
> One thing he has to do
> And from his heart to say
> "Die rather than sin!
> Rather than sin, die!"

When Frs. Margil and López arrived at Tuxtla Gutierrez they were all but overcome with exhaustion and Fr. Margil had to be given the last rites. But the sturdy missionaries recovered and continued their odyssey with crowds of Indians following them carrying branches of trees in their hands. By September, 1685, they reached the ancient capital of Guatemala, Santiago de los Caballeros, today known as Antigua. The two missionaries then carried their apostolic labors throughout the present countries of El Salvador, Honduras, Nicaragua, and Costa Rica. When they arrived at Cartago, capital of Costa Rica, toward the end of 1688 or the beginning of 1689, more than two years after they had left Antigua, they had walked barefoot more than 1200 miles.

In Cartago Frs. Margil and López heard about the hostile Talamanca Indians and accepted the challenge of founding a mission among them. Alone and unprotected they ventured into Talamanca territory and thanks to their perseverance they were successful in establishing missions among these Indians. After two years they passed the missions on to successors and were on their way to Panama when they received notice on August 25, 1691, to return to Querétaro, from which they had been absent seven years. On their way back, when they stopped in Antigua, Guatemala, they learned that their recall had been cancelled; but at the bishop's request both remained in Guatemala to help the Dominicans in restoring the missions among the Chol and Lacandon Indians. After ten years of happy companionship, Fr. Margil lost Fr. López who was named, June, 1694, superior of the new hospice in Antigua. Fr. Margil took another companion, Fr. Pedro de la Concepción, and resumed his missionary work. In March, 1697, he was elected Father Guardian (Superior) of the Apostolic College at Querétaro; he set out immediately after hearing of this appointment, taking only his crucifix, breviary and Mass vestments with him. He walked the distance in record time of five weeks and when questioned about this, he replied, smilingly, "I take short cuts, and God helps me."

Fr. Margil remained superior of the College until January, 1701. In February he again set out for Guatemala to restore peace in the political struggle that was then going on and to raise the hospice, which had opened in 1694, to the rank of an Apostolic College, similar to the one at Querétaro. On June 13, he founded the *Colegio de Cristo Crucificado* (College of Christ Crucified), and on September 8, broke ground for the new church and friary. He was elected Father Guardian and was active in the construction of the new buildings.

After Christmas, 1702, Fr. Margil left the administration of the college to his vicar and set out for Nicaragua. Routine administration was never to his liking; his restless disposition again urged him to strike out for the open road and preach to the Indians. In March, 1704, he made a missionary expedition southwards and conceived the idea to continue through Panama to Peru. He wrote of his plan to his vicar, Fr. Tomás, who was deeply disappointed and replied: "I hoped to find in your letter the help I needed . . . but what do I find instead, that you are planning to go to Peru. . . . Such an idea is a strong temptation from the devil under the guise of zeal and charity which will result in the ruin of this poor College. . . . With this College in its infancy, not yet

three years old, where does Your Reverence want to go?"
Needless to say, Fr. Margil did not go on to Peru.

In August, 1705, since a new guardian was chosen, Fr.
Margil was free for a time to return to his mission among
the Talamanca Indians, but in the following July he was
instructed to establish a third Apostolic College in the town
of Guadalupe, near Zacatecas, north of Querétaro. He arrived in Guadalupe in the early part of January, 1707, and
was appointed head of the college, which position he retained until 1713.

As early as 1690, the College at Querétaro had established
two missions in eastern Texas. Both lasted only until 1693,
and with the founding of the new college at Zacatecas, it
was determined that another attempt should be made as a
joint venture of both colleges. Each was to establish and staff
three missions. Fr. Isidro Felix de Espinosa was appointed
head of the missionaries from Querétaro, and Fr. Margil
was designated to head those from Zacatecas. Fr. Margil
spent the month of March, 1716, preparing supplies for the
trip to Texas, gathering horses, oxen, goats, etc. On March
24, Captain Ramón, the leader of the expedition into Texas,
set out for Mission San Juan Bautista on the Mexican side
of the Rio Grande river, present-day Guerrero, Coahuila.
Fr. Margil followed the caravan on foot and alone, and
it seems that for some time he had not been feeling well.
About a day's journey from the Rio Grande, it was April
18, he was much too ill to walk any farther and collapsed
on the road. He was taken to Mission San Juan Bautista
on the 19th. The expedition crossed the Rio Grande into
Texas on the 20th and waited six days for Fr. Margil to
join them. But his health was only getting worse and on
the 25th Fr. Espinosa anointed him, preparing him for death.
The expedition, a total of seventy-five persons, set out again
on the 27th, leaving Fr. Margil behind with two companions.
Gradually, his health returned and on June 13th he and his
confreres began their journey across Texas. By this time

Ramón and the caravan were at the Brazos river, and on June 22, they crossed the Trinity river and arrived among the Asinai Indians on the 27th, two months after they had crossed the Rio Grande. Fr. Margil and his companions caught up with the expedition about the middle of July, but by this time the three Queréteran missions, San Francisco, Purísima Concepción, and San José, and one of the Zacatecan missions, Nuestra Señora de Guadalupe, present-day Nacogdoches, Texas, had already been founded. The two remaining missions, which Fr. Margil founded early in 1717, were those of San Miguel, near today's Robeline, Louisiana, and Nuestra Señora de los Dolores, near St. Augustine, Texas, where Fr. Margil took up residence. The six mission stations served the Indians in the eastern part of Texas and western Louisiana.

The Indians received the missionaries with great friendliness, but the missions did not fare well because of the lack of necessary supplies and because the missionaries had not been able to persuade the Indians to congregate at the mission stations. The Indians lived in widely scattered small rancherias forcing the missionaries to go from one to another in order to instruct them. Baptisms were few, except for dying children. Added to these hardships was the fact that war had broken out in Europe between France and Spain. The French had a fort at Natchitoches, Louisiana, and since they had received word of the war before the Spaniards had, they took advantage of the situation. The French soldiers went, June, 1719, to the nearby Mission San Miguel (Robeline, La.), and informed the two Spaniards there, a Franciscan brother and a soldier, that they were prisoners of war and proceeded to despoil the mission of whatever property they could carry. In the confusion both Spaniards successfully escaped and made their way to the mission of N. S. de los Dolores (St. Augustine, Texas), and informed Fr. Margil of what had happened and of the impending peril. The news quickly spread throughout the other stations and since additional French troops were on their way, the Spaniards decided to seek refuge by going westward towards Mission San Antonio. Frs. Margil and Espinosa would have preferred to remain at their missions, but they were urged to seek safety, at least temporarily, until aid could come from Mexico. Before leaving the Indians, the missionaries promised that one day they would return.

The refugees arrived at Mission San Antonio in October (1719), the later Alamo, which had been founded only the year before. As soon as Fr. Margil had left his residence at N. S. de los Dolores, he wrote (July 2, 1719) to the Viceroy, Marqués de Valero, informing him of the events that had taken place in eastern Texas and asked for help and reinforcements. Fr. Margil patiently waited for the reinforcements, but they were not to arrive until April, 1721. The Viceroy chose the Marqués de Aguayo, the lord of vast estates in Coahuila, to lead the expedition and instructed him to raise an army and prepare for the march into Texas. The Marqués was always generous in his service to God and King, and gladly accepting the command of the Viceroy he gathered five hundred soldiers, equipment, and supplies. It was April, 1721, by the time the expedition arrived at Mission San Antonio, almost two years after the missionaries had left their missions among the Texas Indians. Fr. Margil was greatly disappointed that the period of waiting took so long but he could not remain idle. Since Mission San Antonio, the halfway station between eastern Texas and Mexico, had proven so salutary to the refugees, Fr. Margil saw the need for another such halfway station. He sought authorization from the Marqués de Aguayo and in February, 1720, he founded Mission San José, in the present city of San Antonio, and only four miles south of Mission San Antonio. San José was to become the most famous of all the missions in Texas. In the following year, Fr. Margil sent Fr. Patrón to Matagorda Bay and there he established the mission dedicated to Nuestra Señora del Espíritu Santo.

With the arrival of the Marqués' forces in April (1721), the six missions in eastern Texas and western Louisiana were re-established. After the restoration of San Miguel, Fr. Margil made that his residence. The Mission San Miguel, together with the nearby presidio and the settlement of Los Adaes formed the capital of the Province of Texas.

Less than a year after Fr. Margil had resumed his missionary activity in Texas he received word that he had been elected Father Guardian of the Apostolic College at Zacatecas. He had been elected to this same office in 1716, but since the news only reached him after two years had elapsed, and since it would have taken him another six months to reach Zacatecas, he remained in Texas. But this time he had to heed the summons and make his way to the college. He left Los Adaes toward the end of January, 1722, thus bringing to an end a fruitful apostolate of five and a half years instructing the Indians of Texas in the good news of Jesus Christ and arrived in Zacatecas in June after a five-month walk.

Fr. Margil was superior of the college until August, 1725. He spent the following month in a quiet retreat in prayer and penance and then in October entered upon his last missionary journey preaching missions and hearing confessions in various places. His last mission was in Valladolid, today's Morelia. On July 7, he reached Querétaro a very ill man. On the 21st he started out for Mexico City; on the 31st he celebrated Mass for the last time and had to be taken by coach from Cuautitlan to the Mexican capital. As the sun was setting on August 2, he arrived at San Francisco el Grande, in Mexico City, and after visiting the church was taken to the infirmary in the Franciscan friary. Fr. Margil was ready for death and as the friars streamed in to visit him he kept repeating, "My heart is ready." On August 5, the nuns of a nearby convent sent him an image of Nuestra Señora de los Remedios (Our Lady of Succour) which he tenderly kissed and said, "Adios, Señora, hasta mañana"

(Good-bye, Lady, until tomorrow"). On the morrow, which was August 6, 1726, Fr. Margil died peacefully in the Lord before two o'clock in the afternoon. At the time of his death he was approaching his sixty-ninth birthday, and had completed forty-three years in New Spain, having founded three Apostolic Colleges, more than thirty missions and converted an untold number of Indians to God.

Fr. Margil's contemporaries looked upon him as a man of genuine greatness, but in his own eyes he was *La misma nada* (Nothingness itself). It was his custom to conclude his letters with this phrase and sign his name and he did this not because of any epistolary convention but because he honestly meant it. He truly thought of himself as nothing. On one occasion when he was appointed superior of an Apostolic College he said, "Nothing is nothing, and it can do nothing. It is God who will lead this College." In his humility he desired to follow the example of Our Lady who declared in her *Magnificat* that God had "regarded the lowliness (nothingness) of His handmaid" and did "great things" to her. He loved to refer to her as *La Doña Nada* (Lady Nothingness). Fr. Margil was convinced that if he did not recognize his own nothingness he would be worshiping his own ego and thus rob God of the glory that is His due. His renunciation of self was total so that he could be the fit instrument in God's hands, a messenger of peace and salvation to his fellowmen.

But among his fellow Franciscans and the Indians whom he had humbly served Fr. Margil was also a man of holiness. The memory of his exemplary life remained vivid among the Spaniards and Indians of Texas and Mexico, and in 1794, Fr. Bringas de Manzaneda, preaching a eulogy on the anniversary of Fr. Margil's death, gave this summary of his life. "His whole life was an amazing kaleidoscope of leadership as superior, of preaching to sinners, of the founding of colleges and missions among the pagans, of endless journeys of thousands of leagues made on foot, of constant growth in holiness and good example, and of the working of miracles . . .

"All America was the witness and the scene of his virtues and miracles. To trace his journeys among the pagans, turn your eyes to the east and west, to north and south, and you will find him in all these places, leading a very austere life, crossing mountains, struggling with the evil spirit until he has triumphantly planted his foundations. The widely scattered provinces of Nicaragua and Costa Rica, of Honduras and Chol and Panama, of Coahuila and Texas — all of them heard his apostolic voice."

The formal ecclesiastical investigation into his holiness began in 1771 and Pope Gregory XVI on July 31, 1836, decreed that Fr. Margil had practiced virtue to a heroic degree and bestowed on him the title of Venerable. In 1861 his body was transferred from the Franciscan church to the Cathedral in Mexico City and it now rests in the Chapel of the Immaculate Conception. The address of the Vice Postulator for Fr. Margil's cause is Rev. Fr. Benedict Leutenegger, O.F.M., San José Mission, 701 E. Pyron Road, San Antonio, Texas, 78214.

PRAYER
(Private use only)

O Lord Jesus Christ, Your apostle Antonio Margil left his homeland to bring the good news of salvation to the people of Mexico and the United States. He endured every hardship and pain because of love of you. May you graciously deign to reward this your servant Antonio Margil by hastening the day when he will be raised to the honor of Blessed and Saint. We ask that Antonio Margil intercede for us to God for this our special request. Through Christ our Lord. Amen.

FOR FURTHER READING

E. E. Rios, *Life of Fray Antonio Margil, O.F.M.* (translated by Benedict Leutenegger, O.F.M. [Washington, D.C.: Academy of American Franciscan History, 1959]), and *Nothingness Itself: Selected Writings of Ven. Antonio Margil, 1690-1724* (translated by Benedict Leutenegger, O.F.M., and edited by Marion A. Habig, O.F.M. [Chicago: Franciscan Herald Press, 1976]).

CHAPTER 4

VENERABLE FELIX DeANDREIS, C.M.
Founding Superior of the Vincentians in the United States.

4

Many Things in a Short Time
VENERABLE FELIX DeANDREIS, C.M. (1778-1820)

Frederick J. Easterly, C.M.

THE ATTAINMENT of heroic sanctity, required in the Process of Beatification and Canonization is achieved only by unselfish conformity with the will of God. Because of human weaknesses God's will is not always discernible with ease, nor is it accomplished with the perfection desired by the heavenly Father. The attainment of that sanctity, however, is not measured by the perfection of human acts, but rather by the truthfulness and sincerity with which these acts are motivated.

The life of the Venerable Felix DeAndreis, C.M., is an example of a life filled with seeming contradictions but which, upon closer scrutiny, reveals a conformity to God's Providence which influenced not only his life but the destiny of lives of others and the future of the Church and the Congregation of the Mission in the United States of America.

Little information is available about the formative years of Felix's life except that he was born on December 12, 1778, at Demonte, a small village in the Diocese of Cuneo in the Province of Piedmont. His father was a notary; his brother Joseph was a doctor and his brother Vincent a lawyer. It is not surprising, therefore, that the young Felix obtained an education that qualified him to pursue advanced studies in philosophy, history, languages, science, mathematics and music. Such a background assured the young student a secular professional career like that of his father and brothers. But the Providence of God was beckoning in the direction of a vocation to the priesthood. He had contemplated this call as early as his fifteenth or sixteenth year. About this time, he approached Fr. Michael Laugeri, the superior of the Turin Province of the Congregation of the Mission, requesting admission to the company founded by St. Vincent de Paul. The superior was acquainted with the intellectual endowments of Felix and advised him that:

"As Vincentians, the employments of our missionaries are far different from those to which you have hitherto devoted yourself in accordance with your natural inclination; the principal object of our institute is to instruct the poor in the country, and form good laborers for the vineyard of the Lord; its duties, therefore, do not require brilliancy of thought . . . but serious study, and discourses without pomp and ornament. How difficult it would be for a young man like yourself to become accustomed to such things."

Undaunted by the response to his request, Felix willingly accepted the recommendation of Fr. Laugeri to delay his admission to the seminary for one year during which time he would pray, meditate, and devote himself to a life devoid of the intellectual pursuits which seemed to be a source of vanity. In this way he could perceive with greater certainty the divine determination of his future life. Concerning this period of determination, Felix submitted to God's will when he wrote:

"I entered into myself and endeavored to correct whatever I knew to be reprehensible in my conduct . . . and I traced out a plan of a more serious life, having resolved to become a missionary, in order to atone for my sins, give glory to God, work out my own salvation, and by the aid of Divine Grace promote that of others; such was my intention, and I acknowledge it to be from Thee alone, O my God."

The statement not only summarized his life, it strengthened his submission to God's will. One year later he entered the Congregation of the Mission on Nov. 1, 1797, at Mondavi with the full approbation of Fr. Laugeri who, now, was convinced of Felix's vocation.

His seminary studies were a source of satisfaction to him although they were pursued under great difficulties. Napoleon's confrontation with Pope Pius VII disrupted the affairs of the Church. Because of the prescriptions of the Provisional Government which Napoleon imposed on Italy and the Vatican, Felix's ecclesiastical studies were interrupted when the Vincentian house at Piedmont was suppressed. He returned to his home in February 1799; in December of that same year he was able to resume his studies in Turin. When this latter seminary was also suppressed, the young seminarian entered the Collegio Alberoni, the Vincentian seminary at Piacenza. It was here that Felix developed a priestly spirit enriched by the words of St. Thomas Aquinas, St. Bernard, St. Augustine, and St. John Chrysostom; his spiritual life was fortified by the writings of St. John of the Cross and St. Teresa; his Vincentian spirit was strengthened by the study of the life of St. Vincent de Paul and the splendid example of his confreres who were his teachers and instructors. With this background, Felix was ordained to the priesthood on August 14, 1802.

The priestly ministry to which he was assigned was patterned after the early years of St. Vincent who found a great need to evangelize the people in the country areas of France. Fr. DeAndreis devoted himself tirelessly to the village places surrounding the city of Piacenza where, because of the political disturbances, the faithful were all but forgotten. His great consolation was to bring to these abandoned people the truths of redemption and salvation; and his instructions were always followed by long periods in the confessional. Not content to serve only the faithful among the laity, he devoted much time to strengthen and fortify the faith, the courage and the perseverance of the clergy during these difficult days of foreign domination by an anti-clerical and anti-religious regime. His sincerity of speech and his wisdom of words touched the lives of every class and condition of people. His services were ever in demand. But again Providence was determining his future. In between his periods of work with the country people he was called upon, because of his holiness and intellectual ability, to assist or substitute for the professors at the Collegio Alberoni. This occupation of his time and talents was a preparation for his future work of seminary formation at Rome and the New World.

Fr. DeAndreis remained at Piacenza from 1802 until 1806, when two events prepared the young priest to recognize once again the path that Divine Providence was indicating. The first of these was the weather conditions in Northern Italy which adversely affected his health. He experienced periods of illness which were accompanied by severe headaches which forced him to curtail his visits to the people and places in the country areas to which he had become fondly attached; they also prevented him from continuing his classes with the seminarians.

This condition resulted in his transfer to Monte Citorio in Rome which was the second event determining his future. His duties at this Vincentian house were associated mostly with the ecclesiastical formation of seminarians who were members of the Congregation of the Mission and students from the Propaganda Fide College which had been forced to suspend operations from 1789 to 1815.

The zeal of Fr. DeAndreis led him into many related areas associated with one of the purposes and goals as stated by St. Vincent de Paul in the Rules of the Community, namely, "to help ecclesiastics in acquiring the knowledge and virtues necessary for their state." In this situation he was to achieve successes which he had not anticipated in his earlier years. His ambition then was to become a priest in order to become a missionary, possibly in China. The more he became involved in this new ministry, the less unlikely became his missionary dream. And yet Providence continued to guide him.

The work at Monte Citorio involved not only his teaching responsibilities but, whenever the time permitted, he conducted missions for the poor in the country districts of Castelli Romani. Here he instructed the youth as well as the adults; urged the faithful in the practice of the Eucharist and sacramental confession, a renewal of their spiritual lives which would bring them Christ's redeeming grace of salvation. In addition, he conducted retreats for bishops and priests alike; preached retreats for ordinands which were prescribed by Pope Pius VII. And, after the example of St. Vincent's Tuesday conferences, Felix also at the request of Pope Pius VII gathered the clergy of Rome to discuss with them the duties and obligations of the priesthood.

It was on the occasion of one of these conferences that that the Bishop-designate of Louisiana in the United States listened to Fr. DeAndreis as he spoke with a group of Roman clergy. The Bishop-designate was Louis William Dubourg who had been named Bishop of Louisiana. In 1815, before accepting the responsibility, he visited Rome for the purpose of obtaining priests and financial assistance. During his visit in Rome he stayed at Monte Citorio where Fr. DeAndreis was assigned. "How happy I would be," he remarked, "if only I had such preachers in my diocese." Without knowing the desire of Felix to engage in missionary service in a foreign country, the bishop spoke with the young priest and asked that he accompany him on his return to the United States, primarily to establish a seminary in Louisiana. In a spirit of obedience, Felix was enthusiastic on condition that the assignment be approved by his Vincentian superiors. The proposal was strongly opposed by Fr. Charles Sicardi, the Vicar General of the Congregation of the Mission in Rome, who protested that the assignment of Fr. DeAndreis to the United States would do extensive harm to the work of the seminary and the spiritual formation of the clergy in Rome. Not to be deterred, Bishop Dubourg took his plea directly to Pius VII who, after much deliberation, decided in favor of Bishop Dubourg, much to the delight of Fr. DeAndreis who saw in this action not his own will but the Will of God.

Under the direction of Bishop Dubourg, Fr. DeAndreis prepared for the long journey to America. Among these preparations was the selection of Fr. Joseph Rosati, C.M., as his colleague in this new venture. Rosati had been a student of DeAndreis at Monte Citorio. Young Rosati, on one occasion, expressed his admiration of his confrere and teacher in the words of the disciples of Christ on their way to Emmaus, "Were not our hearts burning inside us as he talked to us . . . and explained the Scriptures?" (Luke 24:32.)

The new missionaries, DeAndreis and Rosati, were joined by a group of Vincentian priests and brothers, diocesan priests and seminarians, thirteen in all, who also accepted the invitation of Bishop Dubourg. They travelled to Bordeaux where, on June 12, 1816, they boarded an American brig, the *Ranger,* for the long and treacherous sea voyage. Rosati wrote that despite poor accommodations and, at times, unfavorable weather the ship resembled a floating seminary. DeAndreis prepared a regular schedule of exercises to be observed on shipboard. At a stated time a signal was given for rising; a half hour later meditation was held in common. This was followed by Mass provided the sea was calm enough to allow Mass to be said. During the day, at definite times, the breviary was recited in common; they also had conferences, the reading of the New Testament, and spiritual reading. The seminarians were obliged to devote a portion of each day to the study of theology; while all, both priests and seminarians, studied English.

The missionaries, after more than thirty days at sea, arrived at Baltimore on July 25. They were received with warm hospitality by the Sulpician priests at St. Mary's Seminary. Bishop Dubourg had served at this seminary until his appointment as the Administrator of Louisiana in 1812.

Before leaving Bordeaux, with Providence again leading the way, Fr. DeAndreis learned from Bishop Dubourg that, because of disturbances in New Orleans, the missionaries would settle in the village of St. Louis, in Missouri instead of Louisiana. The change necessitated altered traveling plans which would take them overland from Baltimore to Pittsburgh, then down the Ohio river by flat boat to Louisville, Kentucky, whence they would travel the short distance to St. Thomas Seminary, Bardstown, Kentucky. Here they were welcomed on November 22, by Benedict Joseph Flaget, Bishop of Bardstown.

Despite the anxious desire of Fr. DeAndreis and his companions to reach St. Louis as quickly as possible, their ambitions were not fulfilled until one year later. Bishop Flaget explained that plans would have to be made for a residence in St. Louis accommodated to the needs of the community. Furthermore, the people would have to be prepared for the coming of the missionaries and later the arrival of Bishop Dubourg. Until now this news had not been communicated to the Catholics at St. Louis who possessed only a dilapidated church building and a most inadequate residence.

While at St. Thomas Seminary, Fr. DeAndreis taught theology each day and also attended English classes taught to the newcomers by a member of the Seminary faculty. A good deal of DeAndreis' time was spent in translating his sermons into English; he had already translated them into French. Later he began to preach in English and hear confessions. From time to time he devoted his efforts toward a knowledge of the Indian language in view of evangelizing the American natives west of the Mississippi river. He succeeded in translating the "Our Father" into Indian and had hoped to do the same with the catechism. As a matter of fact, he had begun this when, at the end of September 1817, he received the welcome news that Bishop Dubourg and a group of twenty-nine priests and seminarians would arrive shortly to labor for souls in Louisiana.

At the request of Bishop Dubourg, the Bishop of Bardstown, accompanied by DeAndreis and Rosati, departed for St. Louis for the purpose of determining the dispositions of the people toward the new Bishop, and also to prepare for the establishment of the mission. After a hazardous journey of nine days, they arrived on October 11, 1817 at Kaskaskia, Illinois, about sixty miles from St. Louis. As they descended the hills on the east side of the village they forgot all their experiences in the midst of their great joy at seeing a cross surmounting the church steeple and hearing the "Angelus" ring out as the sun set beyond the hills toward the west. Here, for the first time, the travellers had the opportunity of offering Holy Mass since they left Bardstown. The village was almost entirely Catholic and, in years gone by, had been the center of the Jesuit missions among the Indians. It had become a settlement of French Catholics, they had no resident pastor but were visited every Sunday by Fr. Donatien Olivier who said Mass for them. Fr. Olivier resided at Prairie du Rochers, about fifteen miles away.

Finally, on October 15, 1817, the travellers started out on the last leg of their journey and two days later arrived at

St. Louis. Thus ended a long journey that had begun in Rome in October 1815 and came to a happy conclusion in October 1817. At his earliest convenience Bishop Flaget called a meeting of Catholic families to discuss the question of receiving the new bishop and the missionaries. At first, the people were disinclined to accept a bishop and clergy they had never met. After several meetings the people changed their original ideas and consented to contribute both their labor and their money to do whatever was necessary to make the bishop's coming among them a happy one. DeAndreis was overjoyed at the prospects of working with people who manifested such a holy enthusiasm. When Bishop Flaget returned to Bardstown, he requested Fr. DeAndreis to remain at Ste. Genevieve, Missouri, a village south of St. Louis, where he would act as pastor in place of Fr. Henry Pratte who would go to St. Louis to oversee the repair work to the rectory and the church. Here was the first outlet for the ardent zeal of Felix DeAndreis — that zeal that caused him to follow the inspirations of Divine Providence causing him to break all natural bonds of relatives and friends in Italy and the opportunity for material advancement and success in his native country.

Though his stay at Ste. Genevieve only lasted less than three months, the new pastor continued the noble work of Fr. Pratte. On Holy Days he celebrated two Masses and preached; during the week he busied himself instructing the children, hearing confessions, and visiting the sick. This he did until he was finally reunited in St. Louis with Bishop Dubourg who arrived there on January 6, 1818.

With the installation of Bishop Dubourg in the episcopal city, the work of Father DeAndreis increased in enthusiasm and intensity. As Vicar General of the diocese he had to bear, together with Bishop Dubourg, the cares and responsibilities of this far-flung diocese. Very often, for long periods of time, he had to carry on alone while the bishop was away on visitations or fulfilling other duties. As Vicar General and pastor of the pro-Cathedral, he strove to win souls to the Church and draw back those who had fallen from the Church because of lack of priests to guide them.

To meet the priestly needs of the diocese and of the Congregation of the Mission, a seminary was essential. The primary purpose of the Vincentian missionaries who came to the United States was stated in the contract between Bishop Dubourg and the Vincentians — "to promote and carry out as soon as possible, the erection of a seminary, which, aided by the moderate pension required of the seminarists, need not be long delayed." Nor was it delayed. When Fr. Rosati, together with twenty priests and seminarians, left Bardstown in September 1818, they settled in Perryville, Missouri, on a property donated by the people for a parish church and a seminary. Fr. DeAndreis established the seminary and appointed his trusted confrere and colleague, Fr. Rosati, as the rector of St. Mary of the Barrens Seminary, the present seminary of the Vincentian Fathers in the American Province of the Midwest, which in later years gave rise to Kenrick Diocesan Seminary in St. Louis.

On December 3 in that same year, DeAndreis began the first novitiate of the Vincentians in the United States, on the feast of St. Francis Xavier, the special patron of the American Vincentian mission. The novitiate included two priests and a seminarian who had accompanied DeAndreis on the journey from Europe.

Out of these activities on the part of Felix DeAndreis arose the eminent Archdiocese of St. Louis which dominated the history of the Church in Mid-America; he laid the foundation of a seminary system resulting in hundreds of bishops and thousands of priests over the years; and he launched a program of Vincentian activities which has grown from a single mission into a net-work of five American provinces serving from the east to the west coast.

When Felix DeAndreis died on October 15, 1820, less than two years after his arrival in St. Louis, his life fulfilled the phrase "many things in a short time." In his book *Sanctity in America,* Archbishop Amletto Giovanni Cicognani, the Apostolic Delegate to the United States, and later Cardinal, wrote of the Venerable Felix DeAndreis in these words:

"His labors were indefatigable even up to his death . . . his spirit inspires the training of young ecclesiastics who are to continue in the twentieth century the work he began in the early part of the nineteenth. Father DeAndreis was not only a pioneer of Catholic education in the West but also in very truth a zealous apostle of the infant Church in the United States."

The cause of Fr. Felix DeAndreis was introduced before the Sacred Congregation of Rites in June 1918, under the authority of Pope Benedict XV, and the official documents relating to the cause were sent to Rome in 1925.

PRAYER
(Private use only)

Lord Jesus Christ, Savior of the world, who for the conversion of the nations have founded Your Church and established the Holy Order of the Priesthood, and who in Your beneficent Providence were pleased to call to the same Holy Priesthood Your faithful servant Felix DeAndreis, and to endow him with so many apostolic gifts and virtues, deign, we beseech You, O most gracious Lord and Savior, to glorify this same Felix DeAndreis by signs of Your infinite power and goodness manifested in his favor, so that in the judgment of Your Holy Church, he may be found worthy to be enrolled among Your Saints. May this our humble petition be graciously heard by You, O Lord, who in unity with the Father and the Holy Spirit live and reign forever and ever. Amen.

FOR FURTHER READING

Frederick J. Easterly, C.M., *The Foundation of the Vincentians in the United States, 1816-1835* (Washington, D.C.: Catholic University of America, 1938).

CHAPTER 5

VENERABLE DAMIEN DeVEUSTER, SS.CC.
Martyr Missionary to the Lepers of Molokai, in 1889.
(Courtesy of Cause of Mother Marianne of Molokai, Syracuse, N. Y.)

5

A Greater Love

VENERABLE DAMIEN DeVEUSTER, SS.CC. (1840-1889)

Joseph N. Tylenda, S.J.

THE MERCHANTMAN, *R. W. Wood,* slowly slipped from its pier at Bremerhaven and began its tedious five-month journey across half the world to Honolulu in the Sandwich Islands. It was October 23, 1863, and on board its deck were several missionaries who intently watched the city fade into the horizon. Each sensed that this was his last glimpse of Europe. When the vessel made its way towards the English Channel to enter the Atlantic the missionaries, among whom was the young Damien DeVeuster, were agonizingly aware that Belgium, their homeland, was on port side and there they had left forever parents and family, friends and neighbors. Damien foresaw that he would never again see the beloved faces of his parents nor again hear their familiar voices. In embarking from Bremerhaven he left everything behind to be totally free to proclaim Christ.

Once the ship entered the open waters of the Atlantic the missionaries settled down to establish a daily routine for themselves — times for Mass and prayer, recitation of the Office and spiritual reading. Since Damien was still unordained he had to continue his studies towards the priesthood. He put his missionary zeal to an early test in attempting to convert the members of the ship's crew who were Protestant, but this disappointment taught him that missionary activity does not unerringly result in conversions. Their passage through the Atlantic was made slow at times when they had to wait for nature to send favorable winds, but adventure finally met them after they had passed Cape Horn and maneuvered through the Straits. A savage storm caught them in its midst and its monstrous waves beat against the vessel without interruption for ten despairingly long days. Cruel currents forced them southward from their established course and foundering became an imminent possibility. While the storm raged Damien and fellow travelers — now suffering acutely from seasickness — prayed for the ship's safety. The storm finally abated and when they advanced into the open Pacific the ocean lived up to its name.

After twenty-one weeks on board ship, in the early morning of March 19, 1864, the feast of St. Joseph and Damien's baptismal patron, the anxious passengers enthusiastically disembarked at Honolulu and gratefully stepped on dry land. The missionaries immediately advanced to the cathedral and celebrated Mass thanking God for the safe passage. Damien was instantly struck by the luxuriant un-European beauty of the island and discerned that he now had to make this land his new home.

Damien was born on January 3, 1840, in the small village of Tremeloo about six miles from Louvain, Belgium, and was the fourth and last son — the seventh of eight children — born to Francis DeVeuster and Anne Catherine Wouters. At his baptism he was named Joseph, the name suggested by his godfather who proudly bore that name. The DeVeuster family lived on a small farm and its success was the result of the father's labor with that of his children. Joseph's education was restricted to the elementary level and when he arrived at age thirteen his days were spent working on the farm; he spent five happy years helping his father and grew into a sturdy and stocky young man. He found enjoyment in manual labor, perhaps because it gave leisure to his mind to think about God. The farming, carpentry, and whatever else he had learned in Tremeloo all came in handy on the island of Molokai, for little did he realize that his working the farm was really training for his future work with the lepers of Kalawao Settlement.

It is impossible to pinpoint a date when Joseph first began to think of the priesthood. But since three members of his family, two sisters and a brother, had already entered religious life, it would have been natural for him to reflect whether he should likewise follow that path. His brother Auguste, nearly three years older, had but recently entered the Congregation of the Sacred Hearts of Jesus and Mary at Louvain, and was known in religion as Pamphile. To all appearances Pamphile was cut out to spend his time in intellectual pursuits while Joseph was custom-made to manage the farm. With this in mind his father sent him in the spring of 1858, when he was eighteen, to Braine-le-Comte to supplement his education, i.e., become better equipped to manage the business end of the farming enterprise. While at school Joseph attended a mission preached by a Redemptorist in one of the local churches and the desire that he had kept within himself to follow in the footsteps of Pamphile now burst forth with complete conviction. He spoke of his vocation with Pamphile and intimated that he was inclined to follow the Trappist manner of life — a life of penance and manual labor attracted him — but Pamphile, no doubt understanding Joseph more fully than he did himself, talked him out of the Trappists and suggested he enter the same congregation as he had done. He gave further encouragement assuring him that he would have no difficulty in being accepted. If there were to be difficulties it would be with his parents who after having given three children to the Church might want to keep someone at home to work the family farm.

Joseph's parents recognized the genuineness of his call and acquiesced to his desires. On his nineteenth birthday, January 3, 1859, Joseph and his father paid a visit to the monastery of the Sacred Hearts Fathers in Louvain where Pamphile was stationed. The father was under the impression that Joseph was merely going to be interviewed, but when he returned for him Joseph pleaded to remain at the monastery. There was nothing the father could do; he knew this was God's will so he returned home to break the news to his wife.

Since Joseph's education was somewhat deficient when compared to that of the other candidates, he was accepted for the brotherhood rather than the priesthood. Joseph, nevertheless, saw this as the Lord's doing. On February 2, 1859, he was received into the novitiate, given the habit of the congregation and the name Damien. Since Pamphile lived in the same house studying theology in preparation for ordination, Damien, still alive with the desire to be a priest, asked his brother to teach him the rudiments of Latin. Pamphile jumped at the opportunity and proved to be a successful teacher for Damien did so well that the superior reconsidered the former designation and now included Damien among the students for the priesthood. On October 7, 1860, Damien made his profession in the congregation, binding himself by the vows of poverty, chastity, and obedience, and commenced his study of philosophy and theology. In Louvain Pamphile and Damien shared the same room and the brother soon became aware of Damien's exercises of penance. Rather than sleep in bed Damien habitually slept on the hard floor. It was also his custom to rise once a week in the middle of the night and spend the hour from two and three before the Blessed Sacrament. During these years of study Damien developed a strong and virile devotion to St. Francis Xavier, the great missionary of the East; and since the Sacred Hearts Fathers maintained missions throughout the world, he eagerly hoped that one day he would be called to imitate this great saint. In 1863 Pamphile was ordained and his First Mass brought joy and consolation to his family as it did to Damien who, though still in minor orders, knew that his ordination was not far off.

Word spread among the students at Louvain that the missions in the Sandwich Islands, today's Hawaiian Islands, had urgent need of missionaries and Pamphile and Damien discussed their chances of going to such an exotic land. To their joy the newly ordained Pamphile was chosen but shortly after this announcement a typhus epidemic broke out in Louvain and Pamphile volunteered to minister to the sick. He visited them in their houses, comforted them, brought them communion and anointed them until he himself unfortunately fell victim to the dread disease. Damien, practical minded as ever, perceived that his brother would never recover in time to make the scheduled departure date. Knowing that passage had not only been booked but also paid for, and without consulting Pamphile, Damien clandestinely wrote to his major superior in Paris offering himself, even though not yet ordained, to take the place of his sick brother. Whether he expected an affirmative answer or not is unknown, but he was jubilant when such did arrive and he rushed to his brother's bedside, triumphantly waving the letter before him, crying out, "I am going in your place." Damien made a hasty visit to his parents in Tremeloo, then made his way to Bremerhaven and left Europe on October 23, 1863.

Since Damien had not yet completed his priestly training

when he arrived in Honolulu he spent the first several weeks finishing his abbreviated studies. He was ordained on May 21, 1864, and appointed to a parish in the Puna area in the eastern portion of the island of Hawaii, the largest of the archipelago. Fr. Damien's parish, though somewhat large, had but a few hundred Catholics who were widely spread about, and to carry on his priestly work he had to learn the various dialects in use on the island, become accustomed to life in the saddle, and where the horse could not travel he had to learn to rely on his own feet. His association with this parish lasted only eight months. A colleague of his, whose health was not as robust as Damien's, had the neighboring parish — a vast expanse — that embraced the Kohala and Hamakua districts, i.e., about a quarter of the entire island. Since the colleague had not the stamina nor sturdiness to visit so extensive an area the two priests, at Fr. Damien's suggestion, exchanged places, Fr. Damien gladly taking on the more difficult task. This is precisely what he enjoyed, a new challenge for the Lord.

Fr. Damien's new parish had a couple of thousand Catholics who were so scattered that it took him six weeks to complete a tour of his stations. But thanks to God, he enjoyed such vigorous health that his missionary trips were as exhilarating as they were exhausting. When he visited a station he would catechize, baptize, hear confessions, perform marriages and celebrate Mass. Then he would be off to another station. At the larger stop-overs he eventually enrolled the help of young boys in building simple structures that served as chapels for the Catholics of those localities. Fr. Damien spent eight years on the island and most of it was the fatiguing life of an itinerant missionary.

Though Fr. Damien always had his beloved Hawaiians near him, with whom he lived and worked, ate and drank, conversed and prayed, nevertheless, he terribly missed the company and conversation of fellow priests. They were not that numerous on the island and he had to wait three or four months before he could chat with any one of them. In his loneliness he requested from his superiors a companion, not only to help him in caring for the growing number of Catholics in the Kohala-Hamakua districts, but also to lessen the painful isolation that he so intensely felt in his soul. He even suggested that this companion be his brother but, unfortunately, Pamphile was involved in educating the younger members of the congregation in Louvain. In 1868 a colleague finally arrived and Fr. Damien gave him the Hamakua district, keeping Kohala for himself.

Several years prior to Fr. Damien's arrival leprosy had begun to spread rapidly through the islands and by the time of his coming it had achieved monstrous proportions. The government acknowledged that something radical had to be done to prevent its further advancement, and in 1865 it decreed the forcible transportation and segregation of those afflicted to the newly established Kalawao Settlement. The settlement was located on the northern side of the island of Molokai, on a point that jutted into the calm blue water of the Pacific Ocean. It was two and a half miles deep and about three miles wide at its rear where steep, almost perpendicular, cliffs rose 4000 feet forming a natural barrier to insure the isolation of the victims. Its scenery was the most beautiful of the islands and enjoyed the choicest climate and had the most fertile soil. It was precisely the excellence of the land that led the government to choose this location for the settlement since it hoped the inhabitants would engage in farming and be self-sufficient. But, unfortunately, the government forgot that as the disease progresses the victims first lose their fingers then their hands, and how could such as these till the soil. Because of the dreaded isolation on the settlement and the fact that there was no known cure many families refused to inform on their afflicted relatives. Instead they tried to care for them at home and when the case became too advanced they hid them in caves or forests — any place where they thought they could live without being detected. Fr. Damien had come into contact with many such cases during his nine years in Hawaii; he well knew the suffering they endured and witnessed, much to his distress, how the body disintegrates under the malevolent power of the disease.

In the spring of 1873, Bishop Louis Maigret invited his clergy to attend the blessing of a new church in Wailuku on the island of Maui giving his priests a chance to visit with one another and talk about their common work. In speaking to his assembled priests after the ceremonies, the bishop commented on the deplorable state of the leprosy victims in the Kalawao Settlement, of whom the Catholics formed a minority. Because priests rarely visited the island, perhaps once a year and only for a few weeks, the Catholics were habitually without the ministrations and consolation of the Church. The lepers needed a priest but the bishop felt that he could not order anyone to undertake such a hazardous mission. If someone were to volunteer to visit the island at least periodically this would definitely relieve the isolation of the Catholics. In response to the bishop's request four priests generously volunteered to serve the lepers on a rotational basis, each staying for a period of several weeks. The bishop gratefully accepted the plan and the first of the four to go was the thirty-three year old Fr. Damien.

That very day a steamer was in the harbor ready to leave for Molokai with fifty lepers aboard. Fr. Damien and his bishop boarded the vessel and headed for the colony. The date of his arrival among the lepers was May 10, 1873, a memorable date, for ever afterwards the names of Damien and Molokai have become inseparable. Just a few weeks before his departure for Molokai, and unknown to him, the secular press in Honolulu issued a humanitarian appeal for someone to go to the settlement. It read in part: "If a noble Christian priest, preacher or sister should be inspired to go and sacrifice a life to console these poor wretches, that should be a loyal soul to shine forever on a throne reared by human love." Several days after Damien's arrival the same paper noted, "We care not what this man's theology be, he is surely a Christian hero." Fr. Damien, however, was of a different mind than the author of the editorial. He did not go to Molokai out of human love, he went because he was filled to overflowing with a greater love, with a divine love for his poor afflicted brethren.

When Fr. Damien set foot on the settlement the sight before him was unexpected. The faces he saw were disfigured by running ulcerated sores; hands were without fingers and feet without toes. Those greeting him were half-naked and the meager clothing they wore were rags, dirty and foul smelling. About him he saw no houses but only crumbling thatched huts that served as miserable shelters for the lepers. Was it to this that he had come? Nevertheless, because of the great love he carried within him he could not turn his back on these wretched humans. He himself was without a house but he found a pandanus tree near the church of St. Philomena, erected by a predecessor, and there he spent his nights until he built a shack that was to become his residence.

His first tour of the settlement was depressing. He observed that the food supply was inadequate for the six hundred lepers and their attempts at farming were unsuccessful. The cattle was thin and the chickens scrawny. The water supply was located at such a distance from the huts that most were physically unable to carry water to their hovels and hence they rarely washed and had to live in huts that were defiled and polluted. He also sadly perceived that a great number were addicted to an intoxicating drink brewed from the root of a plant that grew on the island; there was much stealing — the less ill took advantage of the seriously ill — and even immorality. He came to realize that even though he had come to care for the spiritual needs of the two hundred Catholics in the settlement he could not restrict his ministry to them alone but would have to use all his talents in trying to make the lepers' last months on earth more bearable and somewhat humane.

Within two weeks after his arrival Fr. Damien sent word to his superior in Honolulu expressing his willingness to relinquish his parish in Kohala and remain permanently on Molokai. Later he wrote to Pamphile about his first days among the lepers. He humbly admitted that in the beginning there was much repugnance in working with them and that he had to close his nostrils while hearing confessions since their decaying bodies gave off such noisome odors. But he was becoming used to it and began to smoke a pipe to counteract the foul smells that continually surrounded him.

Fr. Damien had much work to do and to put his plans into motion he made a trip to Honolulu to seek supplies for the colony: more food for his people, lumber and tools for construction, and pipes to better the sanitation system. His early training in Tremeloo on the family farm proved a great asset to him. With the lumber he and the "healthy" lepers began to transform the miserable wind-swept huts into clean habitable cottages that successfully protected them from the strong gusts and driving rain. He not only directed the construction but also carried the heavy lumber to the sites where it was needed and instructed his helpers in the basic elements of carpentry. Years later visitors to Molokai would see a neat white village and not the wretched scene that was his when he first arrived. With the pipes he introduced the water supply into the center of the settlement where everyone could get water for all their needs. He also aided in planting vegetables; but the farm, unfortunately, was never large enough to support the colony since the lepers, in their maimed condition, were unable to care for it properly. While involved in building the colony he also learned how to clean and bandage sores, apply ointments and prescribe pills. To the lepers of Molokai Fr. Damien was priest and doctor, carpenter and plumber, but above all he was the tangible evidence of God's love among them.

It was by ministering to their diseased bodies that Fr. Damien was able to touch their souls. Within two months of his coming he had two-thirds of the six hundred inhabitants under his spiritual care; about half of these were undergoing instruction prior to baptism. Among his Catholic faithful he formed a group of altar boys and a choir — at times it was necessary to have two individuals sitting at the organ just to have enough fingers to play the required notes — and started a group which would spend time in adoration of the Blessed Sacrament. Death was a common experience on the island and rather than leaving the bodies dumped on the edge of the settlement as had been the custom, Fr. Damien marked off a cemetery and enclosed it with a white picket fence. At the end of his first eighteen months he had celebrated two hundred funerals. Since death was ever present among them he inaugurated a coffin society whose object was to collect money ($2.00) to buy rough lumber to build a coffin for the poor, and he introduced a funeral society which participated at the funeral Mass and accompanied the body, together with musical band, to the cemetery. During his sixteen years on Molokai he buried more than 1600 lepers.

Fr. Damien's concern was not limited to the leper colony alone. Beyond the precipitous wall of rock that formed the southern boundary isolating the lepers was the rest of Molokai whose Catholics were likewise without a priest. Periodically he made the treacherous climb and hazardous descent of these cliffs to minister to their needs. He longed for a priest-companion but those who had come were not congenial. They themselves had been diseased, and in temperament were too unlike Fr. Damien so that in the end they proved to be incompatible. They may have lessened his labors, but they never lessened the anxiety within him. Eventually an American layman came to help and he spent the rest of his life continuing Fr. Damien's work.

Fr. Damien's presence and labors on Molokai were greatly appreciated by the Hawaiian royal family. A single individual burning with a greater love succeeded where a government had failed! In recognition of his self-sacrifice to the afflicted lepers of the settlement Princess Liliuokolani personally went to Molokai (September, 1881) to visit with and to thank him in the name of the nation. When she returned to her palace in Honolulu, she made him Knight Commander of the Royal Order of Kalakaua. The honor meant absolutely nothing to Fr. Damien, but it did show that he meant much to the Hawaiians. The newspapers took up his praises, and his success in the Kalawao Settlement was broadcast throughout the world.

It was in 1881 that Damien first began to feel pain in his feet, but he was not sure that he had contracted leprosy. He knew there was always the possibility, since he was negligent in taking the ordinary measures to prevent contagion. He thought nothing of touching the lepers or handling the tools they had just used. There was always the chance of infection while cleaning open sores or in breathing in the foul air while hearing confessions. By 1885 the telltale signs began to appear on his face, sores and pustules that refused to heal. The disease now began to take control of his body. In July, 1886, he went to Honolulu to learn about a new Japanese treatment for leprosy named after a certain Dr. Goto. When he returned to the settlement he requested of the Board of Health the supplies necessary to initiate the Goto treatment at Kalawao. He managed to build a workable treatment center, and admitted that after three months of treatment he did feel better. But it was not a lasting cure. With Fr. Damien's visit to Honolulu it became public knowledge that he was a leper. The newspapers carried this news as avidly as they had when he received royal honors. Without prior knowledge of Fr. Damien's condition, his brother and mother, now eighty-three years old, in Belgium read the shocking and greatly exaggerated account in their newspaper; and so distressed did his mother become that she died soon afterwards, clutching her son's photo close to her heart.

Throughout his first thirteen years at the settlement, Fr. Damien longed for a kindred soul, and is known to have said, "Being deprived of the companionship of my colleagues of our dear Congregation is more painful to bear than leprosy." Towards the end of July 1886, the long-desired colleague arrived. Ira Barnes Dutton, an American Civil War veteran on the side of the North, learned about Fr. Damien and his work while visiting New Orleans and he determined this was how he could "help my neighbors and fill out a penance which I feel necessary." Without invitation or previous announcement the American suddenly appeared on the Kalawao shore on July 29. He was forty-three years old, three years younger than Fr. Damien, and introduced himself as Joseph, the name he chose when he was converted to Catholicism. Fr. Damien gladly accepted him as a fellow worker and immediately took to him. They labored marvelously together and Joseph, now dubbed "Brother Joseph" became Fr. Damien's closest and most cherished associate; and he continued his labors among the lepers of Molokai for forty-three years after his mentor's death.

In October, 1888, Fr. Damien began to feel great weakness and discerned that the disease was in its later stages. But despite his grave illness, when the three Franciscan Sisters of Syracuse, N.Y., landed (November, 1888) at Kalawao, their hospital outside Honolulu having closed, Fr. Damien made certain he would be at the shore to greet them. The superior of the group was the selfless Mother Marianne Cope, who spent the next thirty years of her life among the lepers.

On March 19, 1889, Fr. Damien celebrated the silver anniversary of his arrival at Honolulu; but a few days later, it was the 23rd, he was confined to his bed and began to prepare himself for death. Throughout this final illness he never lost his natural cheerfulness and told those who cared for him, "The good Lord is calling me to celebrate Easter with Him." And thus it would be. His lepers came to see him, have a final word with him and hear a last exhortation from their holy priest. On Monday of Holy Week, April 15, 1889, the leper priest died with a smile on his lips, confident that the work he had begun would continue through the ministry of Brother Joseph and Mother Marianne.

The sisters prepared the body for burial and it was taken to St. Philomena's church where the lepers silently approached to have a final glimpse of the holy man who had lived as one of them, and had so given of himself because of the greater love he carried within his heart. On Tuesday the funeral Mass was celebrated and he was buried in the cemetery among his lepers and according to his instructions under the same pandanus tree that gave him shelter when he first came to Kalawao sixteen years before.

Fr. Damien was an international figure during his life and equally so in death. In 1936 the Belgian government requested that his remains be brought back to Belgium and there they were reburied at Louvain. In 1959, when Hawaii achieved statehood, the new state chose to place a statue of Fr. Damien in Statuary Hall of the U.S. Capitol as one worthy of everlasting memory among Hawaiians.

The diocesan process leading to beatification began in Malines, Belgium, in 1938. The cause was introduced in Rome in May, 1955; and in July 1977, it was declared that Fr. Damien had practiced virtue to an heroic degree and thus is entitled to be called Venerable. For further information concerning the cause, write: The Director, Fr. Damien's Cause, Box 111, Fairhaven, Massachusetts. 02719.

PRAYER
(Private use only)
O good Jesus, who while on earth, by word and example, so deeply instilled in the hearts of Your children

Your commandment to love one another, vouchsafe, we beseech You, to glorify Your servant Damien, and with him Christian charity itself. May we, in Your divine dispensation, soon see him honored as blessed, who for love of You, gave his life for the most wretched of his brothers. Grant us, therefore, the favor we ask through his intercession. Amen.

FOR FURTHER READING

Gavan Daws, *Holy Man: Father Damien of Molokai* (New York: Harper & Row, 1973); John Farrow, *Damien the Leper* (New York: Sheed & Ward, 1937).

CHAPTER 6

SERVANTS OF GOD (left to right): Brother Anthony de Badajoz, Father Michael de Añon, Father Pedro de Corpa, Father Blase de Rodriguez, Father Francis de Beráscola, the Five Franciscan Missionary Martyrs of Georgia, as depicted by a modern artist.

6

The Martyrs of Georgia

FATHER PEDRO DE CORPA, O.F.M., and His Four Companions (+1597)

Alexander Wyse, O.F.M.

THE STATE OF GEORGIA is commonly thought of as the continuation of the English colony founded by James Oglethorpe in 1732. But it would be a perverse lapse of memory to forget that for more than 150 years before Oglethorpe appeared on the scene, there had been an earlier chapter in the history of the region.

Spain had been the dominant force then, with her influence extending far to the north and to the south. Along with the Florida peninsula, as well as parts of present-day South Carolina and Alabama, what we now call Georgia formed an outpost of the Spanish empire. The oldest city in the United

States is St. Augustine, in northern Florida, founded on September 8, 1565, as the center of this extensive colony.

Pressing reasons of a political nature did indeed motivate Spain in that venture; yet another, a spiritual, consideration was likewise in view. "As we have in mind the good of the salvation of those (Indian) souls," wrote King Philip II in his patent, "we have decided to order that religious be sent to instruct the said Indians . . . that by association and conversation with them, (the Indians) might more easily be taught our Holy Catholic Faith and be brought to good practices and customs and perfect behavior."

Within a year of the establishing of St. Augustine, three missionaries of the still young Society of Jesus arrived, of whom one was almost immediately slain by the natives. News of this martyrdom reaching Europe occasioned a burst of extraordinary apostolic zeal among the sons of Ignatius, and shortly another group, considerably larger, came to assist the first one. Ecstatic with the vastness of the mission field before them, the Jesuits began to push ever farther northward, eventually reaching present-day Virginia. There, however, in early February, 1571, in a bloody massacre at Axacan (near Fredericksburg) eight of them were tortured and killed.

It was then that a request was made for Franciscan friars to undertake the work of evangelization. Arriving in 1573, for about two decades the friars of St. Francis confined their efforts largely to the immediate environs of the garrison towns. Then in 1595 a dynamic octogenarian, Fr. Francisco Marrón, who had had missionary experience in Peru, Guatemala and Mexico, came with a second group of twelve apostles.

From headquarters at Nombre de Dios, as the mission at St. Augustine was called, in twenty years the friars founded eight missions stretching to the north, first among the Timucuas (inhabitants of the northeastern area of our State of Florida) and then among the Guales (in present-day coastal

Georgia). So flourishing was this missionary enterprise that shortly it was organized into a *custodia* (vice-province), which in 1612 was to become the Province of Santa Elena.

The Guales lived under a sort of confederation uniting their settlements in a miniature empire centered around the Golden Isles. The head of the tribe, called the *mico,* was an overlord who not only enjoyed prestige and external signs of respect, but also received periodic tribute — in the form of pearls and ornamental shells — from the subject villages. In this little world, he clearly was a personage of importance, whose favor would be vital to the spread of the Gospel, just as his example was a telling factor in setting the tone of the society over which he presided. The office of mico was transmitted by heredity — not pure primogeniture, but a relationship of blood. Brothers or nephews or cousins might receive the title as readily as the sons of the deceased mico.

One of the surprising features of Guale society was that it was basically matrilineal — their kinship, their blood ties, were traced from a common ancestress through the female line. Women could, and sometimes did, occupy even the office of mico. Yet, despite that strong feminist tradition, generally women were held in low esteem. Nothing more clearly demonstrated this cultural disparity than did the institution of polygamy, accepted without question. Indeed, monogamy was quite the exception among the Guales, there being no moral or social stigma in a man's taking a second or even a third wife. By thus sanctioning the assumption that woman is little more than the means of man's carnal satisfaction or (at best) the breeding machine producing warriors for defense of the tribe, not only did polygamy contribute to the degradation of half the population, but, like a hidden cancer destroying the roots of family life, it vitiated every promise of genuine human development.

The friars were therefore tireless in their efforts to teach the Indians the inherent beauty and necessity of monogamy.

Such natives as were disposed to embrace Christianity were obligated, as a condition of Baptism, to accept by an explicit profession this teaching of the Master. It was not an easy promise to make — as the Jews of old had told the Savior Himself, and as human experience in every century confirms. But it remains an exigency of Christian regeneration that the man and woman joined in marriage are permanently and inseparably two in one flesh. In the mission villages established to receive these converts every provision was made for a gradual strengthening in their Christian profession, not least for their practice of the virtues of family life.

At Tupiqui on the mainland, at Mission Santa Clara, was the veteran Fr. Blas de Rodríguez, who had opened up the work among these people in 1587. By reason of his fatherly bearing, Fr. Blas was held in high esteem by all, even the natives. From Tupiqui he also had authority and jurisdiction over the other mission stations among the Guales. In his years among these Indians he had acquired a sensitive understanding of their mentality and psychology, becoming an authority on their customs and language. Also on the mainland, at Mission Nuestra Señora de Guadalupe, near the village of Tolomato, there was another veteran of long experience in the Florida-Georgia region, Fr. Pedro de Corpa. He had spent almost ten years among the Guales, whose language he had mastered and customs and mentality he understood profoundly.

A third friar in this territory since 1587 was the lay Brother Antonio de Badajoz. Although not instructed in philosophy and theology as the priests, and already along in years, he was graced with a facility in the Guale language and endowed with a shining candor and simplicity of soul. Stationed at the mission on Guale Island, off the coast almost opposite Mission Santa Clara de Tupiqui, as companion to the priest in charge, the good lay brother helped with the material aspects of the mission which was being built from the ground up, and also acted as interpreter for the padre in his instruction of the neophytes and the baptized. Fr. Miguel de Añon was in charge of this Mission, Santa Catalina de Guale. Having come to the New World less than two years before, he possessed an affability that more than compensated for his as yet halting command of the difficult native dialect. Born of a prominent family, he was what the Spaniards call *muy simpático*. His mere presence and his modulated voice breathed a charm that delighted both his fellow religious and the savages. He was a young man, recently ordained, when he arrived in Guale-land in 1595.

At Mission Santo Domingo de Asao (on present-day St. Simon's Island) was another fascinating friar who had arrived with Añon: Fr. Francisco de Beráscola. Raised in affluence (his father was an official of his native Basque town), he had volunteered for the Florida mission in the full vigor of his twenty-nine years, expecting — and meeting — physical hardships for the spread of the Gospel. In Florida but a short time, he was asked to accompany an exploratory mission to the heart of Tama territory (the western part of modern Georgia). His towering stature and his physical strength (which among the friars earned him the playful nickname of "the giant from Cantabria") caused admiration in the natives. He was especially close to the young blades, the youths in their teens and early twenties, whom he delighted by joining in their native sport, a strenuous game much like English rugby. On Asao Island he was alone, but his imposing presence and ready camaraderie with the young people won him a ready acceptance as the spiritual guide of the village.

From time to time these friars came together for a fraternal gathering. Such a get-together was an occasion to discuss the pastoral problems they were facing in their separate missions. Overshadowing all others was the serious scandal which had arisen in the village of Tolomato, where Fr. Pedro had had to make a hard decision. Juanillo — baptized and integrated into the Christian community — had repudiated his marriage vows by taking a second woman to live in his hut. The matter was of more than ordinary import, for Juanillo was the grown son of the mico. The evil example of the heir apparent to the headship of the tribe now seemed like a threatening conflagration, advancing to destroy the fledgling community of believers, slowly being weaned from the acceptance of polygamy.

In private conversation Fr. Pedro had asked Juanillo to recall the solemn promises made at baptism to put on Christ and in all things to live according to His law. The priest's exhortations, however, had no positive result: the back-slider continued to flout the law of Christian marriage. Fr. Pedro consulted the experience of Fr. Blas, the superior of all the area missionaries, who, too, endeavored to bring the recalcitrant young brave to a sense of duty as a Christian and prospective leader of his people. Still Juanillo refused to respect the demands of Christian marriage. As co-administrator of the Christian community, Fr. Pedro had no recourse but publicly to denounce the scandal and to proclaim that Juanillo's aspiration to his father's position would not be honored in the scandalized community.

In an act tantamount to apostasy, Juanillo withdrew from the village, joining the pagans, who having determined not to enter the Church, had continued to live outside the missions. Nurturing his dark desire for revenge, he laid plans to destroy the new religion intolerant of the old order; and in this he found willing accomplices among the resolute disbelievers. Some dissatisfied Christians, including chiefs of several neighboring villages, joined them and the unbaptized natives.

On the night of September 12, 1597, these warriors sneaked into Tolomato. At the first sign of daylight, after Fr. Pedro had opened the church and begun his customary preparation for Mass, they burst into the church. Hate drove them to a fury, as they fell on the kneeling friar and ruthlessly bashed in his head with a tomahawk. A final brief prayer came to the lips of the horribly wounded missionary, and then, without the least sign of resistance, Fr. Pedro de Corpa gave up his life.

As his blood slowly seeped into the sandy soil, the murderers, as if to dramatize the real purpose for which they had perpetrated the hideous deed, rounded up women from the village and, in the presence of the martyred priest, gave themselves over to an orgy of immoralities. The body was further desecrated by the now insane mob. Hacking and chopping off the battered head, they stuck it on a pole and, to the accompaniment of lewd shouts and ribald profanities, carried it to the town landing, where travelers paddling through the strait could see it exposed in contempt and derision. The headless torso, a duo of the sacrilegious rebels carried into the woods, burying it so successfully that it was never more discovered. The mob completed its sacrilege by burning the church and destroying the sacred images.

As the next object of their rage the murderers selected the superior of the Franciscans, Fr. Blas, who too had vainly tried to recall Juanillo from his lapse into polygamy. Crossing the sound that separates Sapelo Island from the mainland, they headed north for Mission Santa Clara. Juanillo and his warriors reached the mission in the morning just as the priest was about to begin offering Mass. Fr. Blas's natural dignity, his fatherlike bearing, at first disconcerted the barbarians, winning for him a blessed concession. He requested permission — which they agreed to grant — to say Mass, after which, he promised, he would not impede them from carrying out their bloody intent. With what fervor we can imagine, to the loud laments of some pious women converts the priest for the last time in his life renewed the sacrifice of Calvary with which, in a short time, he was to associate himself in victimhood.

"My sons," the friar said at the end of the Mass in a sort of prolonged meditation, "for me it is not difficult to die.

Even if you should not cause it, the death of this body is inevitable. We have to be ready at all times, for we, all of us, have to die some day. But what does pain me," he continued, looking around and recognizing in the crowd some of the Indians he himself had instructed and baptized, "is that the Evil One has persuaded you to do this offensive thing against your God and Creator." His voice trembling, he went on: "It is a further source of deep grief to me that you are unmindful of what we missionaries have done for you in teaching you the way to eternal life and happiness. It is not too late, however, my children," he concluded in that gentle voice for which he was famous; "God in His mercy will pardon you if you repent and give up your evil design."

Far from a plea to be spared the ordeal awaiting him, Fr. Blas's words were rather an invitation to the insensate Guales to return to reason — and to grace. Incited by Juanillo, however, they soon allowed their fury to blaze anew. Ransacking the priest's house for anything they thought of value, and in the church destroying whatever they could lay their hands on, the Indians held him bound in ropes for two days — for the friar a grace-filled opportunity to prepare for meetnig his Lord. Finally, on September 16, the torturers crushed his head with a tomahawk. The body was left exposed to be devoured by the vultures and the beasts of the forest. When after several days no bird of prey or animal had touched it, a faithful Christian secretly took it and buried it in the woods.

While the atrocities were being carried out at Tolomato and Santa Clara, Juanillo sent a messenger across the bay to Mission Santa Catalina, ordering the chief to kill the two missionaries who served that island mission. To make sure the order had been carried out, the rabble now took to their canoes and crossed eastward. It was the 17th of September, the feast kept by Franciscans in memory of the Imprinting of the Wounds of Christ on St. Francis' body.

The local chief had refused to carry out Juanillos' command. Instead, confiding to Bro. Antonio what was afoot, he pressed him to escape with Fr. Miguel — in a canoe which he, the chief, would provide — to San Pedro Island, where all the Indians were Christian and whose chief had refused to join in the revolt. In his ingenuousness disbelieving the story, Bro. Antonio remained at his post. When on the 17th the bloodthirsty band did appear, the chief knew the two friars' doom was sealed.

With Bro. Antonio faithfully assisting him to the end, Fr. Miguel celebrated the Mass of the feast, that feast of Christ's Wounds shared by Francis of Assisi. Poignant were the words he read: "May I never boast of anything but the cross of our Lord Jesus Christ! Through it the world has been crucified to me and I to the world." Strength for their coming torture, and consolation, they found in the words of the Gospel: "Whoever wishes to be My follower must deny his very self, take up his cross each day, and follow in My steps. Whoever would save his life will lose it, and whoever loses his life for My sake will save it." Mass over, the two friars spent hours in devout recollection and preparation for death. Renewing their Franciscan vows, they voluntarily accepted their impending sacrifice, offering their lives for the conversion of the people they had come to serve and save.

The Indians descended on the chapel, and Bro. Antonio was dispatched first, and then Fr. Miguel, both with blows from the tomahawk. The chapel, the house, the mission compound still under construction, were ransacked for anything that seemed worth robbing. The bodies were, in turn, desecrated and profaned before being buried finally by some Christians at the base of the large cross which Fr. Miguel — the zealous young priest starting out in his first mission — a short time before had erected as the sign of salvation and the promise of eternal life. "May I never boast of anything but the cross. . . ."

The Guales now moved on to Mission Santo Diego de Ospo (Jekyl Island); there they found another friar, Fr.

Francisco de Avila. Though they treated him with utmost cruelty, they did not kill him, but wounded him and took him captive — an abominable nine-months torture of unspeakable privations and humiliations. Deprived of the grace of witnessing by death to his faith, he is not numbered among the martyrs of Georgia, as are the four already mentioned and one other: Fr. Francisco de Beráscola.

The cacique of Asao was one of those who had joined Juanillo in the savage rampage. He knew that the missionary at Mission Santo Domingo was not at home, that he had gone to St. Augustine to get some needful things for his charges. Daily reports from the north kept reaching the island: this missionary had been slain, and that; this mission was in ruins, and that. The news had a demoralizing effect on the community still learning the meaning of Christian fortitude. In view of the destruction of so many missions and the slaughter of the missionaries, the Mission Santo Domingo Indians feared to resist Juanillo and their own cacique: they weakly were intimidated into backing the rebellion, even though to do so meant betraying their cherished friend and spiritual father, Fr. Francisco de Beráscola.

Some days later — perhaps it was the 18th — Fr. Francisco returned from his errand to the south, unaware of what had been happening. Simulating the affection they had shown him for now well over a year, ten young men came out to greet him as his boat pulled up at the landing, and, Judas-like, they embraced him. Unsuspectingly he set himself to share with them the news of his successful trip to the villa of St. Augustine, when they suddenly abandoned their pretense. Lashing him to a tree, they beat him mercilessly; after which, they imprisoned him in their own cruel form of a jail — a cage used for trapping animals. After three days of starvation and constant beatings, they brought him before the cacique, who condemned him to be burned to death. When the fire was ready, a violent rainstorm extinguished the blaze. Not impressed with what less superstitious people might well have viewed as divine intervention, the Indians set upon the "giant from Cantabria" with an intense fury. Perhaps they were giving vent to a latent envy of his physical power and strength, as with an axe they hacked his strong and athletic young body. Soon he was dead, the fifth friar to give his life in the matter of days.

Dying in obscure Indian villages on the Georgia coast, in the last years of the sixteenth century, these men are not persons whose story is widely known. In that sense they perhaps typify the thousands of no-longer remembered missionaries who came to the New World from France, Portugal, Spain — from Spain especially — to spend themselves in bringing Christ's teachings to the nations of this hemisphere. What does distinguish them, however, from the rest of that army of anonymous apostles is that it was their lot, by their death, to bear heroic witness to the doctrine they had preached in life. In this sense they stand out, and their courage deserves to be recognized and their names to be honored.

They stand out also by reason of the motive which brought about their deaths. They were slain out of a hatred for and violent rejection of Christ's teaching on the sacredness of marriage. Their death was therefore patently a profession, in the fullest possible measure, of the law proclaimed by the Master for His followers. They had come to teach it in His name, and their teaching they sealed with their blood.

The five martyrs of Georgia are glorious witnesses to this Christian dogma on marriage. In our own day, in our tortured society, when — to our woe — marriage, even Christian marriage, is so roundly attacked and its sanctity flouted, their example is a timely lesson and a blessed boon. They died for the truth that Christian marriage, the sign of Christ's unbreakable union with humanity, and the symbol of His love for His Church, is sacred and is beautiful by reason of the lifelong fidelity and love and unity which must distinguish it.

"Husbands should love their wives," the Holy Spirit has

said through Paul the Apostle, "just as Christ loved the Church and sacrificed Himself to make her holy. . . . A man must leave his father and mother and be joined to his wife, and the two will become one body."

The Vice Postulator for the Cause of the Georgia Martyrs is Fr. Alexander Wyse, O.F.M., P.O. Box 34440, Washington, D.C. 20034.

PRAYER
(Private use only)

O Lord Jesus Christ, reward the apostolic zeal of Fathers Peter de Corpa, Blase de Rodríguez, Michael de Añon, Francis de Beráscola, and Brother Anthony de Badajoz, who labored for the spiritual well-being of the Indians in Georgia and gave their lives in defense of the Christian faith. Through their merits and intercession, grant the favor I humbly ask of You, so that for the glory of Your Name, they may be raised to the honors of the altar. Amen.

FOR FURTHER READING

John Tate Lanning, *The Spanish Missions of Georgia* (Chapel Hill: University of North Carolina Press, 1935); Luís Gerónimo de Oré, O.F.M., *The Martyrs of Florida, 1513-1616,* translated with Biographical Introduction and Notes by Maynard Geiger, O.F.M., *Franciscan Studies,* No. 18 (New York: Joseph F. Wagner, Inc., 1936); Maynard Geiger, O.F.M., *The Franciscan Conquest of Florida, 1573-1618* (Washington, D.C.: Catholic University of America, 1937); Marion A. Habig, O.F.M., *Heroes of the Cross: An American Martyrology,* 3rd edn. (Paterson, N. J.: St. Anthony Guild Press, 1947).

CHAPTER 7

SERVANT OF GOD FATHER EUSEBIO FRANCISCO KINO, S.J.
The Padre on Horseback, a pencil sketch by Frances O'Brien.
(Courtesy of the American Heritage Center, Tucson, Arizona.)

7

Ever Northward the Blackrobe

FATHER EUSEBIO FRANCISCO KINO, S.J. (1645-1711)

Ernest J. Burrus, S.J.

FEW MISSIONARIES in the annals of the Church have been blessed with so many and varied talents, human and divine, as Fr. Kino. He was an explorer of distant lands, a builder of churches and homes for his Indian charges, a founder of towns and flourishing cities, a farmer who introduced unknown grains and vegetables, a cattleman who brought in horses, mules, cattle, sheep and goats into a vast region, a priest of God who preached Christ's word and made known his person. He was no less a doer of deeds than a recorder of them through his letters and books, and an illustrator of them through his sketches and maps.

With such ability and his untiring efforts, is it any wonder that he extended the rim of Christendom several hundred miles to the north and northwest from his mission center in northern Mexico? That he aided in the establishment of an entire chain of missions in Lower California, springboard for the settlement of Upper California?

But all his genius and zeal would have gone for nought had he not possessed a deep insight into the souls and character of his humble but enigmatic native charges. From the seemingly primitive Guaycuros in southern Lower California to the far more sophisticated Pima, Papago, Opata and Yuma in northern Sonora and southern Arizona, Kino succeeded in sounding a responsive chord in every heart and in winning a sympathy and co-operation almost unique in missionary annals. Animated with a spirit worthy of St. Francis Xavier, his patron, Kino devoted three times as many years to extending God's kingdom as the Apostle of the Orient. Northern Mexico and southwestern United States became the scene of his successful endeavors for thirty years: from 1681, the year of his arrival in Mexico, until his death in 1711.

Several countries have vied in claiming him. Italy was his birthplace, Austria was his early intellectual home. Germany matured his mental and spiritual formation. Spain enlisted his missionary zeal. Mexico was the theater for thirty years of his amazing expeditions and enduring accomplishments. Southern Arizona in the present United States saw him explore for twenty years, gather its natives into communities, build their missions, and establish the settlements to become our modern towns and cities. Need we wonder, then, that a grateful State would choose Fr. Kino as one of its two representatives in the National Statuary Hall?

Keeping before us this vision of Kino's greatness and accomplishments, let us learn more about the life and deeds back of them.

He was baptized in Segno (near Trent) in northern Italy, his birthplace, on August 10, 1645, presumably the same day he was born. He was christened Eusebio after his grand-father. The spelling of his family name (Chino) was changed to "Kino" when he went to Spain; this was done to pre-serve the pronunciation of the Italian original. Eusebio re-ceived his elementary education in Segno and later in nearby Trent, where he studied at the Jesuit College. The fidelity of his forefathers to the emperor (conferring nobility on the Chinos) and the boy's excellent scholastic record at the Tridentine college won him a scholarship at the Jesuit school in Hall, near Innsbruck, Austria.

While pursuing his humanistic studies there, an event oc-curred which was to set the course of his entire life. Eusebio fell desperately ill — presumably, of pneumonia, all too fre-quently fatal at the time. The best physicians despaired; but not Eusebio. He promised the Lord that, if he recovered, he would enter the Society of Jesus and volunteer for the foreign missions in order to spend his life evangelizing those who had never heard of the Savior. As an earnest of his sacred pledge, he added "Francesco" to his name, in honor of St. Francis Xavier, Jesuit missionary to the Orient.

On graduating from Hall in 1665, he kept the first part of his promise by entering the Order, at Landsberg, Bavaria, Germany. Nor did he forget the second part of his vow: to volunteer for the foreign missions. He said that he was indif-ferent as to which he would be sent; however, he could not help but prefer those of China, where a close relative of his had worked most successfully. Eusebio wrote to the Jesuit Generals at least six times, reminding them of the solemn promise he had once made. A seventh letter acknowledged with gratitude the permission he had pleaded for during more than fifteen years.

But we have run ahead of our account. The two years of novitiate at Landsberg were followed by three of philosophy and science at Ingolstadt. Then, for three more years (1670-1673), he was "Master" Eusebio, as he taught literature at his Alma Mater in Hall, Austria.

He returned to Ingolstadt for four years of theology leading to the priesthood. But young Kino had shown such exceptional talent in his studies that he was allowed two radical changes in his course. First, he was assigned to teach mathematics and science to his fellow Jesuits at the University of Ingolstadt; and, then, before completing theology, he was sent to the University of Freiburg for more advanced studies in his special fields. Some thirty years later, he recorded in his diary how "tempting" was the offer, made by the Duke of Bavaria, of a full professorship in the University of Ingolstadt, and he thanked God for the grace of preferring to teach the Indians their catechism over lecturing to university students.

The long-awaited day of ordination arrived. Bishop Wilhelm Benz conferred the priesthood on him in Eichstätt, Bavaria, on June 12, 1677. Kino was nearly thirty-three; but his long course of training was not yet at an end. In Oettingen, Bavaria, a final year of formation awaited the young priest so impatient to be on his way to distant missions. Before Kino could devote full time to the last phase of his training, he was informed by the Jesuit General that he had been accepted for the foreign missions. The day was unforgettable: March 30, 1678.

Would it be in the east or in the west that Kino would devote his life as a missionary? His heart was set on the east, the scene of the apostolic work of his patron, Francis Xavier. It was for the east that he had studied mathematics and cartography to be used at the Chinese imperial court. But his fellow Tyrolese, Anton Kerschpamer, also preferred the Orient, and Kino was not one to be selfish even in heroism. They agreed to cast lots — Kerschpamer drew the coveted Philippines, gateway to the Far East; Kino drew Mexico; and thus the course of their lives was set by a bit of pious gambling.

He revisited his native Segno en route to Genoa. It was

farewell forever to his mother and two sisters; his father had died before his ordination.

Bad weather and poor seamanship conspired to delay his ship from reaching Cádiz, Spain, in time to board one of the ships in the fleet bound for the New World. On July 14, as Kino neared the Spanish harbor, he saw before him the flotilla as it dipped over the horizon with the setting sun.

First Cádiz, for a few days, then Seville for nearly two years, and then Cádiz again — this time for some ten months — were to be Kino's home in Spain. The long wait was not lost in useless fretting: he perfected his knowledge of Spanish, he read far more widely in mathematics and science, and made many instruments he would need in the mission field, especially compasses, astrolabes and sundials. He was preparing himself to delineate the most accurate maps of vast regions in North America.

On July 11, 1680, he set sail from Cádiz on the *Nazareno*. Before the ship could clear the harbor, it ran into a sand bar. Rescue came soon, but passage on another ship to the Indies would make Kino wait more than six months. Finally, on January 27, 1681, the stranded Jesuit contingent set sail from Cádiz in a special dispatch boat. Despite the terrible risk of sailing without the protection of a convoy, all the missionaries felt fortunate at not having to wait at least a year and a half longer before they could board the next regular fleet for the New World. On May 1, they put into Vera Cruz, Mexico — a trip of over ninety days. The route climbed dizzily as they neared the high passes leading into the valley of Mexico and the capital of New Spain, which they reached about June 1, more than three years after leaving Oettingen, Germany, the starting point of their voyage.

Mexico City at the time was busy with the preparations of Admiral Atondo y Antillon's expedition to Lower California and soberly reflective from the report of the twenty-one Franciscan missionaries and of the hundreds of colonists slain in the recent Pueblo revolt in New Mexico.

Kino was appointed chaplain (with fellow Jesuit Fr. Goñi) and consultant scientist to the Lower California expedition. For more than a century and a half, the boldest *conquistadores,* beginning with Cortés, had tried but failed to establish a permanent settlement or mission in the barren peninsula. In fact, no one was even certain whether the forbidding desert was a peninsula or an island.

It took until early 1683 just to cross to the southern tip of the land. Not even the supplies ferried across the stormy Gulf of California from the fertile Mexican mainland could maintain the expeditionary party and the impoverished natives. Site after site was tried along the Gulf coast and farther inland. All the animals they shipped in had to subsist on the fodder brought in from the mainland. Trees and plants took root only to wither and die from the persistent drought. Jittery soldiers cut down in cold blood the natives suspected of plotting to revolt.

True, much geographical information accumulated from bold expeditions far inland and across the peninsula. The two missionaries acquired a working knowledge of the key languages. Kino compiled the most accurate and detailed maps of the region ever attempted. More and more was learned about the various tribes, their religious beliefs, and strange customs. But none of all this information helped fill empty coffers nor hold out well-founded hopes of successful settlement.

Before the end of 1685, orders arrived from Mexico: "Abandon California!" On his arrival in Mexico City in mid-January of the next year, Kino went to expound to the archbishop, the viceroy, and his provincial superior his new and more inclusive plans for the future.

Kino was not the man to waste time and effort regretting what might have been. He was quick to draw up a more practical and ambitious plan than the one he had to abandon. Accordingly, he would now proceed to the northwestern Mexican Jesuit missions, extend their apostolate to include the unconverted tribes far beyond the established centers, and then from their lands return to Lower California.

Never again would he depend on an unreliable national treasurer who could counter his request for needed funds, "Sorry, but there is no money available." Kino would make his missions not only economically independent but also so prosperous that he could help to establish many others.

On November 20, 1686, Kino set out for the distant north of continental New Spain. As he rode on his fifteen-hundred mile trip, he took with him a precious painting given to him by an eminent Mexican artist friend, Juan Correa. Only the best was good enough for his future Indian charges. It represented Our Lady of Sorrows (Nuestra Señora de los Dolores), which would give him the name to his mission center and home for the rest of his life — a quarter of a century.

En route, at the large Mexican city of Guadalajara, he requested and obtained a twenty-year exemption for his prospective Indian converts from forced labor in the mines or on the farms and ranches. For Kino, the natives were not inferior, but fellow human beings who had not enjoyed the same social, political, intellectual, and religious advantages as the Europeans. Not a single belittling word can be found in all his numerous writings. On his many maps the names of the Indian nations are written in large letters and brightest colors to remind us that what counts in those vast territories are not the fertile valleys or productive mines but the people themselves.

So long as God would grant Kino life and strength, he explored to discover hitherto unknown tribes and lands. Wherever warranted, he left cattle to support the natives, whom he taught to plant wheat and vegetables in addition to their maize, beans, and squash, and to build more substantial homes. Such were the preliminary steps to establishing small settlements, where the Indians gathered, and received religious instruction. In the larger communities, Kino founded schools for the children, whom he taught reading, writing, counting, and singing. He instructed the adults through their native languages, but the children through Spanish in order to incorporate them more rapidly into national life.

Throughout the vast Spanish overseas empire, the most extensive known in history, Spain had relied on three institutions to insure the tranquil life of its citizens, especially along its threatened frontiers: towns, missions, and garrisons. Inasmuch as Kino had established such an extensive peaceful territory among the northwestern nations, hundreds of miles beyond his mission of Dolores, he would have preferred to do without any armed force; but, as the merciless Apache and their allies murdered the Christian natives and raided their prosperous ranches, he was forced to invoke the aid soldiers would give to repel the frequent and bloody incursions.

Kino even pleaded with religious and civil authorities to be allowed to work among the hostile Apache. Had his wish been granted, he might well have saved northern Mexico and southwestern United States some two centuries of massacres and destruction.

Kino understood the unique importance of the rivers in his vast mission territory. They furnished the life-giving water for the crops; along their banks, the missionary could travel from one settlement or mission to another. Unceasingly, Kino rode to explore unknown lands to the north and northwest and to consolidate the centers already founded.

In 1690 he crossed into the present United States, dealing first with the tribes closest to his home mission, but soon he extended his efforts to include the Indians along the Gila as far as its junction with the Colorado. San Cayetano de Tumacácori, San Javier del Bac, San Cosmé de Tucson, and San Agustín de Oyaut became the main centers in Arizona. At the confluence of the two majestic rivers, is where Kino wanted the Spanish and Mexican authorities to establish a town and, with it as a firm base, push far into Upper California. He pleaded for more missionaries and helpers to assist him in the new centers to be established. Timid, small minds could not keep pace with him, especially when he envisioned both Californias settled by many Christian natives, with harbors from which ships sailed not only to Mexico but also to South America, the Philippines, China, and Japan. Through Arizona, goods would be sent to and from Canada and even Europe. Time, experience, and many tragedies would reveal to religious, civil, and military authorities the wisdom and practicality of his prophetic vision.

Kino was overjoyed when his religious superiors sent him a Sicilian Jesuit, Fr. Francisco Javier Saeta, to help him. The new missionary rode northward from Mission Dolores to help out at Caborca, a settlement where Kino had left cattle and supplies not only for the natives but also for exploring parties en route to discovering a land bridge linking the mainland with Lower California.

Fr. Saeta turned to the many tasks awaiting him: building an adequate church and home, learning Pima (the main native language), and alleviating the crushing poverty of his charges. Prospects seemed bright for the future when, on Holy Saturday, sudden tragedy struck. Disgruntled natives from outside the mission slew the defenseless missionary. Fearful of reprisals, even the innocent fled. Nervous soldiers were quick with the sword and gun.

After he succeeded in winning the confidence of entire tribes and in pacifying the terrorized region, Kino mounted his horse for the long trip to and from Mexico City, where he would contact local authorities, the king in Madrid, and the Jesuit General in Rome, in order to save the entire northern enterprise. The burden of every message was, "Those guilty of Father Saeta's death were a few outsiders. Do not punish the vast majority who are innocent." Undoubtedly, this was the gravest crisis Kino had ever faced. The intensity of his feelings is revealed in his desperate cry, "Dearer to me is the salvation of my natives than that of my own soul."

Added to the peril of being withdrawn from his mission field because of the assassination of Fr. Saeta, were the false accusations brought against him by those incapable of understanding his unusual missionary methods. His higher superior in Mexico resolved to keep him from returning. Fortunately, at this decisive moment a letter from Tirso González, Jesuit General in Rome, reached the Mexican Provincial. The message is an incomparable defense of Kino's line of action and of the man himself:

"Father Kino has been led to believe that he was summoned to report on the missions and to discuss with the viceroy the means of re-activating the California enterprise. But the letters of your predecessor state that the real motive was to get him out of the missions and keep him in the province.

"If this is so, I cannot possibly approve such a decision, inasmuch as it deprives those missions of a most devoted worker who has toiled there with untiring zeal and boundless enthusiasm. Such has been his success that were he now employed at other tasks, he should be freed from them and sent to the missions; so far am I from approving your withdrawing him from them!

"Accordingly, your Reverence will let him return without fail to the missions of the Pima Indians, so that he can continue to work among them, unless the renewed entrance into California has received royal approval; in which case, he is to go there, taking with him the fellow missionaries he needs for so wonderful an enterprise.

"Now, I find two main charges against Father Kino; in fact, they are the only charges ever brought against him. The first is that, carried away by his enthusiasm and zeal, he is superficial in his work, hurrying as he does from one task to another. It is said that he baptizes the natives without sufficient instruction in their obligations as Christians. If we consider how much Saint Francis Xavier attempted in such a short span of time, we must admit that saints use quite a different yardstick from the one applied with such caution by ordinary mortals; for them, the might of God has no limits. I am convinced that, if superiors do point out some specific fault to Father Kino, he will amend it and follow their instructions.

"The second charge brought against him is that he is excessively severe on his fellow workers. Now, from the evidence reaching us in Rome, this charge is utterly unfounded. First, because no one has ever complained about him; secondly, because there is scarcely anyone in all the foreign missions who speaks with greater deference and respect of other missionaries; nor does anyone ever show greater kindness than Kino. Such evidence, then, utterly destroys any charge of harshness towards his fellow workers.

"Accordingly, your Reverence will allow him to return to the missions. You will let him work there inasmuch as 'the just man is not to be hemmed in by any law.' I am convinced that Kino is a chosen instrument of the Lord in those missions."

Fortunately, Kino returned to the northern missions to work there during the more than fifteen remaining years of his life. During these years, Kino succeeded in accomplishing two tasks by which he is best known to posterity: (a) he aided Fr. Juan María Salvatierra, S.J., establish the first permanent missions in Lower California; (b) he proved scientifically that the region, hitherto commonly considered to be an island—the largest in the world—is really a peninsula.

He not only encouraged Salvatierra to undertake the voyage that led to the establishment of a mission, town, and presidio at Loreto, but he supplied the missionary with the needed supplies. That was in 1697. For the next fourteen years, as the missionaries in Lower California extended their initial beachhead, Kino kept up a steady flow of supplies from the productive missions on the mainland: cattle, draft-animals, grain, grapevines, fruit trees, vegetables. Seventy years later, when Junípero Serra was authorized to advance into Upper California, it was from the bases solidly established by Kino in Lower California that he was able to do so.

From Kino's abundant writings, especially his extensive and detailed diary, we learn about some forty expeditions he undertook to explore lands and establish missions. The longest expeditions were those he made to discover a land route to the barren peninsula. Shipping cattle and supplies across one of the world's stormiest bodies of water was expensive and uncertain. Kino's most detailed and accurate maps record his heroic efforts to discover the desired route. Sometimes he traveled accompanied by a few devoted Indians; at other times, he was escorted by Officer Juan Manje or a few soldiers.

For the missionaries a map was an essential tool. It marked the route from one mission to another; it showed lands of the natives, those already in the fold and those still to be converted; it recorded the waterholes which meant the difference between life and death; it illustrated the accounts they sent to their religious and civil superiors, reflecting more accurately their endeavors than any written report.

While a keen chill was still in the early March air, Kino mounted his horse — he could not know that it was for the last time — to answer the summons of a fellow Jesuit, Fr. Agustín Campos, at Magdalena, one of the first centers founded by our missionary. As he was singing the High Mass of dedication of the chapel for the natives, named St. Francis Xavier, his patron, death stilled his generous and noble heart. The day was March 15, 1711. Fr. Campos had his brother buried beneath the altar where he was celebrating his last Mass.

His mortal remains were left undisturbed until some fifteen years ago, when the Mexican government appointed a team of archaeologists to discover and enshrine them. After identifying them, they had a glass mausoleum erected over them. Not merely the town square facing the village church is a monument to its most renowned son, but all of Magdalena, renamed in honor of Fr. Kino: Magdalena de Kino.

If love of the neighbor, in the name of Christ, is the true gauge of sanctity, then Kino holds a high place in God's presence. His long life among the natives of North America is the eloquent expression of that love. His sincere preference for the salvation of the least of his brothers and sisters over his own is proof of eminent sanctity. He was deeply convinced that as his work was supernatural in nature — the salvation of souls — so too must the means be supernatural. This explains why he spent much of the day and night in prayer.

His was a Scriptural spirituality. The principles he found in the constant reading and meditation of God's Word sustained his own ideals and convictions, as they also strengthened him in all adversity. His special devotion was the Sacrifice of the Mass. Day after day, he recorded in his diary, "I began the day with Mass." Occasionally, "God be thanked, on this long expedition of twenty (thirty) days, I did not miss Mass a single time; on Sundays, I said two Masses."

PRAYER
(Private use only)

Dear Father Kino, as I reflect on your life, spent in generous love of your underprivileged brothers and sisters, I feel inspired to become less selfish. Since I believe that, if I can be certain that you are now in the presence of the Lord Whom you served so wholeheartedly, I too would love and serve Him more faithfully in imitation of you, I pray that Holy Mother the Church, under the guidance of the Divine Spirit, will soon see fit to raise you to the honors of her altars. Amen.

FOR FURTHER READING

Herbert Eugene Bolton, *Rim of Christendom: A Biography of Eusebio Francisco Kino, Pacific Coast Pioneer* (New York: Macmillan, 1936); Ernest J. Burrus, S.J., *Kino and Manje, Explorers of Sonora and Arizona: Their Vision of the Future* (Rome: Jesuit Historical Institute, 1971).

CHAPTER 8

etrato del Rev. Padre Fray Junípero Serra A
Alta California, tomado del original que se conser
Convento de la Santa Cruz de Querétaro.

SERVANT OF GOD FATHER JUNÍPERO SERRA, O.F.M.
Founder of the California Missions, a portrait painting copied from
the original in the Friary of Santa Cruz (former Missionary College)
in Querétaro, Mexico, and kept at the Missionary College of
San Fernando, Mexico City.

8

Always Forward!

FATHER JUNIPERO SERRA, O.F.M. (1713-1784)

Antonine Tibesar, O.F.M.

IN THE 1700's when the British Lion and, to some extent also, the Russian Bear were sniffing along the western coasts of the present United States, Spain decided to implement its plan to move into Upper California. The Bay of Monterey, the landfall and watering station for the important Manila Galleon on its voyage to Mexico, had to be safeguarded. It would be the last territorial expansion of the then vast Spanish Empire.

Presidio and mission were now to enter our State of California. The soldier to secure the land and the missionary to care for and instruct the natives. Captain Gaspar de Portolá led the one. The missionaries were led by a Franciscan friar, whom the eminent Herbert E. Bolton, called "one of the greatest frontiersmen of the Americas," bespectacled, given to baldness as he grew older, considered small even by the small people of his native Majorca. His name was Fray Junípero Serra. Physically small Junípero may have been, but there was nothing small or weak in his spiritual make-up. Strengthened with giant determination, a "two-fisted fighting man on behalf of the missions and the Indian" in Bolton's phrase, Serra's motto was "always forward." It was his personal paraphrase of St. Francis' dying admonition: "Brothers let us begin for up to now we have done nothing." Thus motivated, this small man with the sonorous voice accomplished so much that today his statue by public vote stands in our National Statuary Hall while the Church authorities consider his cause for the honor of the altars.

Who was this man whose life has so influenced so many?

After the death in babyhood of their first two children a third child, a boy, was born to Antonio Serra and Margarita Ferrer, on November 24, 1713. That same day the boy was baptized, Miguel Joseph, in the parish church of St. Peter in the farming village of Petra, Majorca. A sister, Juana, was born three years later but a fifth child died in infancy. The survivors, Miguel and Juana, were united by a strong affection as revealed later in a letter of that boy then Fray Junípero Serra to Fray Miguel de Petra "the son of my dear Juana." This letter offers one of the few glimpses into the potential reserve of love and affection hidden in this sickly and slight boy. The joyful romps on the broad central plain of Majorca with his sister soon ended. Childhood was brief then in Majorca. Miguel had to go to school. Fortunately, the local elementary school was located in the Franciscan friary of San Bernardino, only two blocks from his father's two-storied stonehouse. There Miguel went to learn Latin, reading and writing and simple arithmetic. One of the friars also taught music much to Miguel's delight, for he was permitted now to sing the office with the friars on important feast days.

All too soon, the boy's intelligence and his parents' wish

to give him a better education occasioned Miguel's transfer to Palma, the capital, to begin his secondary education in his middle teens.

Miguel began the undergraduate course of philosophy taught in the great Franciscan monastery of Palma for both lay students and the young friar clerics. As a lay student, Miguel boarded with a priest attached to the cathedral who taught him to pray the breviary every day.

To the surprise of no one, as soon as Miguel reached the minimum valid age for entrance into any religious order, he requested permission to enter the Franciscan Order at Petra. When it was proved that, despite his frail appearance, Miguel was indeed sixteen, he became a Franciscan novice in Petra in September, 1730. He changed his name from Miguel Serra to Fray Junípero Serra.

The novitiate was a happy year. Too frail and small (his skeleton indicates that he was five feet two or three inches tall) for the physical tasks assigned to the other novices, he was instead appointed to serve the daily Masses. His free time was devoted to reading, especially the lives of the saints. He selected one as his favorite San Francisco Solano from the neighboring province of Andalusia who had died in Lima in 1610 and was canonized in 1726. This occasion was turned into a national festival by royal order with festive sermons, parades and fireworks. All this must have impressed the young man of Petra. Solano became Junípero's model. He too would become a missionary. The desire to bring pagans to Christ began to dominate his life and prayers.

First he had to complete his studies: three years of philosophy and three of theology before he could be ordained. Even before these courses were finished, Junípero was appointed to teach the undergraduate students in philosophy in the same school attended by him a few years before. After his ordination, the young priest continued his own studies in the Lullian University. He received his doctorate in theology there in 1742.

In 1744, the young friar doctor was accepted as the tenured professor of Scotistic theology by his alma mater. To judge by a student's notes, Serra's lectures were clear, well organized and very orthodox. Among his students were Fr. Francisco Palóu and Fr. Juan Crespí, later his companions in California. Palóu for a time even became the professor of the undergraduate courses in philosophy.

Writing was repugnant to Serra, as he himself later stated, even though for most of his life his administrative duties kept him "chained to a desk." His natural propensity and intellectual gifts enhanced by a beautiful and sonorous voice drew Serra to the task of a preacher; a missionary to his people on the island. His periods of university vacations were devoted to this avocation. He was noted as a preacher for formal occasions at the university, but his pleasure was to speak to the ordinary people of the countryside. Indeed, he was preaching a Lenten course to the farmers of Petra when later permission came for him to go to Mexico. This alternation of studious quiet and active personal ministry must have given a pleasing pattern to Serra's life. Indeed, it could have been so satisfying that it could have blotted out the earlier desire to forsake home to bring Christ to the pagans. Fortunately, Serra escaped that temptation.

As the pleasant years passed, it was noticed that the young professor spent longer hours in quiet prayer each night. He had long been accustomed to spend some time at night in voluntary prayer. Now the time began to lengthen — even at times into hours. Some time later, a rumor slowly spread among the Franciscans of Petra that some one had volunteered to go to the missions. This surprised them for Majorcans were not accustomed to go to the Americas. Indeed, the mainland Spanish royal officials tended to consider them too attached to their little island to be good missionaries. Serra was to surprise not only his fellow Majorcans but the Spanish royal officials as well.

Rumors often remain only rumors. But in Serra's case they

blossomed into truth. On Palm Sunday, 1749, while Serra was preaching at Petra, Fr. Francisco Palóu arrived with the news that they had been chosen to go to America and were to report to Cádiz. Both hurried back to Palma, resigned their chairs at the university and set sail on the first ship (an English one) for that port of embarcation on April 13, 1749. At Cádiz, the two Majorcans learned that they were to be assigned to the College of San Fernando in Mexico City. A mission college is a specialized institution within the Franciscan Order intended to train friars to work in the home missions and among pagans.

The trip from Cádiz was boring rather than dangerous. But while traveling on foot from Vera Cruz to Mexico City, where Serra arrived in January 1, 1750, he contracted a painful sore in his leg which was to handicap him the remainder of his life.

Normally, a new arrival spent an entire year at the college in prayer and study. Serra's spiritual maturity and leadership qualities were soon recognized. After only six months, in June, 1750, Serra and Palóu were sent to the Sierra Gorda Missions, a pagan enclave of five missions of about 3,500 Pame Indians in the Sierra Gorda, a mountain range centering at the conjunction of the modern Mexican states of Tamaulipas, Hidalgo, San Luis Potosí and Querétaro. In 1751, Serra was named head or president of these missions. The learned doctor had to go to school again to learn how to win pagans for Christ.

Serra learned his missionary lesson well and it remained with him to his death. He found first of all that he had to speak with his people in their own language to win their confidence. Also, a command was soon forgotten but a request from the missionary for the Indian's help in any task usually evoked a happy response. So, whenever possible, Serra spent his mornings among his people at Jalpán: helping to carry a heavy beam for the church, or stones for its walls, or with a hoe in the community field. In the best sense, he learned to be a father to his people. They responded by developing a well-rounded community with fields, flocks and herds that caused the admiration of the neighbors: prosperous and so progressive that Archbishop Lorenzana requested the transfer of the five towns to his diocesan clergy. This was done in 1770 after Serra had been recalled to develop another difficult mission in September, 1758.

For some time the viceregal officials in Mexico City had been alarmed by the devastating raids of the Apache Indians who were penetrating ever deeper and more frequently into the more northern Mexican provinces. If these were unchecked it was feared that the ranching and mining enterprises there might be ruined. The traditional answer was to plan a presidio-mission complex behind the then-frontier to thwart, if possible, the raiders or, at least, to warn the inhabitants farther south that the raiders were coming. It was decided to build this complex on the San Sabá River in central Texas near Menard. Serra was presumably to be the president of the mission. Hence he was recalled to San Fernando College to consult with the government officials and those of his college and to draw up plans for this new mission. While these plans were going forward in Mexico City, some soldiers and a few friars were sent ahead to begin the construction of a presidio and a mission. This they did on April 18, 1757. But even before the final plans could be completed, the Apache Indians raided and destroyed both the presidio and mission on March 16, 1758. The news of the disaster reached Mexico City only after Serra had returned from the Sierra Gorda. Texas' loss was to be California's gain.

While the authorities assessed the situation at San Sabá, Serra remained at San Fernando as a member of the community. During this time, Serra determined to train his body to become a submissive instrument of his will: he slept on a bed of planks covered by a single blanket, used the discipline with regularity, wore next to his skin a sack cloth or coat of bristles held together with pieces of wire, and accustoming himself to a bare minimum of sleep, kept vigils far into the early hours of the morning. During nine years, 1758-1767, Serra preached to the baptized peoples in the dioceses of Mexico City, Guadalajara, Puebla, Oaxaca and Morelia. Serra appreciated these opportunities to serve the Catholic people. But his yearning to bring Christ to others, who did not know Him, remained. For this, he had come to Mexico and had trained his body and spirit. His desire would be satisfied in a manner beyond his fondest imaginings very soon.

The expulsion by the Spanish King of the Jesuits from New Spain in 1767 created the immediate problem of the need to find replacements. This was especially true of the missions in Lower California. The viceregal authorities deputed the College of San Fernando to take charge of these missions. Serra was to be the president. He arrived at Loreto on April 1, 1768. Twelve friars were selected to help him among them Fray Francisco Palóu and Fray Juan Crespí, his former pupils.

Within less than the year of the arrival in Lower California, the Spanish government decided to occupy Upper California (roughly the modern State of California). The area was well known to the Spaniards for they had frequently visited there and the Manila Galleon visited the Monterey Bay area on each trip to Mexico. To the Spaniards, California was synonymous with paradise — a land of sun and enchantment. Yet there were no European settlements of any kind. For Serra, best of all, it was a land of pagans! As a practical man, Serra wished to retain control of the missions in Lower California as a base for supplies and possible emergency help; but he consented to the government plan to form Lower California into a separate mission, to be later placed under the Dominicans. For him the pagans of Upper California proved a stronger attraction. His diary of the trip north pictures him with the eagerness of a small boy, standing on tiptoe trying to look over the horizon to see the first shadowy glimpse of Upper California. When he arrived after a difficult journey he knelt to kiss the ground. On the way north he had founded San Fernando de Velicatá, still in Lower California but in a pagan area. It was really his first mission.

For Serra, as president or head of the missions, the move into Upper California brought with it problems of enormous complexity. Under the Spanish system, the military administered the territory and guaranteed peace and order. Serra had to care for the needs of the people who would gather in the missions; to feed, house and, to some extent, clothe them. Yet there was not a board or nail, no horse or wagon, neither mule nor cattle of any kind. Wheat or barley or corn were unknown. Tools would have to be brought from long distances and skills developed to use them, plants and seeds imported and acclimatized. For, if the missionaries were to instruct those wild children of nature thoroughly in the truths of the faith and in the ways of Christian living, somehow these neophytes would have to be settled near the mission control. The Indians could no longer be permitted to wander in search of food as they had been accustomed. Yet, they had no extensive cultivated fields. It was a huge task which called for a leader of prudence, sensitivity and determination. The results prove that Serra possessed these qualities. When he arrived in California in 1769 there was only possibility. By the time of his death in 1784, the possible had become reality.

It all began when Serra, accompanying Governor Portolá's expedition, left Velicatá and walked despite his painful leg to San Diego. Here on July 16, 1769, was established the first mission within the present state of California.

Before Serra's death, eight more missions were founded, with about 4,600 Christian Indians, as follows: San Carlos Borromeo, June 3, 1770; San Antonio, July 14, 1771; San Luis Obispo, September 1, 1771; San Gabriel, September 8, 1771; San Juan Capistrano, November 1, 1776; San Francisco, October 9, 1776; Santa Clara, January 12, 1777; and San Buenaventura, March 31, 1782. All preparations had been completed for the foundation of Santa Barbara mission by April 1782 but a lack of missionaries prevented its realization during Serra's life.

In the autumn of 1772 Serra had a number of differences with Pedro Fages, commander of the presidios of Upper California, concerning the extent of military jurisdiction over the missions. Serra was especially worried by the lack of specific norms regulating the demands of the soldiers and presidio officials for Indian labor. Without such rules, Serra and the mission Indians were at the mercy of the whims of the military. The Indians were to work but only at tasks of concern to them. Determined to appeal to the viceroy, Bucareli, Serra departed for Mexico City where he arrived February 6, 1773. He was instrumental in persuading the viceroy to maintain the port of San Blas, to promote the Anza expeditions from Sonora to California, to bring in horses, cattle, and settlers, and to increase supplies to the new province. He presented his case in the form of a *representación*, or legal brief, which, in thirty-two points, covered almost every phase of the mission enterprise in California. Practically all the petitions he made were granted. Indeed, the *representación* became the basis for the Echeveste Regulation of 1773, the first body of legislation for the province of California.

At Serra's request, Pedro Fages was removed from office as commander of the presidio. But his replacement, Fernando de Rivera y Moncada, proved even less satisfactory. There was a clash of temperament between the president of the missions and the new commander. Zealous and dynamic, Serra was anxious to get on with the founding of missions. Indecisive and dilatory, Rivera was inclined to find fault with plans that had not originated with himself and was immutable in the decisions at which he finally arrived. Bucareli favored Serra's plans for expansion over Rivera's preference for cautious maintenance of the status quo.

In 1778 Serra received from Rome faculties to confer the sacrament of confirmation. For over a year he used them without molestation. Then Governor Felipe de Neve, resident at Monterey since 1777, insisted that, as representative of the commandant general of the Internal Provinces, he had the right to affix his own *pase* to the document granting these faculties. Serra disagreed. The missionary was unable to confirm publicly, however, until the dispute was resolved in August, 1781.

As soon as the confirmation of the validity of the indult to confirm reached Serra, he was anxious to resume the administration of the sacrament in order not to deprive his Indians of that grace. By that time he was approaching seventy years of age and he had suffered from severe pains in his chest for some time — possibly some form of heart trouble. He looked so tired and weak that the friars who lived near him all tried to dissuade him from undertaking another visit to the missions.

That was impossible. As he often stated, "among the pagans is my life, and there by the grace of God I hope to die." The time and place of death were in the hands of God. So Serra set out by ship for the south and began his confirmations at Mission San Diego on September 14, 1783. Thereafter he walked northward mission by mission — the fifth time he had walked that *camino real* of about a thousand miles. Twice he almost died but on December 17, 1783, he returned to his own mission at Monterey in time to celebrate Christmas with his own. Then, almost at once he set out again for the more northern missions. He administered his last confirmation at Santa Clara on July 6, 1784. It was entered in his personal confirmation register as confirmation 5,309. The indult to confirm lapsed ten days later on July 16, 1784.

Possibly at about this time Serra was informed by the superior of the San Fernando College of the royal decree ordering a reorganization of the missions. In accordance with these decrees, the Bishop of Sonora and California, proposed that the missions of both Californias should be entrusted to the Dominicans. Serra and his fellow Franciscans were to leave. At this first news, no one knew if the royal decrees were already in effect or if the decrees were mere proposals. At any rate, the college asked for Serra's immediate reply. He was too sick to plan a trip to Mexico. But Fr. Francisco Palóu, his dearest friend, had just received permission to return to the college for his health. Serra wrote to him at Mission San Francisco and requested that he come to Monterey at once to say good bye and help him die.

Palóu hurried overland to San Carlos and arrived in the afternoon of August 18. Standing near the door of the chapel, Palóu listened as Serra led his Indians in their afternoon instruction and hymns. The familiar voice was as strong and full as ever. Palóu remarked to the accompanying soldier that the old one could not be very sick. But, indeed, he was. Serra had made a retreat in preparation for death and had written letters of farewell to all his missionaries. So, the soldier replied, "Father, we must not be too confident. He is very sick. But when it comes to praying and singing, this saintly father is always well."

Serra welcomed Fr. Palóu, his companion and dearest friend of more than forty years, with warmest affection. In the distant past at the Petra monastery they had encouraged each other to volunteer for missionary work in America. His friend had come to help him again.

They spoke indeed of important matters concerning the missions which Palóu was to deal with when he got to Mexico — among them the probable coming of the Dominicans to Upper California. Although this transfer was later cancelled by the royal authorities, Serra died believing that it would be carried out. Palóu was to write: "In spite of such an unexpected and heavy blow, I did not discover in our father [Serra] the least sign of trouble or sadness but a great calmness and inner peace, for he said: 'Let the most holy will of God be done, for this vineyard of His and since He so orders it, doubtless these workmen are more suitable. . . ' "

With that and other items of important business disposed of, Serra took advantage of Palóu's presence to prepare for death. The stifling breathlessness coupled with the pain in his chest rarely permitted him to sleep or even to lie on his plank bed. He spent a day in seclusion and then made a general confession. On August 27, 1784, Palóu went to his little room before dawn to find Serra praying his Matins as had been his custom throughout his life. He admitted that his strength would not permit him to celebrate Holy Mass with proper devotion and requested Palóu to consecrate a host for him. Later that morning Serra asked to receive the Holy Viaticum. For this purpose he insisted on walking to the Church. Once there, Serra knelt, vested in surplice and stole, and as Palóu held up the consecrated host, he began to sing the *Tantum Ergo* in a voice so sonorous and vibrant that the attending soldiers and Indians burst into tears. The remainder of the day was spent in seclusion. During the night of August 27-28 Palóu administered Extreme Unction and then began the prayers for the dying as Serra sat on a low seat supported by his Indians sitting on the floor. Later that morning the presidio carpenter came to receive instructions for his coffin. At about that same time the captain and chaplain of a ship that had just anchored in the Bay of Monterey came to call. Serra's sense of courtesy remained with him to the end as he got up to welcome his guests with a warm *abrazo* and ordered the church bells to be rung in their honor. After some moments of pleasant conversation, Serra thanked them for coming to his funeral. When the guests had left, Serra requested Palóu to give him the Indulgenced Blessing — to his great consolation. After sharing a cup of broth, the two friars recited the Hours of the breviary proper to the time of day. Then Serra concluded "Now let us go to rest." A short time later, Palóu came back to check on Padre Serra. He found him lying on his bed with his missionary cross about a foot long in his crossed arms on his breast — as he had always been wont to sleep. Fr. Palóu noted that it was about 2 p.m. of August 28, 1784. Truly, Serra's life was "always forward."

The diocesan investigation into Fr. Junípero's holiness began in the Diocese of Monterey in 1934 and the proceedings of that investigation were submitted to the Sacred Congregation of Rites in Rome in 1950 where the cause is under study. For further information: The Cause of Padre Serra, The Old Mission, Santa Barbara, California, 93105.

PRAYER
(Private use only)

O Lord Jesus Christ, reward the apostolic zeal of Your servant, Padre Serra, who, leaving home and fatherland, labored for the salvation of souls in Mexico and California. Graciously deign by evident signs and prodigies to glorify him, so that for the exaltation of Your Most Holy Name, he may be raised to the honor of the altars. Grant that through his merits, I may obtain the grace I desire. Amen.

FOR FURTHER READING

Maynard Geiger, O.F.M., *The Life and Times of Fray Junipero Serra, O.F.M.* (Washington, D.C.: Academy of American Franciscan History, 1954); Antonine Tibesar, O.F.M., *Writings of Junipero Serra* (Washington, D.C.: Academy of American Franciscan History, 1955-1966).

CHAPTER 9

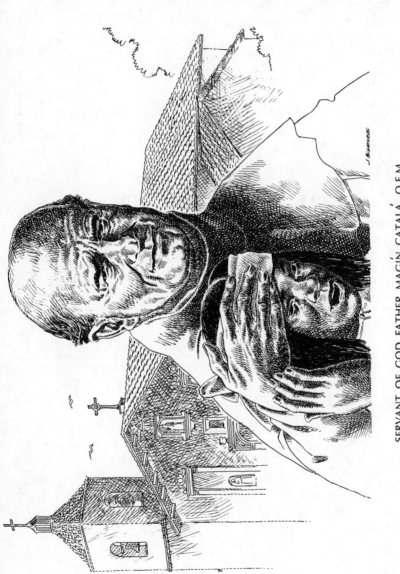

SERVANT OF GOD FATHER MAGÍN CATALÁ, O.F.M.
The Holy Man of Santa Clara Mission, California
A drawing by José Cisneros. (Courtesy of Franciscan Herald Press, Chicago.)

9

Beloved of God and Men

FATHER MAGIN CATALA, O.F.M. (1761-1830)

Joseph N. Tylenda, S.J.

MISSION SANTA CLARA was the eighth of the twenty-one missions founded in California by the pioneering Franciscans. Fray Thomas de la Peña, with a group of Spanish soldiers and their families, left Mission Dolores (San Francisco) in early January, 1777, and walked forty miles southward to a designated site in a fertile plain on the banks of a river that later received the name Rio Guadalupe. The chosen location was called Thámien by the native Indians living there — a name suggested by the groves of trees that lined the banks of the river — but the new arrivals named the settlement after the other great saint of Assisi, St. Clare, the young maiden who left home to join St. Francis in his search for gospel simplicity and perfection and became the foundress of the Order of Poor Clares.

Mission Santa Clara remained in existence fifty-nine years and reached its zenith under the leadership of Fray Magín Catalá, who came to it sixteen years after its foundation and remained with it for the next thirty-six years of his life. Six years after his death the mission was secularized by the Mexican government and the mission church became a parish church. No other missionary was as intimately connected with Santa Clara as was Fray Catalá, the humble Franciscan who was esteemed and reverenced as "prophet," "miracle worker," and known as "the holy man of Santa Clara."

On January 31, 1761, twin baby boys were taken to the parish church of Santa María Mayor in Montblanch, in the province of Catalonia, Spain, for baptism; one was named Magín José Matías, the other Pedro Antonio Juan. The boys, who were born but a day or two prior to their baptism, were the sons of Dr. Matías Catalá Roig, a public and royal notary in Montblanch, and Francisca Guasch Burgueras. Almost nothing is known of Magín's early life and youth, but records in Lilla, near Montblanch, show that it was there that he was confirmed on August 10, 1767, by Archbishop Juan Lorio y Lancis of Tarragona.

The young Magín had been acquainted with the Franciscan friars and their religious manner of life sufficiently attracted him to want to become one of them. On April 4, 1777, at age sixteen, he entered the monastery of St. Francis in Barcelona, and a year later pronounced the three vows of religion: poverty, chastity, and obedience. Magín's study of philosophy and theology in preparation for the priesthood was done in Barcelona, and when those scholarly years were completed he was ordained in Gerona in February, 1785. His twin brother, Pedro, likewise joined the Franciscans and spent his entire religious life within Catalonia.

It was during his years of study that Magín heard and read about the missions his fellow Spanish Franciscans maintained and staffed in Mexico and California. While letters arriving from the missionaries graphically described their adventures in the New World, they also told of the remarkable success they had in evangelizing the Indians. It is not known when Magín's desire to go to the American mission took hold of him — was it during his years of study, or was it only after ordination — in any case, he volunteered and was happily accepted. Having left his beloved family and Catalonia, he traveled across Spain to Cádiz on the Atlantic, and together with eight friars set sail for the New World sometime in September or October, 1786. Since the missions in the New World were under the protection of the Spanish crown, missionaries were approved not only by their religious superiors but by an official governmental agency as well. Fortunately, a governmental report is extant describing Fray Magín's physical appearance. He is said to have been of good physical build, about five feet, eight inches tall, with dark hair and a divided beard; his eyes were grey and he had a thick nose as well as a scar next to his left ear.

The eager missionaries arrived at the Apostolic College of San Fernando in Mexico City, most probably at the end of 1786, where they began to study mission methods and Indian languages. Fray Magín remained at the college for the next six years, and may have been employed there, or may have used it as headquarters from which he traveled to the surrounding towns and villages preaching missions and instructing the Mexicans in the faith. His activity during these six years will, unfortunately, always remain unknown since the college's archives had been destroyed by the Juárez faction in 1864.

Fray Magín's opportunity to go to the missions finally came in 1793 when his superior assigned him and Fray José Espí, who had crossed the Atlantic with him six years previously, to Upper California. Both arrived at Monterey by the ship *Aránzazu,* and directly went to visit Fray Lasuén, mission superior and worthy successor of the great Fray Junípero Serra. The superior appointed Fray Espí to Mission

San Antonio but asked Fray Magín to wait another year before giving himself to the Indians in the missions. Since it was a governmental regulation that all Spanish ships had to have chaplains aboard for the spiritual welfare of the crew and exploration party, the superior appointed Fray Magín chaplain for the duration of *Aránzazu's* expedition to Nootka Sound in today's Vancouver Island, Canada. The obedient Franciscan set aside his burning personal desire for the missions and accepted the chaplaincy to the soldiers and sailors. On July 2, 1794, the *Aránzazu* again docked at Monterey and since Governor Arrillaga planned another voyage to Nootka Sound he asked Fray Magín to continue as chaplain. But since he had been appointed to serve the Indians on the mission, Fray Magín felt he could no longer postpone his primary duty and, thus, he respectfully declined the Governor's invitation.

In August, 1794, Fray Catalá was at Mission San Francisco and the records reveal that he performed a baptism on August 25th and officiated at a funeral on the 30th. He then moved southward to Mission Santa Clara where his name appears for the first time in the baptismal register as having baptized a male infant on September 1, 1794. The child's number in the register is #2510, indicating the number of baptisms at the mission since it opened in January, 1777. Fray Magín's coming to Santa Clara began an association with the mission that was to last until death in 1830, and since then the names of Magín Catalá and Santa Clara have been inseparably united.

The mission compound that Fray Magín saw when he arrived in 1794 was not the construction of the original founders. The mission of 1777 had been built on the banks of the river but due to periodic flooding, the missionaries, after a few years moved the mission to a new site, two miles to the southwest. A new church was begun in 1781 under Fray Murguía's direction and was dedicated by Fray Serra in 1784. It was in this church that Fray Magín began his missionary apostolate in California.

When Fray Magín arrived in Santa Clara, Fray Sanchez was superior of the mission; and when he was transferred to Mission San Gabriel in October, 1797, Fray Catalá succeeded him, a position he held until 1830. His assistant was Fray José Viader, who had come to the mission in 1796, and who was to succeed Fray Magín in 1830.

Shortly after his arrival at the mission Fray Catalá was afflicted with inflammatory rheumatism that increasingly debilitated him to the extent that he found great difficulty in getting around. Undoubtedly, it was this infirmity that kept him from frequently visiting the neighboring missions. A few such visits are recorded but they are most infrequent considering his thirty-six years at Santa Clara. His infirmity, however, did not prevent him from going as far as the San Joaquin Valley, some hundred miles distant, to search out unconverted Indians to attract them to reside in the Christian mission or in one of the Indian villages or rancherias that surrounded it. The few trips to the San Joaquin Valley must have been especially fatiguing and perhaps agonizing since he had difficulty in riding a horse, and if he walked, he did so with a limp. Faced with his poor state of health, Fray Magín left the care and management of the material aspects of the mission — the farm, livestock, and various trades at which the Indians worked to make the mission as self-sufficient as possible — to Fray José, while he reserved for himself the spiritual side of mission life, instructing the catechumens and catechizing the neophytes, administering the sacraments and visiting the sick.

The population at Mission Santa Clara was quite large. There were as many as a thousand Indians and Spaniards living immediately outside the mission compound, besides the ten Indian settlements a short distance away. All of these were dependent on the mission for their religious and temporal needs. During Fray Magín's early days at the mission, the Indians from pueblo San José, founded in 1797, walked the four miles under the burning California sun to Santa Clara for instruction and services. Noting the inconveniences that these Indians had to endure in order to attend religious services, Fray Magín, with two hundred of his Indians, planted countless black willows along the roadside, from Santa Clara to San José, so that when the trees grew to maturity they would form a naturally shaded road for the Indians. Contemporary accounts have described this alameda as the "handsomest" in Upper California, and Mission Santa Clara as the cleanest and best operated. It was on this same covered roadway that the missionaries and Indians held their religious processions on the great feasts of Easter, Corpus Christi, etc. In 1803, Fray Magín built a chapel for the Indians at San José, but many still walked to Santa Clara for their instructions.

Life on the mission was well regulated; there were set hours for prayer and set hours for work. The day began with early Mass and prayers, followed by breakfast. Then chores were assigned — farming the fields, taking care of the livestock, or working at one of the trades. Again in the evening there were prayers for the assembly. Fray Magín gave two instructions daily for the catechumens and neophytes, one in Spanish and the other in the language of the Indians. During these he would explain the chief doctrines of the faith, the Mass, the sacraments and religious customs. He taught them their prayers and their hymns. Through the years the Indians have passed down several hymns that were Fray Magín's favorites. On Sundays and holydays he preached a Spanish sermon at morning Mass then in the afternoon delivered one in the Indian tongue. On Fridays in Lent the entire mission assembled for outdoor Stations of the Cross, walking halfway up the beautiful tree-lined alameda. In May they daily recited the rosary and the Litany of Loreto.

While his rheumatism was still in its early stages, Fray Magín developed insomnia which had so weakened his health that in March, 1797 he was forced to ask his superior to return to Mexico. Since he was so capable a missionary, Fray Lasuén hated to see him leave the mission and asked him to remain a bit longer, hoping the insomnia would pass. The request was again made in 1798 and permission was granted to leave at the end of the year. But because of the shortage of missionaries and with no one to replace him, Fray Catalá agreed to stay on another year. In 1800 he once more presented his request and permission was again granted, but his great love for the Indians overcame his just concern for his health. Then in 1801 he improved remarkably. But in 1804 his rheumatism became more inflammed, so that he could only limp along with pain. At times he needed a servant to help him get around. Despite his ill health, Fray Magín never gave up visiting the sick or comforting the afflicted; he thought nothing of his pain when he went to the outlying Indian rancherias to offer his flock spiritual advice and consolation. Fray Magín's dedication to the Indians at Santa Clara was but the outward expression of his dedication to God.

The mission's records show that during Fray Magín's stay at Santa Clara, from January, 1795, to December, 1830, there were 5,471 baptisms (infants, children and adults), 1,905 marriages and over 5,000 burials. Of this number of baptisms, Fray Magín personally baptized 3,067 between September 1, 1794 and October 27, 1827. After this date he was too feeble to administer the sacrament.

As the mission grew in size so did the need of a new church. Fray Magín and Fray José, with the indispensable talent of the Indians, built a new one in 1818-19, this was the fourth church at the mission. In 1825 they built another, the fifth and final structure. This last structure had been remodeled (1861, 1887), then destroyed by fire (1926) and replaced (1929) with today's attractive edifice.

In 1821 Mexico became independent of Spain, and California fell under Mexico's jurisdiction. In 1824 the government ordered all male inhabitants to swear allegiance to Mexico and its constitutions; but since the missionaries were Spanish, most thought it wrong to take the oath before the king of Spain had officially acknowledged Mexico's sovereignty. Therefore, on July 6, 1828, Fray Catalá wrote to the civil authorities of California stating that in conscience he could not take the oath but he would be faithful and obedient to the government and its officials. This action on the part of the Mexican government was but the first of several which would eventually mean the dissolution of the Franciscan missions in California.

During the last two years of his life, Fray Magín suffered intensely. He was no longer able to ascend the pulpit to speak to his faithful, nor was he strong enough to stand at the Communion rail and preach. Rather than omit any opportunity of explaining the faith, he had a chair placed at the rail where he sat during his instructions. His hearers found him a forceful preacher, who spoke with great conviction and fearlessness, and who was rather severe on gambling, immodest dancing, and extravagance in dress. It was not unusual for him to bring his audience to tears.

On February 9, 1830, thinking that death was soon to come, Fray José anointed his companion of thirty-three years. But Fray Magín rallied and lived for another nine months during which he continued his Sunday sermons and weekday instructions, a phenomenon he continued within a day of his death. At daybreak on November 22, 1830, at age sixty-nine, and having served Mission Santa Clara for thirty-six years, Fray Magín Catalá died to the world and began his life in God. His devoted associate, Fray José, who remained with him during his last hours, recorded the following in the church register: "His whole life was exemplary, industrious and edifying, and more so his death." With the Indians from Santa Clara and San José attending, Fray Magín was buried on the following day and his body was placed on the left side of the sanctuary of the mission church he had built.

Fray Magín's manner of life was quite austere. He observed the rules of the Franciscan Order with love and exactness. It was his custom not to eat until noon, and then he would only take a gruel of corn and milk; he did the same in the evening. He abstained from meat, fish, eggs, and wine. He spent long nights before the Blessed Sacrament in the mission church, or before the large crucifix which still has a place of honor in the restored edifice. Once during Holy Week he knelt before this crucifix and unmindful that several people were also in church, he spoke to the figure on the cross: "When, O my God, shall I see Thy glory? How much longer shall my banishment last in this valley of tears?" And to the astonishment of those in the church, they heard the reply, "Soon thou shalt see God in glory." Eyewitnesses have also attested that they had seen the Savior of that crucifix bend down to embrace Fray Magín and lift him above the ground.

It was not uncommon for him to interrupt his instructions or sermons and ask his audience to pray for someone who at that very moment had an accident and was dying. Subsequent reports always indicated that Fray Magín was correct. He did the same when his mother died in Spain; and when official notification of her death arrived six months later, it was learned that she had died the very day that he had revealed it.

The prophecy that made the greatest impression on his hearers was the one in which he predicted that a large city would one day rise on the site of Yerba Buena; that great houses would be built there, and when prosperity would be at its height, it would be destroyed by earthquake and fire. The town of Yerba Buena yielded to the city of San Francisco, and in 1906 it was indeed destroyed by earthquake and fire.

Three years after Fray Magín's death, the Mexican government in California began its systematic process of secularizing the missions. Mission Santa Clara was dissolved in 1836, one of the last to suffer secularization. The Indians' lands and livestock were dispersed and sold, and they were left to their own resources. The mission church became a parish church. In 1851 the church, the only memorial of Fray Catalá's great mission, passed into the hands of the Jesuit fathers who had come to Santa Clara and used it as the center of a seat of learning which has since grown into the present University of Santa Clara.

Because of the manifest devotion that the Indians continued to show toward Fray Catalá, the Jesuits at Santa Clara informed Archbishop Joseph Alemany of San Francisco of the missionary's reputation for holiness. In August 1884, the investigation into Fray Catalá's life and fame for holiness was undertaken and the results of that process were later sent to the Sacred Congregation of Rites in Rome. In 1907 his remains were transferred from an unmarked grave to the foot of the altar of the large crucifix before which he had spent such long hours of prayer. The marble plaque, erected at that time to indicate the place of burial, wonderfully describes the Servant of God: "Beloved of God and men, whose memory is in benediction" (Ecclesiasticus 45:1). In 1908, the Sacred Congregation of Rites authorized a second investigation into Fray Catalá's life and virtues and the testimony gathered in this second investigation was likewise sent to Rome where the cause now rests.

PRAYER
(Private use only)

O God, Who sent Your holy servant, Father Magín Catalá, to preach Your gospel to the Indians, and inspired him to glorify Your Blessed Name among them by the example of his eminent virtues; we humbly beseech You to honor him on earth with the testimony of miracles performed through his intercession; to grant to us by his merits all manner of blessings; and to fill our minds with the light of Your truth; that walking always in the way of Your commandments, we may come to eternal union with You: through Christ our Lord. Amen.

FOR FURTHER READING

Zephyrin Engelhardt, O.F.M., *The Holy Man of Santa Clara* (San Francisco: James H. Barry, 1909).

CHAPTER 10

SERVANT OF GOD MOTHER THEODORE GUERIN, S.P.
Foundress of the
Sisters of Providence at St. Mary-of-the-Woods, Indiana.

10

With Courage and Faith

MOTHER THEODORE GUERIN, S.P. (1798-1856)

Sr. Joseph Eleanor Ryan, S.P.

THE SEA BREAKS ENDLESSLY against the rugged shores of Brittany; high winds sweep across its caves, crevices, and barren rocks, its sandy tracts marked by monuments from prehistoric times. It is a land of mystery and its people a race apart: upright, dauntless, sensitive and spiritual, generous and devoted, and possessed of a faith that is proverbial. From such a land, from such a race, came that "apostolic woman" who was to be a pioneer in the evangelization of the American Midwest, Mother Theodore Guerin.

Anne-Thérèse Guerin was born in Etables, Cotes-du-Nord, Brittany, on the feast of the Holy Angels, October 2, 1798. Her father, Laurent Guerin, was a naval officer, her mother, Isabelle Lefevre, descendant of a family long-established in Etables. Even among its Breton neighbors, the Guerin family was noted for its staunch faith and generous charity. Laurent and Isabelle Guerin had four children, two sons and two daughters. Madame Guerin dedicated her elder daughter, Anne-Thérèse, to the Blessed Virgin, and the child as she grew, loved to think of herself as "Our Lady's little girl." She was a lively, affectionate, generous child, a leader among her little companions, obedient and respectful at home. Their home was near the sea, and Anne-Thérèse loved to wander on the shore, climbing the rocks, gathering shells, watching the great waves break, or hiding in the grottoes where, looking out across the sea, she lost herself in thought. The sea, her mother had told her, was the symbol of eternity; that long, deep thought was to remain with her all her life. It was in these hours on the Breton shore that she learned to pray.

Captain Guerin's patriotic service kept him from home for long periods at a time. Mme. Guerin devoted all her energies to the care of her home and the education of her three remaining children. The eldest, Laurent-Marie, had died in infancy. When Anne-Thérèse was nine years old, a young cousin, forced to interrupt his seminary studies for a time, assumed responsibility for her education. Delighted with her progress, especially in Scripture and Sacred History, he obtained for his "little theologian" the privilege of making her First Communion at the then early age of ten.

It was on this occasion that in her childish ardor the little girl confided to her confessor her desire to belong to God alone. It was a desire she never ceased to treasure, together with the confessor's assurance that God would aid her to realize it if only she did not take back the heart once offered.

In the years that followed, that heart was prepared for the sacrifices such consecration would entail. Anne-Thérèse was only fourteen when her father, on his way to bid his family farewell before joining Napoleon's campaign in Russia, was overtaken by bandits near Toulon, robbed and slain. Mme. Guerin was still mourning the loss, a few months earlier, of her youngest child, four-year-old Jean

Laurent; at the news of her husband's death her already-threatened health broke completely. Anne-Thérèse found herself suddenly called upon to assume all the family responsibilities. With exquisite tenderness she nursed and cherished her mother; between household tasks she undertook the care and instruction of her little sister, Marie-Jeanne. As for herself, all thought of pursuing her dream of religious consecration had to be set aside for a while. Not until her mother was restored to health and Marie-Jeanne at an age to replace her in the home, did Anne-Thérèse feel free to follow the inclinations of her own heart.

She met unexpected opposition. Mme. Guerin had grown to depend too much on her elder daughter; she declared that she would not be able to survive a separation. Besides, she pleaded, Anne-Thérèse was already serving God in her service of the poor around her; she had the gift of winning hearts and consoling the distressed; her days were filled with prayer and union with God. Why seek another way to serve Him? For five years her mother resolutely refused her consent. Then, suddenly and mysteriously, she withdrew all opposition. Anne-Thérèse always attributed this change of heart to the influence of her Guardian Angel.

Anne-Thérèse entered the novitiate of the Sisters of Providence of Ruillé-sur-Loir, August 18, 1823. This newly-formed congregation, devoted to works of charity, owed its foundation to the pious and zealous parish priest of Ruillé, Fr. Jacques-François Dujarié, whose early life in revolutionary France reads like a Christian adventure tale. When in 1806, Fr. Dujarié erected at the extremity of his parish a little stone house for the volunteer assistants in his catechetical work, he could not foresee that this "Little Providence" would become the cradle of a flourishing congregation imbued with its founder's spirit of simplicity and self-sacrificing charity. Yet in less than twenty years such a community had emerged. The young woman who entered its novitiate that

August morning was destined to share and help perpetuate its spirit.

Anne-Thérèse's early years in religion, under the watchful guidance of a remarkable superior, Mother Marie Lecor, passed like her childhood in ordinary duties accomplished with extraordinary fidelity. She had already learned to walk in the ways of the interior life, was accustomed to hours of silence and prayer, to self-denial and the performance of humble tasks. From the first, her superiors recognized her promise. As Sr. St. Theodore, she received the habit on September 6, 1825, and pronounced her vows two days later, September 8. One year later, the young religious was placed in charge of the community's largest and most difficult mission, in the parish of St. Aubin, Rennes. This mission in the most abandoned district of the city challenged all the charity, zeal, and prudence of the young superior. Yet so well did she meet the challenge, so well did she succeed in winning the seemingly ungovernable children, and through them, their parents, that in the words of one chronicler, "This quarter which had been so long the abode of ignorance and all its regrettable consequences, was not long in becoming the pride of the inhabitants."

As allies in her formidable task, Sr. Theodore had enlisted the Guardian Angels of her pupils — a practice she was to continue and earnestly recommend throughout her life. She recognized, too, the place that genuine love and concern play in any endeavor to save souls. "You must love the children if you wish to win them for God," she would tell her community later. "To win children to virtue the road of precept is long, but the way of example is short."

No one of those to whom Sr. Theodore ministered ever had occasion to doubt her love and concern. Her eight years in Rennes inspired gratitude and esteem in all who knew her. Hence the surprise and genuine regret expressed on all sides when at the retreat of 1834, she was assigned to another mission.

It is part of the life of religious obedience to accept humbly such changes, which are nevertheless very often painful. For Sr. Theodore in this instance there was an added pang. She knew that the superiors whose affection and unreserved confidence she had hitherto enjoyed, had been moved to their decision by misinterpretation of her filial charity and deference toward the Reverend Founder, then beset with difficulties. For a religious so completely dedicated to the interests of her community, this misunderstanding was a harrowing trial. Despite the heartache, she set out with docility for her new assignment, a small establishment in the country town of Soulaines, near Angers. Sr. Theodore poured her whole ardent soul into all that she did, in the hidden mission of Soulaines as well as in the important establishment in Rennes, all unaware of the future work for which Providence had chosen thus to prepare her. In Soulaines, where the classes were small, the life unharried, she recaptured the quiet she loved, and found time for prayerful study of the spiritual masters whose guidance was in the future to serve her so well. In order to be of assistance to the sick poor of the region, she obtained permission to study medicine and pharmacy under a competent physician of Angers. The knowledge thus obtained was also to prove invaluable. Meanwhile, the field of her usefulness steadily widened; the poor and the sick of the surrounding countryside became her confident and happy protégés, who called on her in every need. The school thrived, also. Sr. Theodore received for her excellent work, letters of commendation and a medallion decoration from the Ministry of Education. She earned besides the undying gratitude of pastor and parishioners by obtaining for them from the leading citizen, M. Perrault de la Bertaudière, the gift of a beautiful new church.

While her charity, zeal, and availability to every need were helping to enrich the lives of the people of Soulaines, many of whom attributed to her instruction and prayers their own conversion or deepening of faith, an entirely new and unexpected mission was being prepared for her. The newly-consecrated Bishop of Vincennes, Indiana, Celestine de la Hailandière, visited Ruillé in August, 1839, seeking sisters to carry on the works of charity in his vast and needy diocese.

The diocese of Vincennes, established in 1834, comprised besides the entire state of Indiana, the eastern third of Illinois. A biographer of Simon Gabriel Bruté, its first bishop, compares the phenomenal progress made in that area in the ensuing twenty years to a rapid transition from pre-medieval to contemporary times. When Bishop Bruté took up his charge there were no schools outside the old Indian missions and Vincennes; there were only three priests besides himself to serve the huge diocese. Like other bishops of the American frontier, he had need to seek aid abroad. When he died after five years, exhausted by his gargantuan labors, one of the priests whose services he had enlisted, now his successor, was repeating the appeal to France. The Sisters of Providence of Ruillé had never considered foreign missionary work, but the superiors heard in the bishop's eloquent plea a summons that their zeal could not ignore. Mother Mary asked for volunteers among the sisters.

Sr. Theodore did not for a moment consider herself eligible for such an awesome assignment. Would not the precarious state of health which had been hers since her novitiate be a burden on the mission rather than an asset? To do any good in a foreign land, one would need a command of the language; at her age, could she hope to acquire such mastery? Those chosen for such an undertaking must be possessed of special abilities, of outstanding virtues and invincible courage. Her humility did not permit her to recognize these qualities in herself.

In Mother Mary's opinion, however, one sister only possessed the talents and the virtues required not merely to share, but to lead such a mission, and that was Sr. Theodore.

When she was approached, as a humble and obedient religious she set aside her misgivings, sincerely acknowledging her nothingness and placing all her confidence in the Providence of God. The missionary band included two other professed sisters and three novices. Sr. Theodore would be "Superior of the Motherhouse and Superior-General of all the houses later established."

The group left Ruillé the evening of July 12, 1840; after Mass before dawn on July 16 they set out from Le Mans for Le Havre. In the *Journal of Travel* which Sr. Theodore kept for her sisters, friends, and benefactors in France, she describes the emotions of the sisters as from the deck of the *Cincinnati* they watched their homeland fade into the distance. Both fear and fascination invested the thought of the land that awaited them. To the French of that era, familiar with the romances of Chateaubriand, and the novels of Cooper in translation, America was an exotic country populated for the most part by savages still in the Dark Ages of heathenry. Missionaries looked forward to hardships, perhaps martyrdom in their efforts to establish there a Christian civilization. M. Theodore describes the amazement of the French sisters at their first sight of the beauty and development of the New World. They were, of course, to meet a different face of America as they traveled farther west, one that she would describe as "wild, uncultivated, a world which seems to be in its cradle."

There was no one from Vincennes to meet the sisters. M. Theodore looked in vain for a messenger from the bishop at whose bidding they had come. It was not until they reached Madison, Indiana, that they had their first short visit with him, a visit that gave them little enlightenment or encouragement.

At last, after three long months of travel by sailing vessel, trains, steamboats, stage, they arrived in the late afternoon of October 22, 1840, at the dwelling that awaited them. "What was our astonishment," she wrote in her *Journal*, "to find ourselves still in the midst of the forest, no village, not even a house in sight!"

Their guide and chaplain, Fr. Stanislaus Buteux, pastor in the area, led them across a ravine to where, amid the trees, in the frame house of farmer Joseph Thralls, four postulants awaited them. The six sisters and four postulants were to share this small house with the Thralls family. They would have for their use one room and half of the garret.

They had agreed that their first visit would be to the Blessed Sacrament. Eagerly they followed the priest, who offered to lead them to the church.

"The church! I send you the picture," she wrote. "Yes, dear friends, that is the dwelling of the God of the Universe, in comparison with which the stables wherein you shelter your cattle are palaces. There it is that every day the Lamb of God is offered up, a sacrifice for the living and the dead. There He reposes night and day in a small *custode* in which the priest can scarcely put his two fingers. No tabernacle, no altar. . . . This then, is the church of the place, which is also our chapel. It serves moreover as the dwelling of the priest, and still it is only about thirteen feet wide and fifteen feet long.

"Having prayed, wept, and thanked Almighty God for past favors and begged His assistance for the future, having prayed for you, dear Sisters, and for you all, dear friends and benefactors in France, and having placed ourselves under the protection of the Blessed Virgin Mary, we went to embrace the postulants who were awaiting us."

The sisters spent their first bitter Indiana winter thus isolated in the forest, their extreme poverty lightened by their superior's cheerful abandonment to Providence. By purchasing the little farmhouse containing their exceedingly cramped quarters, they obtained space for a chapel and the whole attic for dormitory. To the first four postulants another was added one month later, when the Vicar-General, Fr. Augustin Martin, arrived to preach their first retreat.

M. Theodore began at once their religious formation and the spiritual conferences which were to become a legacy to the congregation. These conferences were sometimes to take the form of catechism lessons, since in pioneer days many of the young women who presented themselves as postulants lacked knowledge of fundamental truths of faith. M. Theodore never lost her love for sacred silence and her gift for imparting it to others.

Lacking the resources of older European orders, religious communities in America at this period found themselves faced first of all with the prosaic necessity of earning a living. For the teaching communities, this meant opening an academy where the tuition of pupils helped make it possible to maintain classes for those who could not pay. One of M. Theodore's first cares, then, was to hasten the completion of the convent under construction so that it might serve as a boarding school while the sisters continued to live in their cabin. Thus they might commence as soon as possible the work for which they had come. "We must make a beginning," she wrote, "and trust in Providence. If it is God's work, it will not fail, for we shall leave it in the hands of our Blessed Mother."

St. Mary's Academy opened July 4, 1841. M. Theodore noted in her *Journal* that this day was Saturday, and that the name of the first pupil was Mary. This was the first of many such notations. She loved to exclaim in gratitude, "All the good that has come to us has come through Mary!" Her childhood devotion to the Mother of God had matured with her. It was one of the marks of her spirituality, one of the characteristics she tried to cultivate in her community. Every feast of Mary was lovingly observed; every community project was confided to her care.

Those who confide in Mary are never disappointed. The enrollment in the Academy, small at first, increased steadily. At the same time, the community was growing in numbers; in less than a year, ten young Americans were sharing the poverty and joyful simplicity of the sisters' life. Not only did the priests of the diocese, eager for assistance in their parishes, direct their young penitents to St. Mary's; those who had met. the sisters on their way to Indiana or had heard of their undertaking became their advocates. Thus the gifted young Anna Moore came recommended by the Vicar-General of New York, Fr. Felix Varela; the educated and talented Eleanor Bailly, who was to succeed M. Theodore as Superior General, arrived from her French Canadian homestead.

With all the zeal of her apostolic spirit, and her superb gifts for educational leadership, M. Theodore devoted herself to the establishment of the school and to the charge that was dearest to her, the formation of her community. The sisters cherished her daily conferences, one of her means of imparting zeal for God's glory, love of prayer, charity and union, and her own vibrant faith and consequent devotion to the Church and the Holy See. "Always be children of the Church!" she begged her sisters.

Notes of her conferences, carefully preserved by the sisters, help to explain the amazing extent of her contribution to the growth of the Church in America. An observer of American Catholicism in the nineteenth century, commenting on the important part played by religious communities of women, signalizes the work accomplished by the religious of St. Mary-of-the-Woods, upon whom, it seemed, all the pastors of the diocese reposed their hopes. The immense field for evangelization was M. Theodore's preoccupation. It was a temptation to send out laborers too soon, but she did not wish to build on sand; hence she spent herself to prepare her community spiritually and intellectually. Thoroughly convinced of the nobility of her vocation, she never tired of reminding her sisters of the grandeur of their calling. "God in calling us to the religious life had not wished only to sanctify us," she told them, "but He has called us to work with Him for the salvation of our brothers. O, what a beautiful vocation is ours! Have you sometimes thought, my dear Sisters, that you have been called to do on earth what Our Lord Himself did? He instructed, and you instruct. He was surrounded by little children, and you — you pass your life among them." Such a vocation called for unremitting effort and self-conquest: "It would be necessary for us to possess all the virtues in order to be able to teach them to our pupils. . . . Remember that you are visible Guardian Angels of these little children, and that you must behave toward them as do their Guardian Angels. Recall that our Lord loves them, and if you do them good, He will love you also. Think sometimes of that beautiful day in Paradise, when the true Sister of Providence will see herself surrounded by all the children she has taught to love God."

Although her first concern was for the spiritual formation of her sisters, she did not lose sight of the fact that this perfection could only be attained through the fulfillment of their duties. She gave them the benefit of her own talent and experience, conducting model classes for them, following their progress closely.

She had neglected no opportunity since landing in the United States to observe the customs of the people she had come to serve, the conduct of schools, the diverse conditions of the country. With amazing foresight she combined her own experience in France and her observations in America to fashion an educational system admirably suited to the needs and aspirations of young American women. It was characteristic of her broad vision to secure for her institute at St. Mary-of-the-Woods as early as 1846 a charter from the Indiana legislature establishing its place in the higher education of women in Indiana. Even at that date the school was beginning to attract pupils from all over Indiana, and from other states; it was beginning also to enjoy the reputation that was to distinguish it. In the words of Booth Tarkington, whose mother had attended St. Mary-of-the-Woods,

"I think my mother's days at 'Old Saint Mary's' were the happiest of her life . . . the recollection of them was bright and vivid sixty years afterward. Something rare and fine was brought from France to Saint Mary-of-the-Woods, and none of those who were students there remained unaffected by it."

This elusive quality, derived in no small measure from the example of M. Theodore, marked also the other schools she opened in the diocese. She herself accompanied each group of sisters named to an establishment. Once they were settled, she encouraged them by her letters and her visits. The first establishment outside St. Mary-of-the-Woods Academy and the free school in the village was St. Joseph, Jasper in 1842. That same year saw two sisters in St. Francisville, Illinois. In 1844, M. Theodore opened the academy in Madison, which was to triumph over intolerance and persecution, and in 1846 the justifiably esteemed St. Augustine Academy, Fort Wayne. In 1849, four sisters inaugurated St. Vincent Academy, Terre Haute. 1853 saw schools opened in Evansville and North Madison. In 1854, M. Theodore conducted sisters to Lanesville in southern Indiana, where at one time Mass had been offered once a week by the Kentucky missionary, Fr. Stephen Badin. During the last year of her life, 1855, she established sisters in Columbus, Indiana; preparations for a mission in Indianapolis were incomplete at the time of her death.

Like all labors undertaken for the salvation of souls, this work was not accomplished without trials. In the words of the Foundress, "Our congregation has grown in the shadow of the Cross. I hope that our heavenly Father will never deprive us of this precious mark which distinguishes his children."

There were adversities inseparable from a missionary enterprise in its beginnings: poverty, fatigue, misunderstanding, tolerance. These M. Theodore welcomed, and helped her daughters to embrace, as signs of their union with the redeeming Lord. Most excruciating of all her sufferings were those that accompanied the treatment she received from one whose assistance and support she needed most, and whom she respected and revered the most — her bishop.

Few of her sisters even partially realized the extent of these sufferings. Bishop de la Hailandièrè has been described as a pious and dedicated prelate, whose unfortunate temperament caused keen suffering for himself and for all who had dealings with him. In her attempt to establish her work in his diocese, M. Theodore endured obstacles, accusations, rebuffs, and finally banishment from her community and the threat of excommunication. Soon after her arrival, he began to deplore the close bond that united the American foundation to its motherhouse in France, and to evince a determination to conduct the community according to his own ideas. When in 1843, after a devastating fire, M. Theodore undertook on his recommendation a quest for alms in France, the bishop seized the occasion to assume control, using his authority imperiously without regard for either the Rule or the opinions of the sisters left in charge. Upon M. Theodore's return to Indiana after a hazardous voyage and a long illness in New Orleans, she had to summon all her humility and tact to reply to the charges his autocratic suspicious nature had contrived. From that spring of 1844 until the late autumn of 1847 her ordeal intensified. Just as the fate of the community hung in the balance, the cross was lifted; Bishop de la Hailandière's long-proferred resignation from a task to which he felt himself unequal was accepted by the Holy See and his successor named.

During the six-month episcopate of Bishop John Stephen Bazin (November, 1847 - April, 1848) life and hope were restored to the struggling community. When on Easter Sunday the new bishop died, a martyr to his pastoral duties, M. Theodore was at his bedside. His successor, Bishop Maurice de St. Palais, continued the fatherly interest of Bishop Bazin. After the years of sorrow, M. Theodore could explain: "If we had never borne the name of daughters of Providence, we ought now to assume it." The years of trial had helped to establish the community in faith, fraternal union, confidence in God and love of the Cross. By 1852 appeals were being made from every side. The congregation had also happily increased in numbers, and the need for a larger, permanent motherhouse became imperative. The cornerstone was laid on the feast of Corpus Christi, June 13, 1852; Bishop de St. Palais presided at the solemn Mass on August 7, 1853, as the sisters gathered for their first retreat in their new home, as yet only partially completed. "Everyone is happy in seeing what the Lord has done for us," noted M. Theodore, "and especially that we can offer Him a more suitable habitation. Our hearts are truly grateful." Her devotion to her Lord in the Tabernacle, founded on her ardent faith, permeated her life.

The academy pupils added to the joy of their teachers by sharing their fervor. The girls joined the sisters in the retreats customary in preparation for feast days, and even returned to prepare for important events in their later lives. Conversions occurred regularly among the non-Catholics, prejudices broke down, and more and more the pupils "crossed the bridge" from academy to novitiate to join the sisters whose lives inspired them.

During the years that remained to her, M. Theodore, in spite of continually failing health, devoted all her efforts and her abilities to the development of her community and its works throughout the diocese. On May 30, 1855, she reached St. Mary's exhausted from her last visit of the missions. Early in June she sent out her last retreat circular inviting all the sisters to "come as soon as possible to give me the consolation of seeing you all fervent and closely united." She was unable to make that retreat. During intervals of partially-restored vitality that fall and winter she occupied herself with plans for the completion of a chapel to be dedicated to the Immaculate Conception.

The rigors of a severe winter, the strain and sadness of the last illness and untimely death of Sr. St. Francis Xavier, Mistress of Novices, left M. Theodore without physical resistance. On Monday of Holy Week, March 17, 1856, she made the last entry in her *Journal,* "I am obliged to keep my bed. What a beautiful week to be upon the Cross! O good Cross, I will love you with all my heart!" Many times the prayers and sacrifices of the sisters had won her back from near-death. This time there were brief respites, but no lasting improvement.

Convinced at last that death was imminent, the chaplain, their "good Father Corbe," administered on May 12 the sacraments of the sick. She lingered until early morning, May 14, 1856. "The extraordinary beauty on the face of this good Mother," wrote Fr. Corbe to a friend in France, "proclaimed that God had already glorified His servant. Her countenance became luminous, shone with purity and happiness. Never had I seen it so beautiful . . . it is thus that the saints die, or rather that they fall asleep in the Lord in the evening of their lives filled with good works."

She was buried the next day. The sisters carried her body to the little cemetery; on a white cross above her grave were inscribed the words, "I sleep, but my heart watches over this house which I have built." Well persuaded of her maternal vigilance, not only her sisters, but all who have known her, continue to seek and receive her help. During her lifetime it had been written of her, "There was in her whole person an extraordinary charm. No one ever knew her without loving her, and no one ever spoke to her without carrying away a lasting remembrance."

This esteem has grown throughout the years. Confident in her intercession, clients of M. Theodore from all parts of the world visit her tomb, translated in 1907 to the crypt beneath the Community Church of the Immaculate Conception. The introduction of her cause in Rome was approved on February 19, 1956, and is now under consideration in

the Sacred Congregation for the Causes of Saints. For those
interested in M. Theodore's cause, please write: Sisters of
Providence, Saint Mary-of-the-Woods, Indiana 47876.

PRAYER
(Private use only)

Lord Jesus! Only Master of truth and life, who taught
the world the way of salvation, grant us the grace which
we humbly ask, through the intercession of Your faithful
servant, Theodore Guerin, who spent all her life to make
you known and loved. May this grace be consolation
for soul and body, and may it unite us ever more to you
and to one another in time and in eternity. Amen.

FOR FURTHER READING

Katherine Burton, *Faith Is the Substance* (St. Louis: Herder, 1959);
Sr. Mary Theodosia Mug, S.P., *Life and Life-Work of Mother
Theodore Guerin* (New York: Benziger, 1904).

CHAPTER 11

SERVANT OF GOD FATHER SAMUEL MAZZUCHELLI, O.P.
Missionary of the Northwest and Founder of the Dominican Sisters of
Sinsinawa, a portrait painted in Rome by Podeti in 1825, when
Friar Samuel was 18 years old.

11

Wherever God Calls

FATHER SAMUEL MAZZUCHELLI, O.P. (1806-1864)

Sr. Mary Nona McGreal, O.P.

ONE OF THE FIRST Italian missionaries to come to the United States was Samuel Mazzuchelli of the Order of Preachers. Had he lived today he would have rejoiced to carry out the teachings of the Church of Vatican II, which he anticipated as cherished ideals. He understood, as did few of his contemporaries, the significance of the local Church, the servant role of bishop and priest among their people, the necessity of Scriptural preaching and instruction, the missionary aspect of pastoral ministry, the use of the vernacular in worship, the need for adult catechesis as well as Christian education for all ages, and the contribution of the gifts of women to the life and growth of the Church. The

155

keynote of his own vocation was that of the universal Church: the summons to evangelization.

Samuel Mazzuchelli, the youngest son of Luigi Mazzuchelli and his wife Rachele, was born in Milan on November 4, 1806, a year after the invading Napoleon had crowned himself with the iron crown of the Lombard kings. The comfortable family home lay just behind the beautiful Duomo of a thousand pinnacles. There Samuel's mother died when he was six years old and his father sent him to school in Lugano, Switzerland, with the kind and competent Somaschi Fathers, founded by St. Jerome Emiliani.

No one knows what drew the young Mazzuchelli, at age 17, to enter the Order of Preachers. There were no friars left in Milan and very few in Italy since their houses had been confiscated and the friars dispersed. Like other religious orders in Europe, the Dominicans seemed doomed to extinction because of political oppression and related causes. Understandably, Samuel's father was strongly opposed to his entrance into the Order of Preachers. Nevertheless, the youth asked admission and was received into the Dominican Order on December 6, 1823, in the little town of Faenza on the Adriatic coast and made his profession a year later. Immediately afterward he was sent to Rome to study at the ancient convent of Santa Sabina on the Aventine hill, the site given to St. Dominic when he was founding his Order six centuries earlier. In 1825 the convent was returned to the friars after it had been confiscated, and it was opened as a house of studies for the Lombard province.

As though it were not enough to open a house in such troubled times and see only a handful of students come to it, the friars of Santa Sabina were soon alerted to the urgent needs of the Church in the United States. In 1827, Frederic Rese, the Vicar General of the new and struggling American diocese of Cincinnati came to Rome. He had been in Europe for more than a year, begging for missionaries to go to the fur traders and Indians in the wilderness of the Great Lakes region, a region under the spiritual care of the pioneer Dominican missionary bishop, Edward Fenwick. Having few priests and no funds he sent the Pope a cry for help, describing Cincinnati as the poorest diocese in the world.

The first to answer Bishop Fenwick's call for mission helpers was the student Samuel Mazzuchelli. Although only a sub-deacon, he set out for America in June, 1828, a traveling from France by sailing vessel. He marked his twenty-second birthday on the Atlantic before disembarking at New York in mid-November, and traveling by stagecoach and river boat to Cincinnati. On December 1, 1828, Bishop Fenwick warmly welcomed his brother to the rough, courageous life of the itinerant missionaries.

The young Italian cleric studied English and prepared for the priesthood in a long-cabin priory and the little church of St. Joseph, the first in Somerset, Ohio. There he learned the kind of call he had answered, and had the first glimpse of what would be demanded of him for the sake of the gospel. Writing, some time later, he described a striking example of the zeal he found at Somerset. Speaking of the few priests there and their difficult ministries, he related:

"In March, 1830, at nine o'clock on a pitch-black night, while a torrential rain was falling, a man knocked at the door, asking for a priest to carry the Viaticum to a gravely ill person ninety miles distant. Father O'Leary, a simple and holy man, not in the least disconcerted by the storm and darkness, made ready to go, mounted his horse, and as if the sky were clear and sunny set out cheerfully, to arrive at the deathbed the following day. Such happenings were then common in Ohio."

Such example, along with his studies, prepared Samuel to be ordained by Bishop Fenwick on September 5, 1830, in the diminutive cathedral of St. Peter of Chains. From there he was sent, before his twenty-fourth birthday, to the most distant missions of the vast Cincinnati diocese which reached as far as the Canadian border on the north and went beyond the Mississippi river on the west. He made Mackinac Island his headquarters, the home base of his many journeys — by snowshoe, canoe, or overland on foot — visiting the scattered people of the northlands.

Who were his people? They were Indians, Whites, and persons of mixed race who were bound loosely to one another by the fur trade, and experienced the vestiges of former conflict among Indians, traders, and soldiers at the outposts of the Old Northwest. Dispersed throughout the region which is today's Wisconsin and upper Michigan — an area larger than all Italy — these people were served by a single newly-ordained priest. He was following in the footsteps of the French Jesuits, whom he called the "unforgotten Padres," but only a few Indians retained the memory of those zealous missionaries who had been recalled when the Society was suppressed in the mid-eighteenth century.

The Indians who still lived on their ancestral lands were largely Chippewa or Ojibway, Menominees and Winnebagos. Entering their wigwams to share their life and bring them the news of Jesus Christ, Fr. Mazzuchelli, out of respect for a culture more ancient than and far different from his own, made himself one with them. Recognizing his mendicant poverty, the Indians offered him food, sleeping mats and the traditional welcome. When they requested to be admitted into the Church he would ask them to help him catechize their people. He devised a plan for Christian education whereby families would learn together, in their own language, the needed skills and the truths of the gospel. The plan was not supported by the government, but his way of teaching and preaching endeared the young priest to the Indians. He composed and printed for them a liturgical almanac in the Chippewa language and a Winnebago prayerbook which he sent to President Jackson in a plea for justice for Native Americans. Among the Indians he introduced the use of the vernacular language in their vespers, and other practices later found successful by the missionary Frederic Baraga, who arrived a year after Mazzuchelli to minister to the Ottawas on the Michigan mainland. They became friends and each referred to the other as his inspiration and spiritual director.

The white fur traders were mostly French Canadians. Although these families antedated the cession of the Old Northwest to the United States and were old in the faith, many had become indifferent to religion because of the lack of a resident priest. Using the French he had learned in Europe, Fr. Mazzuchelli challenged them to bring the Church to life in the northern wilderness. As a sign of this life and to provide for it, he enlisted the settlers at Green Bay, in the winter of 1830-1831, to build the first church of present-day Wisconsin, St. John's.

Among the traders at Mackinac Island was a Protestant clergyman who expressed strong anti-Catholic feelings by launching a series of Sunday sermons denouncing the teachings of the Catholic Church. The Rev. Ferry's campaign began with his opposition to Fr. Mazzuchelli's first Christmas sermon at Mackinac in 1820 and lasted for many months. The young priest, who had never known Protestants at home, met this weekly challenge with assiduous preparation from the Scriptures and other sources, both Protestant and Catholic. Each Sunday he went to listen to Mr. Ferry's sermon, inviting his own parishioners to join him there. On the following Sunday evening he would present his own reply, written in English in a small copybook, all of which are still preserved. Thus, he discovered that the courage needed for journeys in to the wilderness had to be matched by the courage of his faith and conviction.

Despite the opposition of Protestant missionaries, who sincerely questioned the teachings of the Church, one of them did give witness to Fr. Mazzuchelli's heroic ministry. Writing to a Presbyterian mission magazine, Persis Skinner declared:

"There is a priest in this locale, an Italian, who, they say, came from an opulent family of Rome and who, despite the characteristics of Italians of his rank, the softness, the refinement and luxury, is content to take food and room with an Indian and adapt to the conditions of the place in order to propagate the church of Rome. He is a true and faithful servant of his master and manifests a zeal, a patience and a perseverence that the Christians would do well to imitate. In coming to Mackinac he had certainly to sacrifice all that is dear to a man: hearth, family, friends and country, naturally dear to his heart as life itself, and exchange this for a 'home' upon this isolated island with only the company of French in a culture of savages. . . . All personal suffering in order to gain this goal is, according to him, unworthy of consideration."

In 1834, when other missionaries came to minister in the region, the Italian friar left it to them to go elsewhere, but he never forgot the Indians. He pleaded for justice for them with Indian agent, congressman, governor and the President of the United States. He cherished the memory of the faith that was born among them, a faith which continues to this day in their many Catholic descendants. He left among the Menominees the first Catholic Indian school, which was later moved to Keshena and continued by the Friars Minor and the Sisters of St. Joseph of Carondolet, St. Louis, Missouri.

Once a year Fr. Mazzuchelli left Wisconsin on the long journey down the Mississippi to St. Louis to seek sacramental direction and absolution from a fellow priest. In the spring of 1835 he discovered, while on his journey, that the lead-mine district along the river around Dubuque and Galena was being settled by Catholic immigrants who begged him to stay with them. In answer to their request, the Master General of the Dominicans assigned Fr. Mazzuchelli, not yet thirty years old, to be the only priest in the vast region where today three states meet at the Mississippi: Wisconsin, Iowa, and Illinois. Here French was no longer needed; the new settlers, both Catholic and Protestant, grew accustomed to his eloquent English with its Italian accent as he preached, instructed and ministered to these people throughout the Mississippi valley.

In the 1830s steamboats began to bring newcomers up the river from the port at New Orleans, and family wagons trundled overland from the East. With the aid of his Catholics, often assisted by their Protestant neighbors, Fr. Mazzuchelli spent eight years forming new parishes and building churches "where the people could worship and hear the Word of God." Some churches were made of logs, rough or well-hewn — each family brought a tree cut from their forest — and some were of brick or native limestone. Two were prefabricated in one place and later floated down the river to another. A number of churches survive as monuments to the faith of the first settlers and their pioneer pastor, and some are still in use today by congregations in Prairie du Chien and Shullsburg, Wisconsin; Galena, Illinois; and Davenport, Iowa.

Even more important than building church structures was the forming of parishes. More than thirty Christian communities from Green Bay, Wisconsin, to Burlington, Iowa, owe their beginnings to Fr. Mazzuchelli whom they honor as their first pastor. The descendants of the first parishioners, although scattered now at great distances, cherish the memory of him who brought the sacraments to their great grandparents or other forebears. Family stories abound concerning his preaching and teaching, his courtesy to Protestants, his care of the sick during epidemics, his kindness. But the distinguishing quality that appears in every reminiscence is his priestly zeal. Of his preaching and teaching one contemporary stated:

"His long lectures before Mass on the Old Testament and the usual sermon after the Gospel were always most inspiring and listened to by us, his poor ignorant congregation with such wrapt attention that you could hear a pin drop in the church. His language was always so simple and unctuous that any child could understand it. . . . In his lectures in the study hall, the students seemed riveted to the chairs, so wrapt was their attention."

By 1843 three recently-appointed bishops assumed the care of those regions in which Fr Mazzuchelli had initially labored alone. They were Mathias Loras of Dubuque, William Quarter of Chicago, and John Martin Henni of Milwaukee. The Dominican friar believed the time had come to realize his dream of many years, that is, to open a mission center where Dominican fathers and brothers, and later sisters, could support the pioneer dioceses in several ways: forming new parishes, preparing young men for the Dominican and diocesan priesthood, and providing Christian education for the people of the region. From the Holy See and officials of the Order of Preachers he obtained authorization to establish a new province in the upper Mississippi valley, distinct from that of the American Dominicans who came with Bishop Fenwick to Kentucky in 1806.

In 1844, Fr. Mazzuchelli purchased the site for his new project; it was a natural elevation in southwestern Wisconsin which the Indians named Sinsinawa and the settlers called "the Mound." In quick succession he opened a novitiate for Dominican friars, a college for men, and a school for farmers' and miners' children. Recognizing the great need of such schools the people enthusiastically supported Fr. Mazzuchelli's projects. He was, however, disappointed in his hope of obtaining European theologians and professors from the Dominicans to teach the laymen and seminarians enrolled in the college. Several priests who came from Italy proved to be ill-fitted for community life and unwilling to share the hardships faced by missionaries. Discouraged, the founder, in 1849, resigned as head of the Sinsinawa foundation and handed the project over to the Dominican province of St. Joseph in Kentucky. Given the title of Missionary Apostolic, Fr. Mazzuchelli continued to help the fathers at Sinsinawa, but went to live as pastor in the neighboring parish of Benton, Wisconsin. His only desire, he said, was to be a simple pastor and missionary.

Although his dream of a missionary center was not realized, one of the projects which he began before he left "the Mound" was "taking root in the Church" — to use Fr. Mazzuchelli's own words — with slow but steady growth. This was the community of Dominican sisters which he formed at Sinsinawa in 1847, when he gathered four young women of the region to be its first members. Their purpose was to participate in the mission of the Order, preaching and teaching the Word of God, and thus extend his own missionary work to the parishes and dioceses to which they would be called. Here, as in all other facets of his many-sided ministry, Fr. Mazzuchelli emphasized the role of the sisters in service to the local Church. The first four professed members remained at Sinsinawa for several years, going out to teach in the parish and public schools. In 1852 they rejoined their founder at Benton and remained there under his direction until his death in 1864.

With them he founded the Academy of St. Clara (later moved to Sinsinawa) to offer young women of the frontier an unusually high level of education. As superintendent, Fr. Samuel, as he was usually called, set the standard for both teachers and pupils. With the same ardor that caught the attention of his parishioners when he preached, he now instructed their daughters in religion, Scripture, history, natural science, and even English composition.

In frequent sessions with the seedling community of sisters, he formed them in the traditions of Dominican apostolic life. Essential to his vision was the emerging role of religious women. He foresaw that the majority would no longer be cloistered as they had been during previous centuries. His new community, he believed, should be clearly identified with the Third Order and therefore, he adopted for their

Rule that of the Dominican tertiaries, changing it to meet the needs of religious women of simple vows living in community. The Sinsinawa Dominican Sisters became one of the earliest nineteenth-century congregations of Dominican women to live a fully active apostolic life, much the same as the friars had done from the foundation of the Order of Preachers. Since their establishment in 1847 more than three thousand women have responded to the Dominican vocation.

Fr. Mazzuchelli's "yes" to the call to follow Jesus Christ was repeated numberless times; it was his unfailing response to the summons to serve the Lord in His people. His understanding of the missionary vocation of priests was described in his *Memoirs,* an account of the American missions that he wrote for Italians and published in Milan in 1844. He expressed the keynote of his life in these words: "Let us wake up then, and if we are called, set out for any place where the work is great and difficult, but where also, with the help of Him who sent us, we shall open the way for the Gospel."

To answer such a call the young Dominican had set out from Italy with the conviction that "A Christian's native country is wherever God calls him," and that for those sent on mission "a hundred cities, a hundred nations in various regions become our magnificent fatherland." In the New World he found the work great and difficult, indeed, as he journeyed endless distances, suffered from hunger and cold, begged for shelter and food, and encountered lethargy, contradictions and limitless needs. In his austere poverty, which, like St. Dominic, he believed to be necessary for preaching the Word, Fr. Mazzuchelli brought to his parishioners, students, and sisters the spiritual riches of a mind and heart always responding with his patron, the prophet Samuel, "Here I am, Lord."

The final summons for Fr. Samuel came from a dying parishioner. After riding into the country on a bitter cold February day in 1864, he was taken ill with pneumonia and died a week later on February 28. On his deathbed the missionary prayed Psalm 84: "How lovely is your dwelling place, O Lord." It was the song of a pilgrim, the prayer of a priest before celebrating the Eucharist, the psalm used by the Church to dedicate a new church. It brought to a fitting close the life of a man always setting out to bring the Good News to people far from his own home. When one of those attending the dying priest saw tears on his face and commented on them he explained that his long journey was coming to an end, and he wept for joy that he was now going to enter his true country.

Fr. Samuel Mazzuchelli's grave at Benton is regularly visited by pilgrim Americans. From the time of his death until the present the people who knew Fr. Mazzuchelli and those who have kept his memory alive for many generations have revered him as a holy priest, a zealous preacher, teacher and pastor. Many accounts of his pupils, sisters, and parishioners tell of his self-sacrificing charity, his kindness and compassion. The regions where he once worked alone are now served by eight dioceses: Marquette in Michigan; Green Bay, Milwaukee, Madison and LaCrosse in Wisconsin; Rockford in Illinois; Dubuque and Davenport in Iowa. Three of these, namely Milwaukee, Madison, and Dubuque, together with the Archdiocese of Milan, initiated in 1966 the process to petition the beatification of Fr. Samuel Mazzuchelli. In 1976 the writings of the Servant of God were examined and found free of error concerning faith and morals. Meanwhile, the required *Positio,* or documentary review of evidence of his life and virtue, is being written. Manifold favors have been ascribed by many of the faithful to his intercession. Yearly bulletins and other communications are published by the Mazzuchelli Guild, Sinsinawa, Wisconsin, 53824.

PRAYER
(Private use only)
Lord Jesus, You called Your servant, Samuel, even in

early youth, to leave home and all for a Dominican life of charity in preaching your holy Gospel. You gave him abundant graces of Eucharistic love, devotion to Your Holy Mother of Sorrows and a consuming zeal for souls. Grant, we beseech You, that his fervent love and labors for You may become more widely known, to a fruitful increase of Your Mystical Body, to his exaltation and to our own constant growth in devoted love of You who with the Father and the Holy Spirit live and reign one God, world without end. Amen.

FOR FURTHER READING

The Memoirs of Father Samuel Mazzuchelli, O.P., translated by Sisters Jeremy Finnegan and Maria Michele Armato (Chicago: Priory Press, 1967); Sr. Mary Nona McGreal, *Samuel Mazzuchelli, O.P.* (Sinsinawa, Wisconsin: Mazzuchelli Guild, 1973); Jo and Jim Alderson, *The Man Mazzuchelli* (Madison, Wisconsin: Wisconsin House, 1974).

CHAPTER 12

SERVANT OF GOD FATHER FRANCIS XAVIER SEELOS, C.SS.R.
Redemptorist Pioneer and Missionary in the United States.

12

Redemptorist Preacher and Healer
FATHER FRANCIS XAVIER SEELOS, C.SS.R. (1819-1867)

Thomas Artz, C.SS.R.

COULD TWO CANONIZED SAINTS have lived in the same parish house in Pittsburgh, Pennsylvania, in the late 1840s? It seems almost incredible yet it might someday come true. The pastor of St. Philomena's parish at that time was John Neumann who was canonized a saint in 1977. One of his assistants was Francis Xavier Seelos, a young Redemptorist priest. It is possible that within a few years Fr. Seelos may also be formally declared a saint of the Church. His life is an inspiration and reading about him can perhaps inspire others to lead a better Christian life.

Francis Seelos was born January 11, 1819, in Füssen, a small town in Southern Germany. His father worked as a tailor and later became the sacristan of the local parish church. The Seelos family was not known for great wealth

169

or prestige, but it was a devout Catholic family, the type that fosters vocations. Along with Francis, who became a priest, two of his sisters became nuns.

From his early years, Francis wanted to become a priest. Fr. Francis Heim, the pastor of the local parish, was most helpful in getting him started on the road that led to the priesthood. He gave young Francis special training in the Latin language, so important at that time for anyone who wanted to be a priest. When it was clear that the Seelos family could not pay for Francis' education, the pastor found special benefactors who supported him during his years of schooling.

After six years of grammar school in his hometown Francis spent seven years studying at St. Stephen's Academy in Augsburg. In 1839, he entered the University of Munich on a scholarship for the two-year course in philosophy. His desire to be a priest deepened with each passing year in school, but he was never a gloomy or overly pious person. On the contrary, his classmates and friends remembered him as a cheerful and fun loving person. Besides philosophy, Francis also learned how to dance and fence.

Francis began his theological studies at the University of Munich in 1841, and remained there for one year. In 1842 he applied for admission to the Congregation of the Most Holy Redeemer (also known as Redemptorists), and expressed his desire to become a missionary to the United States of America.

Transatlantic correspondence was slow in those days, and it took several months before Francis learned that he had been accepted by Fr. Alexander, the Redemptorist superior in the United States. But by then he had transferred from the University of Munich to the seminary of the diocese of Augsburg at Dillingen. After learning of his acceptance, he left the seminary and went to a nearby Redemptorist community at Altötting, Germany. After a short period of orientation with the Redemptorists, Francis left Germany for the

United States on March 17, 1843. He spent the next month aboard the ship *Saint Nicholas,* traveling with Fr. Ernest Glaunach and two Redemptorist laybrothers.

In April, 1843, Francis arrived in New York to join the Redemptorists. At that time the Redemptorists had been in America for little more than ten years; they numbered but a few dozen priests and brothers working primarily for German speaking immigrants. Francis was sent to the Redemptorist parish of St. James in Baltimore where on May 16, 1843, he was invested with the distinctive Redemptorist habit and began his year of novitiate.

Those were happy days for Francis for he always loved the spiritual life and its treasures. As a novice he now had time to give himself completely to the Lord and to prepare himself for the priesthood. He knew that unless he himself were holy it would be impossible to make others holy. It was for this reason that he prepared so diligently by prayer and penance, always striving to deepen his love for God and his fellowmen and women.

Francis officially entered the Congregation of the Most Holy Redeemer on May 16, 1844, when he professed for life the religious vows of poverty, chastity, and obedience. He was now a Redemptorist. In the following eight months he completed his private studies for the priesthood and on December 23, 1844, was ordained by Archbishop Eccleston of Baltimore.

Fr. Seelos was a priest for less than twenty-three years when God called him to his heavenly reward. Many great things were to happen in that short time. At the time of his ordination he had not yet mastered the English language, nevertheless, he immediately began to serve God and to win souls for the Lord. For several months after his ordination Fr. Seelos remained in the Baltimore area. In August, 1845, he received his first assignment and joined the Redemptorists working in St. Philomena's parish in Pittsburgh.

It was in Pittsburg that Fr. Seelos met Fr. John Neumann,

pastor of St. Philomena's parish. Later Fr. Neumann became Provincial Superior of the Redemptorists in America and then Bishop of Philadelphia. Today he is St. John Neumann. During the years they were in Pittsburgh Fr. Neumann was a saintly example to the young Fr. Seelos of all that holy and zealous parish priest should be.

Fr. Seelos remained in Pittsburgh nine years. In 1851, ordained seven years and only 32 years old, he was made pastor of that growing Pittsburgh parish. The faithfulness that he showed in his duties inspired all priests who served in the parish to give greater glory to God by their service to His people. The parish records show that in a typical year, Fr. Seelos performed some 150 baptisms and 35 marriages. He preached countless sermons, in English and German, and as a confessor he was unmatched.

The people loved their pastor because he inspired them to live better lives. As pastor he was never too busy to speak with or to offer his help to his parishioners. Anyone could come to see him — even early in the morning or late at night — and he tried to do all that was reasonably possible to help. He also made a special effort to have an interest in the school children. Two or three times a week he visited the school often stopping to give a catechism lesson. He spoke to the children in simple words and with great feeling, so they could come to know and love the Lord more deeply. He also started an orphanage in Pittsburgh's Tory Hill section.

While in Pittsburgh, Fr. Seelos became a legend. People came to seek his spiritual assistance. In 1860, when the diocese of Pittsburgh was to get a new bishop, many people, including Bishop Michael O'Connor, the retiring prelate, thought that Fr. Seelos would be an excellent choice. But Fr. Seelos did not become the new bishop — even to be considered for such a position showed how highly respected he was.

In March, 1854, Fr. Seelos was transferred to Baltimore

to become pastor of St. Alphonsus parish. Assisted by seven Redemptorist priests, he was responsible not only for the care of the people in the main parish but also for the spiritual needs of many who lived in the outlying areas of the city and those who were served by mission chapels. In fact, Fr. Seelos, at one and the same time, had to care for four parishes with schools with more than 1300 children.

Besides his many administrative duties he also had responsibilities within the Redemptorist community itself. Still he found time for the individual needs of his parishioners. He spent countless hours in the confessional and preached at missions and novenas.

Fr. Seelos took a special interest in many communities of religious sisters. He served as confessor and spiritual director to the School Sisters of Notre Dame, Sisters of Providence, and Carmelite Sisters in the Baltimore area. These sisters were involved in the very important ministry of spreading the gospel and educating the faithful, and Fr. Seelos helped them prepare themselves spiritually for these works.

As the years rushed by the constant hard work began to take its toll. Fr. Seelos had never been robust and now he began to weaken noticeably. During Lent of 1857 a blood vessel in his neck ruptured and he was near death for several days. It took many weeks before he returned to his normal duties. Fr. Seelos used this time of sickness to great advantage. Even in his busiest of days as pastor he maintained his personal times of prayer, spiritual reading and practices of piety and mortification. Now confined to bed he spent the entire day in prayer, drawing closer to the Lord and recommending to God all the needs of his own parish and the needs of God's people throughout the world.

Throughout his life, even though his health was poor, Fr. Seelos was often called upon to do double duty. For a short while after his ordination he remained in Baltimore and was both parish priest and assistant to the novice master. Later in

Pittsburgh, he had his parish duties and was also in charge of the Redemptorist novices. This meant that in addition to his usual parochial duties he was called upon to instruct the new Redemptorists in the ways of spirituality and community life.

From 1857 to 1862 Fr. Seelos was called upon to do triple duty. In 1857 he was appointed pastor of Sts. Peter and Paul church in Cumberland, Maryland. It was a small parish of less than one hundred families, but it still required much of his time each day and on weekends. More important than the parish was his assignment as director of students. Attached to the church at Cumberland was the Redemptorist seminary, and Fr. Seelos was in charge of the students' spiritual formation and general welfare. He was directly responsible for shaping these young men into holy and dedicated priests. At times there were as many as seventy students in the seminary — they may have been a diverse group, but they were united in their love and esteem for their director.

Besides pastor of the parish and director of the students, Fr. Seelos was also a seminary professor. His years of study in Augsburg and Munich finally came in handy. In his years at Cumberland he was respected as an able professor who always made his subject clear to the students. At various times he taught coures in Dogma, Sacred Scripture, and Church History.

As a superior for sixteen of his twenty-three years as a Redemptorist, Fr. Seelos was a gentle man of prayer. His observance of the Redemptorist rule of life and his dedication to his priestly duties inspired others to a greater obedience and dedication. In his conferences as director of students he instilled in the seminarians a sense of dedication to God and His people, a love for the priesthood, and a desire to live as holy and virtuous Redemptorist priests.

Fr. Seelos believed that it was especially important for the Redemptorist seminarians to learn the traditional custom of devotion to the twelve monthly virtues. St. Alphonsus Liguori made these twelve virtues one of the basics of the rule when he founded the Redemptorists in 1732. The practice was practically, psychologically, and theologically sound.

Each month Redemptorists were exhorted to deepen their practice of a certain virtue. In January, it was faith. One's thoughts were to be centered on hope in February. March was for love of God; April, love of neighbor; May, poverty; June, chastity; July, obedience; August, humility; September, mortification; October, recollection; November, prayer; December, self-denial. Each year the cycle of the twelve monthly virtues would be repeated and renewed. Fr. Seelos learned this way of practicing the virtues during his novitiate. He continued each month of his life to grow closer to the Lord by practicing the special virtue for that particular month and exhorted the seminarians to do likewise.

In the 1860s the Civil War, then devastating the United States, began to cause grave problems for the Redemptorist seminary at Cumberland. The fear that his seminarians might be drafted sent Fr. Seelos to Washington to confer with President Lincoln and cabinet officials. There was also the worry that Cumberland could become a major Civil War battleground, and as a result the seminarians were moved to Annapolis, Maryland. At Annapolis they enjoyed a new and larger building and a greater degree of safety. Fr. Seelos moved to Annapolis in May, 1862; and shortly after arriving, he was relieved of his duties as the director of students, but remained as pastor of the church and seminary professor. He was also called upon to minister to the many soldiers, prisoners of war, and wounded who were in the Annapolis area.

August, 1863, saw Fr. Seelos enter into the work that is most characteristic of the Redemptorist priest. He was appointed the leader of the Mission Band. Now his work would be to bring people back to God and to increase the fervor of those already in God's grace, especially by the ministry of preaching. The home mission was a special series of sermons and spiritual exercises conducted in parishes by missionary priests. The purpose was to renew and strengthen the faith of the people and call those who had fallen away back to the practice of their faith.

For the next three years Fr. Seelos conducted missions in countless parishes in more than a dozen states. He criss-crossed the country moving from the Northeastern United States to Missouri and Illinois and then back again. He preached in the cathedral in Chicago and the major churches of New York City. He won souls back to the Lord in count-less small towns like Morris, Illinois. Each mission lasted only a few weeks, but the good that Fr. Seelos acheived in that short time continued for many years.

When Fr. Seelos stepped into the pulpit to preach his mission sermons the faithful were immediately attracted by his friendly glance and his kindly tones. His sermons were simple and to the point. It was the simplicity of the message and the sincerity of his voice that moved his listeners to draw closer to the Lord.

It was through his sermons that Fr. Seelos won the ad-miration and confidence of the people, but it was in the confessional that his true holiness and priestly zeal for souls were exhibited most clearly and positively. After each mis-sion sermon he went to the confessional spending long hours welcoming sinners back to the grace of the Lord. He gained a widespread reputation for being able to bring peace of of mind to those who were troubled. He gave despairing souls hope, courage, and determination to face the future. Those who had been disturbed by scruples of conscience were often cured of this terrible affliction with only one visit to Fr. Seelos' confessional.

Fr. Seelos remained on the Mission Band until the autumn of 1865, when he was transferred to the Redemptorist parish of Holy Redeemer in Detroit. After all those years as pastor, seminary professor and leader of the Mission Band, he still remembered how to be an assistant pastor. Fr. Van Enstede, the pastor of Holy Redeemer, could not have found a more willing associate. In the parish he was able once again to show special care for his favorite people, the poor and the sick. When St. Alphonsus Liguori founded the Redemptorists he instructed them to serve especially "the most abandoned," and throughout his priestly life Fr. Seelos put these words into practice. His stay in Detroit was brief. After ten months he was transferred to New Orleans.

When Fr. Seelos arrived in New Orleans on September 28, 1866, the Redemptorists had charge of three different churches, caring for the Catholics of three nationalities, French, German, and English. Fr. Seelos was familiar with all three languages, but he spent the majority of his time working in St. Mary's using his native language to help those who came to the United States from Germany.

Outbreaks of yellow fever were a frequent and sad occurrence in New Orleans. In September, 1867, the disease again devastated the city; sick calls came day and night and funerals were frequent. Fr. Seelos worked tirelessly among the sick and dying until September 17, when he himself was stricken by the yellow fever virus.

His holiness became obvious during his final illness. In the face of the most severe pain he did not complain but remained constantly in prayer and seemed to be completely at peace, eagerly awaiting the moment when the Lord would come to take him to Himself. His condition worsened and on October 4 it was clear that the end was near. The Redemptorist priests and brothers, his confreres, gathered at his bedside in prayer while in the church and throughout the city the people prayed for the humble priest they had come to know and love in the brief time that he had been with them. Fr. Seelos died at 5:30 p.m., on October 4, 1867. He was forty-eight years old. He was buried the following day in St. Mary's church, but later his remains were transferred to St. Alphonsus church in the same city. Fr.

Seelos' earthly life had ended, but it surely was not the end of his work in New Orleans. In fact, it seemed to be but the beginning.

While still alive, Fr. Seelos often brought spiritual healing to troubled souls in the sacrament of confession. The Holy Spirit also chose to work through him on countless occasions to bring physical healing to people as well. The healing power of Fr. Seelos seemed to increase after his death, and through the intervening years the favors granted through his intercession have steadily grown. Fr. Seelos' cause is presently under consideration in Rome. The Vice Postulator of the cause is Rev. William Grangell, C.SS.R., and for further information please write Father Francis Seelos Center, 2030 Constance Street, New Orleans, Louisiana, 70130.

PRAYER
(Private use only)

O my God, I truly believe You are present with me. I adore Your limitless perfections. I thank You for the graces and gifts You gave to Father Seelos. If it is Your holy will, please let him be declared a saint of the Church so that others may know and imitate his holy life. Amen.

FOR FURTHER READING
Michael Joseph Curley, *Cheerful Ascetic: The Life of Francis Xavier Seelos, C.SS.R.* (New Orleans: Redemptorist Fathers, 1969).

CHAPTER 13

SERVANT OF GOD BISHOP FREDERIC BARAGA
Missionary Bishop of Upper Michigan and First Bishop of Marquette.

13

Missionary to the Indians

BISHOP FREDERIC BARAGA (1797-1868)

Francis G. McManamin, S.J.

IN 1797, WHEN our republic was engaged in an undeclared war with France, and the vast land known as the "Northwest Territory" was inhabited mostly by Indian tribes, both friendly and unfriendly, Frederic Baraga was born on June 29, in Mala Vas castle, in the parish of Dobrinic, Carniola, a Slovene province of the Austrian Empire. His parents, Catherine and John, were a deeply religious couple. It was a closely knit family of five: Catherine and John, and their three children, Amalia, born in 1795, Frederic, and then Antonia, born in 1803.

Since religion and education were the foundation stones of the family structure, the children received good training in their faith and in secular studies. Private tutors attended them in their younger years, but when Frederic was approaching his teens his parents sent him to a boarding school in the nearby town of Ljubljana. While at school both his mother and father died, and young Frederic found himself the head of the family under the guidance of an uncle. The parents left the children financially secure and hence, Frederic and his sister were sent to the home of Dr. and Mrs. George Dolinar in Ljubljana. The Dolinars had two children, one of whom was Anna, about two years younger than Frederic. A warm friendship developed among all the children and, in time, a romantic attachment grew between Anna and Frederic. Family and friends presumed that eventually the two would marry.

When Frederic completed his education in Ljubljana, Dr. Dolinar encouraged him to study law at the University of Vienna. Frederic took this advice and there also studied English, Spanish, French, German, and Italian, languages he would find very useful in later years in North America.

Meanwhile, Frederic's cherished gift of a graced spirituality deepened during his years in Vienna, especially after his privileged meeting on July 12, 1817, with the Redemptorist saint, Clement Hofbauer. Father Hofbauer so impressed Frederic that the young man said: "This day will always remain indelibly written in my memory for the incredible graces the Lord granted me." His warm friendship with Fr. Hofbauer led him to re-examine his goals and prompted him seriously to consider the priesthood.

After graduation from law school in 1821, Frederic pondered his future and firmly decided on the priesthood. A painful experience awaited him: how to break the news to Anna. Both his uncle and Dr. Dolinar guided him through this difficult time and, when free, he entered the seminary where the course of studies was adapted to suit his academic background. He was ordained to the priesthood on September 21, 1823, two years after his entrance into the seminary.

His first pastoral assignment, St. Martin's church, was

considered an attractive one but all was not serene. The diocese was in the grip of Jansenism, i.e., a heresy that over-emphasized predestination, taught that Christ did not die for every one, and discouraged pilgrimages, prayers to the saints and recitation of the rosary. Even the bishop leaned in that direction. The country, meanwhile, was plagued by "Josephinism," i.e., a theory that the State had supreme authority over the Church. These two "isms" were to cause many anguished moments for Frederic. At his new station Frederic soon became a marked man, for he attracted attention by supporting religious practices at variance with Jansenism. He frequently visited the sick, prayed over the dying, attended the poor, and performed good works highly praised by the people. Warmly received though he was by the flock, his pastoral zeal received sharp criticism from the local clergy. He went so far as to write a prayer book, *Spiritual Food,* for the people, but since his teaching was not Jansenistic, he had difficulty in getting it published.

Opposition countinued to mount. Frederic was finally reported to the bishop for exaggerating devotion to the Blessed Sacrament, introducing devotions to the Sacred Heart of Jesus and the Assumption of the Blessed Virgin Mary. The Jansenists had won the day. Frederic was reprimanded and sent to Metlika near the Croatian border, a region noted for its backwardness. Once again his zeal for souls caused a collision between him and the parish priests. He reached out to the people, rekindled old devotions that had lapsed and renewed their religious fervor. As before, he won the affection of the flock but incurred the wrath of the priests.

Meanwhile, in 1827, Bishop Edward Fenwick of Cincinnati appealed to the European bishops for priests to staff his young diocese. Father Rese, his vicar general, stopped in Paris to solicit aid from the Society for the Propagation of the Faith and then traveled to Vienna. There in conference with Emperor Francis I and Prof. Joseph Pletz of the University, they planned a society very similar to the one in

Paris; the result was the Leopoldine Foundation, an organization named after the emperor's daughter who had been empress in Brasil. While still in Europe, Fr. Rese wrote a brief history of the Cincinnati diocese and emphasized its need for missionaries and financial support, and noted that Bishop Fenwick, hearing the pleas of the Indian in his diocese, was very eager to send missionaries to them. Frederic received a copy of this history and then wrote to his bishop.

"After long and serious consideration and after carefully examining what I think is the Will of God for me, I have definitely decided to go to work as a missionary in North America. In order to put this resolution into execution, I respectfully beg my Reverend Ordinary to be transferred from the Diocese of Ljubljana to the Diocese of Cincinnati in North America."

When the bishop approved Frederic's request, the young priest immediately wrote to Fenwick. Weeks passed, then months, without a word from Cincinnati. Disappointed though he was, he could see in this an expression of God's Will. Writing to his sister, he said: "God could allow my letter to the Bishop of Cincinnati or his to me, to be lost on its long and unsafe transit. . . . His Holy Will be done." But the long-awaited response arrived on September 22, 1830, and he immediately made plans for his departure. The first Sunday in October was the parishioners' "farewell Sunday." They so loved him that it was a sad occasion; the parish priests, on the other hand, were anxious to see him depart and bade him an unfriendly goodbye.

On his way he stopped in Vienna to visit classmates and the Leopoldine Foundation before continuing to Havre de Grace for his departure on December 1. He arrived in New York on the last day of the year and, tarrying there only briefly, he continued on, reaching Cincinnati on January 31, 1831.

Since it was an unfavorable time of the year to journey to

the northern reaches of the diocese to establish a mission among the Indians, Bishop Fenwick assigned Baraga to pastoral duties in the city and its environs, where he was primarily associated with German Catholics. He finally set out for his mission station on April 21, 1831. The bishop requested him to visit the Catholics on the way and then meet him in Dayton, for the bishop wished to accompany him to the missions. As Frederic journeyed along he encountered a number of isolated Catholic families, both German and English speaking. One old Irishman in particular, living long in the wilderness, had not seen a priest in fifty years. Frederic met his bishop in Dayton and together they made their way to Arbre Croche (Harbor Springs, Michigan), where he began his apostolate among the North American Indians.

Frederic discovered that the Ottawa Indians at Arbre Croche were not ignorant of their religion, for a humble Indian, Chief Assiginak, had been instructing them in the Catholic faith. The young missionary set about instructing the natives, baptizing them, hearing confessions and saying Mass. Soon he established a model Christian community that would be the envy of some European monasteries. The Angelus bell would ring at 5 a.m., and the village would assemble at the church for morning prayers. This was followed by Mass. Then the evening bell would bring them in for night prayer and the singing of hymns in their native tongue. After these devotions Frederic gave a short instruction. On Sundays and holy days of obligation, the Indians met four times: early morning prayers, High Mass at 10 a.m., vespers and catechism at 3 p.m., and night prayers at sunset. Baraga wanted to make Arbre Croche a model so that other Indians would embrace the faith and choose to settle in such a permanent community. Soon after his arrival he reopened the school; he and the chief taught the boys, while a half-breed woman taught the girls.

With Arbre Croche as his mission base, Baraga visited

the nearby Indian settlements. His first journeys were short but then he increased the distance as he grew stronger and more accustomed to travel. In the beginning he had to use an interpreter, even for confessions; but as his fluency in the Indian tongue grew he was able to dispense with this assistance.

Describing his labors at Arbre Croche during the fall and winter of 1831, he wrote:

"It is unspeakably consoling and joyful to be to be here. The conversions of pagan Indians, who live around here, are so numerous that in the short space of two months and a half that I have been here, seventy-two Indians, children and adults, have been baptized; among them are venerable old men of sixty and seventy years."

He proceeded to explain his methods: he would enter a wigwam and ask the inhabitants about their religious beliefs. Sometimes he found Catholics, other times pagans. To the latter he tried to show the utility and necessity of the Christian religion. Many accepted his teaching and embraced the faith. "I cannot express with what heartfelt joy and grateful feelings I baptize newly converted pagans," he said, and then added that on one day he "baptized at one time eleven pagans."

Frederic was not content to minister only to the Indians at Arbre Croche but was anxious to reach out to more distant settlements. In May, 1832, with his trusted Indian guides, he set out for Beaver Island. Describing the canoe trip to his new settlement he remarked about the favorable reception his party received from the Indians. Observing Indian protocol, he engaged in "small talk" on the evening of his arrival, and then requested of the chief a conference with the Indian assembly the following day. The next day he spoke to them about the Christian religion and proceeded to instruct them in some truths of the faith. Success smiled on his efforts, for he was able to baptize twenty-two adults on May 11.

A man on the move, Frederic soon journeyed to another settlement, Indian Lake, on the north shore of Lake Michigan. The natives with eager longing had awaited a "Blackrobe" and even went so far as to begin construction of a church in anticipation of a missionary visit. Baraga was warmly received and, having glimpsed the crude church under construction, rejoiced. He helped them complete the building and the next day he dedicated it to the Blessed Virgin Mary. He remained quite a while among these Indians instructing them, saying daily Mass and preaching to them about God's love. Of all the Indians gracing this settlement only one refused to accept baptism. In the tradition of St. Francis Xavier, he requested the Indians, after they were baptized, to bring him all "idolatrous articles" used in their pagan rites for a mass burning. He usually made this a grand ceremony for it marked their transition from paganism to Christianity.

During these early days on the mission Baraga established a pattern of activity that remained basically unchanged until his death. He chose a particular Indian settlement as permanent mission station and there established his residence, a church, a school and other residences for teachers, brothers and sisters should he be fortunate to receive their help. He encouraged the Indians to abandon their nomadic way of life, gather around the church in a permanent settlement, substitute agricultural efforts for traditional hunting and fishing expeditions, and construct homes to replace the primitive wigwam. In time the mission station would assume the look of a traditional parish. He was greatly influenced in his planning by the Jesuit Reductions in Paraguay. Leaving a permanent settlement such as Arbre Croche and beginning the process all over again did bring some regrets, but the prospect of answering the call of "Indians who yearn for the Bread of Life and have no one to break it for them," encouraged him to proceed with his plans.

Meanwhile, Frederic's beloved friend, Bishop Fenwick,

died and was succeeded by John Purcell. Baraga was informed that a new diocese, Detroit, had been carved out of the
territory of the Diocese of Cincinnati, and Fr. Rese was
named bishop. One of the first items on Rese's agenda was
the devolpment of Grand River (Grand Rapids) as a mission
station, and he dispatched Baraga to serve the settlement.
The missionary arrived on the tenth anniversary of his
ordination plus one day, September 22, 1833. Unlike the
friendly atmosphere at Arbre Croche, at Grand River there
was deep seated opposition to Catholicism and the new missionary. A devoted fur trader, Louis Champou, and his
family lived in Grand River and they did everything they
could to prepare the Indians for Frederic's arrival. Nevertheless, unscrupulous fur traders had taken advantage of
the Indians and through the use of "demon rum" had gained
mastery over them. When Baraga reprimanded the Whites
for their behavior they sought revenge by inciting the Indians
against the new priest. In one of his reports he noted that
the Indians often inflicted serious injuries on one another
in their drunken brawls. What disgusted him most was the
outrageous behavior of drunken women who would attack
like raging wolves and mutilate one another by biting off
noses and severing fingers. When the men attacked one
another with large knives, murder was often the result. The
Grand River apostolate was difficult and met with only
limited success. His enemies harassed him repeatedly and
tried to force him to retreat, but he remained faithful to his
charge.

The United States government, a constant threat to the
Indians and their way of life, violated the trust the Indians
felt they had established with it. Through unequal treaties,
the actions of unscrupulous Indian agents, the connivances
of wicked fur traders and greedy Whites, the Indians were
slowly forced from their lands, herded into groups, and
marched farther west and north. Frederic stood as one of
the last barriers to the white man's march onto Indian lands.

At Grand River, Baraga's resistance to government encroachment was so strong that the government pressured Bishop Rese to remove him. His enemies had won the day. When Frederic was relieved of his mission mandate he moved to the Chippewas in the Lake Superior region and first took up residence at Cottrellville, then settled at La Pointe. When he stepped ashore on July 27, 1835, he was the first priest on the Island in 164 years. His work was cut out for him; he began constructing a church, the first ever at La Pointe. His missionary efforts began paying off immediately, but success incurred the wrath of the local Protestant missionaries.

The pattern of missionary activity at Arbre Croche was repeated at this new station. Frederic soon set out for the Indians in distant settlements, such as Fond du Lac where he was ably assisted by a devoted fur trader, Pierre Cotte, who had prepared many of the Indians for the missionary visit by instructing them in the essentials of the faith. Within a few days of his arrival Baraga baptized fifty-one adults.

Returning to La Pointe, he continued his priestly ministry and within five months he had converted 184 Indians. His plans for a school, however, hit a snag for the lack of a teacher, and so he wrote his sister, Antonia, in Austria, and asked her to consider coming to La Pointe. Though successful in his apostolate he realized more could be accomplished had he had adequate financial resources. This prompted him to go on a missionary tour of Europe to solicit aid. It also afforded him an opportunity to have his books published. Besides being an intrepid missionary, Baraga was also a scholar, author and linguist. Like many Europeans, he had an aptitude for languages and quickly learned Indian dialects so that he was able to preach and teach them in their own tongue. He became so proficient in these Indian languages that he wrote devotional books for his converts and dictionaries for students and missionaries.

His journeys in the fall of 1836 took him to Europe where

he visited the Society for the Propagation of the Faith and these generous people authorized funds for the printing of his books. They were written in the Ojibway and Ottawa dialects so that the five tribes, Ojibway, Ottawa, Potawatomi, Menominee and Algonquin, could use them. He remained in Paris ten weeks supervising the printing and collecting funds for his mission. In Paris he met his sister who had accepted his invitation to teach at La Pointe, but she remained in Paris while he continued his tour of Europe. In March 1837, he had an audience with Pope Pius IX and received a very warm reception from the pontiff. Wherever he went — Paris, Lyons, Rome, Vienna — he was showered with gifts for the missions. Finally, he returned to Paris, joined Antonia, and both left for the United States.

While his mission grew and success marked his moves, Antonia tried teaching but was unable to manage. The harsh climate, the difficulties with the Indian language and unexpected disappointments proved too burdensome for her, and so she returned home.

Frederic remained at La Pointe for eight years, then moved to L'Anse where he walked into the middle of an internal dispute about tribal succession. The problem was exacerbated by religious differences among the Indians of whom some where Catholics while others were Protestants. Holding true to his missionary plan, Frederic went to work on the school. Both the mission and the school were highly successful; and this, in turn, alarmed the Methodist missionaries in the area. They pressured the Acting Superintendent of Indian Affairs, Robert Stuart, to have Baraga removed from L'Anse. They wanted to intiate a policy whereby the government would issue one license for a mission and prohibit a second mission to operate in an area where one had already been established. Pressure was exerted on Frederic to move but he refused. Although threats and intrigues met him at every turn, he remained steadfast in his resolve to remain at L'Anse. Discrimination toward the Catholic mission resulted, but Baraga reminded the agent that his actions were shockingly inconsistent with the freedom of religion professed by the United States. When the local troublemakers were removed, dissension ceased.

While ministering to the Indians at L'Anse, Frederic learned that a new diocese had been created in the Wisconsin Territory with its seat at Milwaukee. Part of the upper reaches of Baraga's territory was transferred to the new diocese, but L'Anse remained under Detroit. A national council of Catholic bishops assembled in Baltimore in 1852, and there Bishop Lefevere of Detroit offered a resolution that the territory of the Upper Peninsula of Michigan be raised to the status of a Vicariate Apostolic and recommended Baraga as vicar. The council supported Lefevere's recommendation. Rome approved it and on November 1, 1853, Archbishop Purcell consecrated Frederic Baraga, naming him Bishop of Amyzonia, and Vicar Apostolic of Upper Michigan.

The newly consecrated bishop was aware of the region's desperate need for money and material and in January, 1854, he wrote a letter to the Leopoldine Foundation. He described his territory, spoke of the Indians inhabiting the region and of his many needs and finally asked help to construct his cathedral at Sault Ste. Marie. After this first plea he decided to visit Europe himself to solicit financial aid and personnel. Like his earlier tour, this visitation proved to be a success. Through the reports he had submitted to the Leopoldine Foundation and from his own presence among them from time to time, Europeans knew a great deal about this North American missionary and the extraordinary work he was doing. They wanted to be part of it and were generous in response to his appeals. When he visited Trebnje he met his widowed sister, Amalia, now sixty years old — he had not seen her in seventeen years. In Rome he again had an audience with Pope Pius IX and, while speaking to the pontiff, requested that his Vicariate Apostolic be raised to the rank of a diocese. The pope indicated that he would be favorable should the American bishops support this request, and since they did the elevation was effected. In an exchange of gifts, Baraga gave the pope two copies of his dictionary and received a chalice from His Holiness.

Baraga continued missionary work even after he settled into his new station, Sault Ste. Marie. When the summons went out for the Second Provincial Council of Cincinnati, 1858, he responded, but not with great enthusiasm since his health, though not impaired, was suffering the effects of years of rugged missionary activity.

The Civil War then came to the United States. Upper Michigan was far removed from the battlefields, but it did feel indirect effects of the conflict. Shortly after hostilities began the Third Provincial Council of Cincinnati assembled. Baraga, now a sick man, nonetheless attended, but he was most happy when it was over and he could return home. In 1863, he journeyed as far as Cincinnati to oversee the publication of another Indian work of his. From this vantage point he saw the war's horrifying effects and lamented the "horrible, all-devastating and desolating war." Once home he resumed his episcopal visitations and pastoral duties.

A move was underway to change the bishop's residence from Sault Ste. Marie to Marquette. Because of the remoteness and inaccessibility of Sault Ste. Marie during winter the priests of the diocese promoted this move. Marquette, in the meantime, showed signs of emerging as a commercial and political center and it would be an ideal location for the bishop. Baraga accepted these recommendations, petitioned Rome for the change, and was given permission to move provided he retained his current episcopal title, *Marianopolitanus* alongside the new one, *Marquettensis*. He acquiesced but remarked to friends that he would "never use the two titles, except when writing to Rome. On all other occasions I will always write: Bishop of Upper Michigan."

Advancing years, declining health and a move to a new

city, did not lessen Frederic's zeal, but it did diminish his activity. He attended the Second Plenary Council of Baltimore in October, 1866, and there suffered a stroke. Despite his illness he made his way back to Marquette, but his days of active ministry were over. His health continued to decline and the early weeks of January, 1868, were exceptionally painful for him. Death came in the early morning hours of January 19. When Frederic Baraga died, two dioceses had been established in Michigan carved from Cincinnati. Thousands of Indians had embraced the faith and civilization had come to parts of the wilderness frontier.

During his lifetime rumors circulated that Bishop Baraga was a saint. Whenever he chanced to hear such remarks he abruptly silenced the speaker. He was a humble man and discouraged all such talk. But he was a saintly man! God gave him the special gift of deep prayer. He had the practice of rising early in the morning, at 3, and would spend several hours in prayer before he began his rounds of activity. Penances were his constant companion: fastings, abstinences, chastisements of the body. His breviary was his favorite form of prayer and he read it by campfire light, or while storms lashed against his canoe or walking the paths through the wilderness going from one mission to another. Prayer was an integral part of his life. Bishop Baraga was also a man of love, for it was his love of God that brought him to the neglected Indians in North America.

In recognition of Bishop Baraga's holy life, the diocese of Marquette has opened proceedings leading to his beatification. For further information: Cause of Bishop Baraga, 230 Baraga Avenue, Marquette, Michigan, 49855.

PRAYER
(Private use only)
O Bishop Baraga, because of your great desire to live a life of total commitment to Jesus Christ the Lord,

you dedicated yourself completely to missionary activity to make God known, loved, and served by the poor whom you loved and served. Obtain for me, too, a complete dedication of myself to the Lord. Help me to be more concerned for the needy and those who are discriminated against.

As a man of peace, a man of love, you brought peace and love wherever you traveled. Teach me to share peace and love with my fellow man.

Pray for me that the spirit of prayer which was so intimately a part of your life may also be as deeply a part of mine.

Help me to accept the hardships of life as willingly as you did, as a part of my dying to myself that I may rise with Christ in glory.

Intercede for me with the Lord that He may grant me the graces and favors for which I pray. Amen.

FOR FURTHER READING

Bernard J. Lambert, *Shepherd of the Wilderness: A Biography of Bishop Frederic Baraga* (Chicago: Franciscan Herald Press, 1967).

CHAPTER 14

SERVANT OF GOD MOTHER CORNELIA CONNELLY, S.H.C.J.
Foundress of the
Society of the Holy Child Jesus in England and the United States.

14

No Reserves with God
MOTHER CORNELIA CONNELLY, S.H.C.J. (1809-1879)

Sr. Mary Anthony Weinig, S.H.C.J.

"COURAGE, CONFIDENCE, CHEERFULNESS," a down-to-earth saying of Mother Connelly, is not only advice but a reflection of the qualities her forebears needed in a New World, and a glimpse of the natural foundation for the work of grace in her for whom the grain of wheat dying, and the vine trimmed to the quick were images of fruitfulness.

Ralph Peacock, a Yorkshireman in his mid-twenties, migrated to the United States during George Washington's presidency and settled in Philadelphia, then temporary capital of the new nation, where he became a citizen in 1797. The following year he married Mary Swope Bowen, widow of a Jamaica planter. Her grandfather, Daniel Steinmetz, believed by some to be Jewish, had come from Germany in 1732. His large family belonged to the First German Reformed Church where in 1768 his daughter Susanna married Dr. Jacob Swope; she died the same year after giving birth to Mary. This child growing up during the Revolutionary War would remember her physician father ministering to the soldiers of the Continental Army, and her merchant grandfather aiding them with supplies. At eighteen Mary married an Englishman, John Bowen, in the same church as her parents. Bowen died in 1794, leaving her with two children but financially secure. Four years later Mary and Ralph Peacock were married in Christ Church by the Episcopal Bishop of Philadelphia, William White. Ralph, baptized in infancy in the Church of England, did not form lasting ties with American Episcopalianism; by 1803 he was a pew holder in the Second Presbyterian Church, then flourishing under the able rectorship of Jacob Janeway. Family marriages and burials, but no baptisms, are recorded there until Mary Peacock's death in 1823.

For twenty years, until Ralph died at 50 in 1818, the Peacock family seems to have lived happily at various addresses within the historic square mile around Independence Hall in old Philadelphia. One daughter said in later life that she could not recall a harsh word ever spoken; extant correspondence reveals the lasting warmth of family affection. The household included Isabella and John Bowen, the children of Mary's first marriage, and eventually seven others. It is the youngest child of Ralph and Mary Peacock, born January 15, 1809, and named Cornelia Augusta, who concerns us here.

Almost nothing has come down to us about Cornelia's childhood. Her education consisted partly of lessons at home including painting and music. Her favorite brother, Ralph, she reminisces in a letter, primed her canvas for her; her eldest brother, Dodsworth, who died in 1822, was an artist.

She and her sister Mary Frances, closest in age and "best beloved," enjoyed the theater.

Bereavement came soon. Cornelia was only nine when her father died. Five years later she lost her mother and the home was broken up. The three oldest children were already married, the boys in their twenties were on their own, and the two youngest girls, Mary and Cornelia, were welcomed respectively by their sister and half-sister Adeline Peacock Duval and Isabella Montgomery. Isabella had married Austin Montgomery the year Cornelia was born; the childless couple lavished every care upon the gifted orphan, who grew into a lovely and accomplished young woman.

It is in this setting that significant religious steps were taken. The Calvinist cast of Cornelia's mother's own upbringing, reinforced by the strict discipline of Janeway's Presbyterian congregation, diminished its hold on her children as they came under the influence of the fervent James Montgomery, brother-in-law of Isabella and High Church founder and pastor of St. Stephen's Episcopal Church, which opened in 1823.

Here the Duvals and the Bowens worshipped and their children were christened. Cornelia and Mary were understandably brought into the same orbit. At first it is surprising to learn that these two young women were baptized at St. Stephen's in 1831. We have no record of an earlier baptism, and find a strong reason for Cornelia's needing a certificate of valid reception of the sacrament: in December of this year she was to marry an Episcopalian minister, Pierce Connelly.

Isabella Montgomery not approving of her ward's engagement, Cornelia appealed to her other married sister, Adeline Duval, and the wedding took place in the latter's home, December 1, 1831. Bishop White officiated, as he had for Cornelia's parents thirty-three years before. If feathers were ruffled, Cornelia's loving tact soon restored harmony. It was in the 1830s that a lifelong correspondence began among the members of a close-knit family who until then had lived within a few blocks of each other in their native Philadelphia.

Cornelia was the pioneer, the first woman of the family to set out permanently for unknown territory since her progenitors had come to America from Europe one, two, three generations before. Her twenty-seven year old husband, who had also begun life in a Presbyterian congregation and changed to Protestant Episcopal in his student years, served at St. James' Church, Kingsessing (Philadelphia), where Bishop White ordained him in 1828. Pierce's hopes for a rectorship in Boston not being realized, he accepted a call to Trinity Church in Natchez, Mississippi. Here the newly-married couple moved early in 1832.

Natchez was a city of contrasts — a busy river port through which Mississippi cotton was shipped north and south, a notorious hang-out for gamblers and horse thieves, a residential center for an intellectual, politically influential and wealthy elite. Pierce's pastoral responsibilities, far from being limited to the occupants of the beautiful ante-bellum homes and their slaves (for whom he composed a catechism), extended more than a day's journey south and east. His zeal and success were impressive, his home happy and by Easter, 1835, already blessed with two children, his wife an ideal helpmate with "perfect confidence in the piety, integrity and learning" of her deeply loved husband.

What prompted Cornelia to write this to her sister Adeline was alarm in Philadelphia over Catholic leanings in Natchez. Why had Pierce "meddled with controversy?" "To find out the truth, the blessed truth." The flood of anti-Catholic pamphlets in the Nativist polemic of the 1830s had reached the Mississippi Valley and by their extravagance led the rightminded to look more closely at the faith and practice under attack. This reading, and the providential opportunity to discuss such matters with a new Catholic friend, the French cartographer Joseph Nicollet (there on a surveying expedition for the U.S. government), affected the Connellys profoundly. Nicollet's religious fervor and spiritual insight equalled his erudition. Pierce experienced his quick sympathy; Cornelia found him "our great and good friend." After Pierce resigned his rectorship (August, 1835) for reasons of conscience, Nicollet had "the joy of putting [his] friend in better hands," those of Bishop Rosati in St. Louis, and events moved rapidly.

Encouraged to go to Rome, where Pierce, after clearing up some remaining doubts, was to make his abjuration, the Connellys sold their home and effects in Natchez and prepared for a long sea voyage — and an undetermined future — with a three year old son and a baby daughter of nine months.

This was Cornelia's second journey in faith on her husband's initiative, following what she believed was God's will for them both. And, as four years before she was not deterred by her guardian's objection to her marriage, here too she acted decisively upon clear conviction. She had no theological uncertainties to hold her back; she was received into the Church and made her First Communion in New Orleans before they sailed for Europe in December, 1835.

In October she had written to her anxious family: "Pierce is not a Catholic nor could he be a Catholic priest if he desired it while I live." Pierce's dilemma was real: he still felt he had a priestly vocation; he knew his obligations as husband and father. There would be some comfort in the (1836) advice of Cardinal Odescalchi, Vicar of Rome, that "my prospects of usefulness in embracing the Catholic Faith will be greater as a married man than as a priest . . . the example of my conversion will be kept in sight longer. . . ."

Was Odescalchi's discernment of Connelly's situation aided by the presence of the Catholic wife at her husband's abjuration and conditional baptism in the Cardinal Vicar's private chapel (March 27, 1836)? His view was not shared by all authorities whose decisions shaped the converts' destinies during the next decade.

Meanwhile in Rome, Pierce and Cornelia met many ecclesiastics and lay people who helped and inspired their first months in the Church. The English Earl of Shrewsbury took a kindly interest in the couple, and his saintly daughter, the Princess Borghese, became Cornelia's friend. The spiritual and cultural riches of the city were a feast for Cornelia, and she made time for music, art, and language studies. This proved to be preparation for a future role as educator, and also as wage earner when her husband's salary was insufficient.

Here we quote a particularly perceptive passage from a recent study (Sr. Caritas McCarthy's 1980 Gregorian University dissertation, *The Spirituality of Cornelia Connelly*), and an excerpt from a letter of Cornelia at this period:

"Cornelia, wholeheartedly wife and mother, energetically struggled to demonstrate her place within his [her husband's] commitment as he began to search for a fitting lay apostolate. It was to her own more general ecclesial vocation that she appealed. We cannot but admire the resourcefulness and feel the poignancy of her striving to hold together their marriage, to reconcile seemingly conflicting demands of God, to find an adequate religious mission for Pierce. She wrote to Pierce when he was exploring vocational prospects in England [Spring 1836]: 'Dearest Life, I received your sweet letter from [Paris] the day before yesterday — let me kiss you for it, but at the same time give you a good scolding for being so dull. Dear love I knew it would be so — you try very hard to persuade me you are happy but all the time I know your heart is with me — but this must not be so; give it all to the Church, all, all, and then I shall have it, too, for am I not one of its children without a wish that is not connected with it? Oh, Petty, don't think about want or any affliction that it might please the Almighty God to punish us with; while we have the kingdom of heaven within us will we not be happy in spite of every earthly want, and while we have the faith will we not be able to bear all even to death? Oh love, think not of me — if I still have too much pride I deserve . . . to suffer in the *sight of our relatives* . . . but never think of this my love if your duty to God would be better fulfilled by going home — but I cannot conceive you could be more useful by going back to America . . . can it be possible that a man of your abilities would not be useful to the Catholics of England? At all events, don't give way to depression — the Almighty will not forsake you after having done so much for you — he will give you faith and give you strength to go on in the good work and be useful in the world; and have you not already increased the faith of some and shaken others?' "

England and America were both in some sense mission territory. Support in funds and personnel from Europe was a godsend to the church of the frontier and of the immigrant (and a cause of alarm to the Nativists). Pierce, whether as informal emissary with letters of introduction, as spokesman on his own authority, or simply as proof of a good investment (a "big catch"), was welcomed by interested churchmen and benefactors: by Pope Gregory XVI, by Nicholas Wiseman, then rector of the English College in Rome, by Prince Metternich in Austria. The Connellys' third child was born in Vienna (June 1837). But word of financial losses at home consequent upon the Panic of 1837 terminated their European sojourn. Characteristically Pierce responded with gloom and anxiety, while Cornelia, "dancing with delight" was "more rejoiced than I can say over a return to our peaceful quiet home life."

Back in Natchez by January, 1838, the Connelly's did find it difficult to make ends meet. Pierce was a bank clerk, Cornelia planning to open a Young Ladies' academy to supplement their income, when an invitation to Louisiana seemed apostolically and personally a good move in the spring. Pierce was to teach at the new Jesuit College of St. Charles in Grand Coteau. Cornelia could give music lessons at the Sacred Heart convent nearby. A tiny cottage would be available to them. This "missionary venture on the edge of the frontier" proved a seedbed of graces for Cornelia and a strong spiritual foundation for the work that lay ahead.

There was suffering, the death in early infancy of her fourth child (September, 1839). There was the ever present thought that God might ask the renunciation of her married life: "Oh my God, if all this happiness is not to Thy greater glory and the good of souls, take it from me — I make the sacrifice." Grief totally unforeseen came when her two and a half year old son was accidentally pushed by a big dog into a vat of boiling sugar, and died in her arms — "suffered 43 hours and was taken into the temple of the Lord on the Purification," February 2, 1840. Her notebook, usually laconic, gives glimpses of a soul deeply united with our Lord and totally generous.

Cornelia had been introduced to the *Spiritual Exercises* of St. Ignatius in a retreat she was permitted to share at the convent in December, 1839. Here was sustenance and a means to continued growth, an instrument to help others grow, and a touchstone for her life. The able direction of Fr. Nicholas Point, S.J., and Cornelia's complete openness to God prepared her to see God's leading in what was next asked of her. On October 13, 1840, Pierce, himself in retreat with the Jesuits, told her he was now sure that God was calling him to the priesthood, and proposed that they make no outward change in their lives but live as brother and sister while he took their not unprecedented case to Rome. Cornelia, pregnant with their fifth child, begged him to consider seriously, to discern maturely. If God asked this sacrifice, she would make it.

No one knew of their proposal except their spiritual directors. Cornelia's sister Mary did not suspect. Mary Frances had come into the Church (as did most of her family sooner or later) and was soon to enter the Society of the Sacred Heart at Grand Coteau. To this Cornelia's thoughts also turned as Pierce left for Europe in May, 1842, taking their eldest son, Mercer, to boarding school in England and proceeding to Rome. In a year Pierce was back to fetch her. Both must be present in Rome. There were delays en route, visits, something like the old social life she thought she had relinquished. Was Pierce sufficiently clear in his purposes?

Finally settled at the Sacred Heart Convent, the Trinità dei Monti, in Rome with her daughter Adeline in the school and her small son Frank and his nurse with her in a cottage on the grounds, Cornelia waited and prayed through her dryness of spirit and the suddenly swift progress toward her husband's goal. The pope had taken things into his own hands, granting the decree of separation in March, 1844, and approving Pierce's ordination in July, 1845. Just prior to this Cornelia had made a solemn vow of chastity, first offering to Pierce, before it was too late, to resume their married life. He persisted in his determination.

Cornelia knew by now that her vocation was not to the Society of the Sacred Heart. She had been assured that her vow did not hinder her caring for her children. The boys' education was guaranteed by generous friends. Adeline would remain with her mother. Where and how was not at all certain. But plans for ministry were tentatively drawn up, Fr. John Grassi, S.J., and Pierce assisting Cornelia to outline a rule for an apostolic congregation to be formed possibly in America whose needs she knew. Bishop Wiseman and Lord Shrewsbury asked specifically that she come to England: girls' education was sadly lacking; the fields were ripe for the spiritual works of mercy.

The English plea prevailed. With "the verbal sanction of . . . Gregory XVI, 1846, and the Protection of Cardinal Franzoni" of the Propagation of the Faith, the Society of the Holy Child Jesus — tradition tells us that she heard this name interiorly in prayer — came quietly into action, October 13, 1846, when Cornelia with a few companions, fewer material resources, and a faith that was to be much tried arrived in the industrial town of Derby. The influx of poor Catholic immigrants during the Irish potato famine of the 1840s increased the need of night schools and Sunday schools where the factory girls could learn to read and write. These and the day schools made heavy demands on Cornelia's and her sisters' zeal and charity, which also extended to ladies' retreats, instruction of converts, translation of French spiritual books, and the beginnings of a boarding school.

Yet religious tranquility and order and a spirit of joy and simplicity characterized the convent from the start. All were novices together, but Cornelia was the guide and mother. In a little over a year Bishop Wiseman received her vows of poverty and obedience and installed her as superior general. By 1859 he gave formal episcopal approbation to the adapted and fleshed out rule which was the basis of the constitutions finally approved by Rome only after Cornelia's death.

Vicissitudes tested Cornelia's trust and courage from the first. Her two younger children, contrary to her expectation, were sent to boarding schools, then secretly whisked away by their father. His frustrated attempts to interfere in Cornelia's work were followed by really aberrant behavior. In December, 1848, Pierce began suit in the English courts for restitution of conjugal rights. When Cornelia in 1850 appealed the decision against her and the Privy Council suspended the sentence in 1851, Pierce failed to pursue the case and resorted to a spate of anti-Catholic pamphlets rather like those whose preposterousness had led him to the Church twenty years before. He eventually subsided and ended his days as Protestant Episcopal minister to an English congregation in Florence, Italy, Cornelia's alienated children believing him to be the wronged party throughout.

In nineteenth-century England many would uphold a man's power over his wife and children as property rights. A twentieth-century priest psychologist, Georges Cruchon,

S.J., reads Pierce's emotional state as psychological inability to deal with his disappointed ambition and jealousy of his wife's career — egoism unable to do without the admiring support of a devoted spouse, feelings of rejection involving his relations with his mother. Cornelia knew intuitively the risks entailed in letting Pierce go off alone. Her submission to the arrangements made was not the docility of a Victorian wife but a total sacrifice to God of something good and holy because she believed He asked it of her through the voice of His Church.

God's blessing was evident in her work. Nowhere easy, the labor of foundation was keenly felt in Derby, where through a combination of circumstances involving financial and pastoral misunderstanding her position became untenable; St. Leonards-on-Sea, a second and long-lived establishment, survived storms of counterclaim about the intentions of the donor. The litany could continue through the unpromising American beginnings in Towanda, Pa., the precarious footholds in France. But the apostolate flourished and bore abundant fruit. Her schools were happy places where the children's character and creativity were developed and challenged in an atmosphere of trust and spontaneity. Her teacher training college won high praise. Much that she envisioned was realized after her lifetime. Her death at St. Leonard's in England on April 18, 1879, was the fulfillment of her sacrifice. Her life of accepted suffering is part of her legacy of joy in the Lord.

The cause of Cornelia Connelly's beatification was introduced in the English diocese of Southwark in 1959. The documentation on the life and writings of the Servant of God is nearing completion for submision to the Sacred Congregation for the Causes of Saints. For further information: The Postulator, Sisters of the Holy Child Jesus, 620 Edmunds Avenue, Drexel Hill, Pennsylvania, 19026.

PRAYER
(Private use only)

O God, whom it pleased to glorify the name of Your Son, the Holy Child Jesus, through the obedience which He learned in the school of suffering: be pleased also to glorify the name of Your servant Cornelia who was inspired to found the Society of the Holy Child Jesus in His spirit of sufferng obedience. Through the same Christ Our Lord. Amen.

FOR FURTHER READING

Mary Andrew Armour and Ursula Blake, *Cornelia* (Society of the Holy Child Jesus, 1979); M. Therese Bisgood, *Cornelia Connelly: A Study in Fidelity* (Westminster, Md.: Newman, 1963).

CHAPTER 15

SERVANT OF GOD MOTHER ADELAIDE OF ST. TERESA, O.C.D.
Foundress of the
Carmelite Monastery at Grajal de Campos, Spain.

15

Yankee Courage in a Carmelite Nun

MOTHER ADELAIDE OF ST. TERESA, O.C.D. (1817-1893)

Otilio Rodriguez, O.C.D.

JOAN ADELAIDE O'SULLIVAN was born in Yonkers, one of the more populated suburbs of New York, on October 8, 1817, the fourth of six children of an aristocratic Irish family. Her parents were John Thomas O'Sullivan, a Catholic, and Mary Rowley, an Anglican and niece of Lord Chesterfield. On her father's side she was descended from the O'Sullivans who were the Earls of Bantry in southern Ireland in the sixteenth century, and on whose coat of arms was the motto: "There is no hand as generous and bounteous as the O'Sullivan hand." During the Catholic persecution under Elizabeth I, the family lost its estates and sought refuge in Spain where King Philip III rewarded the courage of the head of the family, Donall O'Sullivan, by promoting him to Knight of Santiago and Earl of Bearehaven. He died in 1618 and was buried in the church of the Noble Irish College in Salamanca, which he had founded and generously endowed. Since persecution continued in the homeland the family left Spain and emigrated to the United States. It was in New York City that Adelaide's grandfather established himself (1783) and where his home became a kind of public chapel for the newly-arrived Irish immigrants until old St. Peter's church, Barclay Street, was opened.

Adelaide had been baptized an Anglican, as were the other children of the family, but when she was four years old, and with her mother's consent, she became a Catholic being baptized by Fr. Benedict Fenwick, S.J., the future Bishop of Boston and close friend of her father. She was a lively and joyful child and took great delight in her religious instructions.

Adelaide's father followed a diplomatic career and was an astute business man who had many commercial contacts with Spain and Latin America. He frequently traveled abroad but tragedy unfortunately struck in 1824 when the ship in which he was traveling was lost at sea. Adelaide was then only seven years old and her father's passing was doubly painful; she not only. lost her beloved parent but also lost him who instructed her in her beloved Catholicism. She eventually found a spiritual guide in Fr. George Fenwick, also a Jesuit and brother of the Bishop of Boston, and it was he who prepared her for her First Communion (1830), and introduced her to the practice of virtue and the exercise of mental prayer.

In 1835 the family moved to Washington, D.C., and was well received among the best families of the capital. Adelaide was eighteen, a well-educated young lady, modest and devout, and one who tried as best she could to avoid worldly entertainments and social gatherings. She entered the famous Academy of the Visitation in Georgetown to complete her education taking courses in literature, music, needlework, etc. But she did not remain long at the Academy. It seems her mother could not adjust to life without her daughter at her side and, furthermore, it was time for Adelaide to become acquainted with Washington's best young men. Suitors came to ask for her hand in marriage, but she successfully avoided them since she had already determined to belong to no one but to Jesus Christ.

The resolute Adelaide, against the wishes of her family, returned to the Visitation Academy, but this time to seek admission as a nun (1837). Within the convent enclosure her spiritual life developed and her devotion to Jesus Crucified became her favorite form of piety. One day while meditating on the words from the Song of Songs (8:6), "Set me as a seal upon your heart," she took a burning iron rod and engraved a cross and three nails on her breast to indicate her irrevocable dedication to Christ. She received the habit of the Sisters of the Visitation and made her profession on November 1, 1839, receiving the name Sister Mary John.

While at the Visitation convent, Adelaide was introduced by her spiritual director, Fr. Felix Valera, to the writings of the great Carmelite nun, St. Teresa of Avila. These writings made such an impression on her that she decided that she had to enter Carmel. But to carry out this decision was not as easy as she had first thought. She would need ecclesiastical approval to transfer from one convent to another and, furthermore, the only Carmel in the United States at that time was in Baltimore, established in 1830, where the sisters did not take solemn vows. But Adelaide desired to imitate St. Teresa in everything, even to the taking of such vows, and so she placed her trust in Providence as she had learned from St. Teresa, "God never puts good desires into the soul without helping her to put them into practice." It so happened that Fr. Varela had a relative who was Prioress at the Carmel in Havana, Cuba. Adelaide applied for admission even though she knew no Spanish. She arrived in Havana on October 15, 1840, and at the request of the archbishop of the city was admitted "on a temporary basis pending final decision either to stay, or leave for another convent or go back to her own country." During her stay at the Havana Carmel she made remarkable progress in the spiritual life; she devoted herself to mental prayer, recollection, and penances for the conversion of her family. Adelaide found great peace of soul and this led her to resolve to become a saintly Carmelite always seeking to do the will of God. She courageously lived her vocation to the full, no matter what the cost. Her health began to decline and she contracted yellow fever; it was only after much suffering that she returned to health.

Since the anticlerical Spanish government of Mendizábal decreed the suppression of religious orders in Spain and her colonies, including Cuba, the Havana Carmel was now forbidden to accept postulants and its novices were forbidden to take vows. Adelaide thus found herself in Carmel, where she wanted to be, but without the possibility of ever pronouncing vows as a Carmelite nun. While she was undergoing this severe test, Monsignor George Viteri, the newly-appointed Bishop of San Salvador, stopped at the Havana Carmel on his way to Rome. Learning of Adelaide's predicament he encouraged her to transfer to the Carmel in Guatemala City where his sister, Mother Mary of the Rosary, was Prioress. This was the only ray of hope that the saddened Adelaide possessed. When Bishop Viteri returned to Havana from Rome, he and Adelaide set out on August 10, 1843, for Guatemala. Adelaide arrived at her destination on September 8, where the Carmelite sisters greeted her most happily and on October 4 of that year she received the Carmelite habit and, according to the Order's custom, took the name Sister Adelaide of St. Teresa.

Sr. Adelaide's determination was rewarded with a peace-filled year, a year of spiritual advancement in every respect; she was prayerful, mortified, docile, fully interested in her

Carmelite formation and much admired by her community. She was admitted to profession on October 15, 1844, feast of her patroness, St. Teresa. Sr. Adelaide was twenty-seven years old, humble and of a peaceful nature, beloved by everyone for her deep spirituality and her natural talents — she was an excellent pianist. Fourteen years after her profession she was appointed (1858) to the office of Mistress of Novices and the choice was a happy one, for she was a living example to her novices of what they ought to become. In life, joy and satisfaction are mingled with sorrow and pain, and Sr. Adelaide's life was no exception; she suffered immeasurably when her mother died (1860) in Lisbon while visiting her son, John, who was U. S. Minister to Portugal.

In 1868 Mother Adelaide was unanimously elected Prioress of the monastery; she alone was the most capable and worthy of that office. She was so greatly esteemed by her sisters that she was re-elected Prioress in 1871. During that year the anti-Catholic hatred of the Revolutionary Junta began to exert itself in Guatemala by expelling the various religious orders of priests and curtailing religious activities. M. Adelaide foresaw the great loss the Church was to suffer and she had the indomitable courage to write to the leader of the revolutionaries, "I think your junta looks like that scene in the Stations of the Cross where Pilate is sitting in judgment over Christ, surrounded by Pharisees." It was inevitable that M. Adelaide would come into collision with the junta.

In February, 1874, the junta decreed the closing of all monasteries and the gathering of all nuns into one convent. M. Adelaide and her community left their beloved Carmel to go to St. Catherine's convent, but the transfer did not result in the abandonment of the religious life as the authorities had hoped. Eventually, St. Catherine's was also closed and the sisters had to seek hospitality from friends and acquaintances. During this period when her Carmelite sisters were dispersed throughout Guatemala City, M. Adelaide received an invitation from the exiled Archbishop of Guatemala, who had been in Havana since 1871. The Havana Carmel requested M. Adelaide to return to them, but she would not go without her community. Later, and because the Havana Carmel could only accept five sisters, M. Adelaide with four others journeyed there (November, 1875), always nurturing the hope that one day she and her sisters would be united again in a place suitable to live the strict rule of Carmel. Havana was but a temporary stopover. The Bishop of Savannah in Georgia invited the sisters to make a foundation in his diocese, and together with her small band of sisters, she left for New York in August, 1877. The community spent two years in Savannah and it now grew to nine members, but Savannah was not the place for them. Having had the encouragement of the Jesuit fathers in Yonkers, it was decided to try a foundation in New York. Yonkers was M. Adelaide's birthplace; and when she and her community arrived (September, 1879), her brother, John, together with the Jesuits gave them a most hearty welcome and took them to the house they had prepared for them. But New York was not to be the permanent home of her foundation. M. Adelaide then went to Toronto (September, 1880), but neither was this Canadian city to be the site of her monastery. Despite these failures, M. Adelaide was much too courageous and adventurous to set her project aside. The spiritual director of the community at this time was Fr. Salinero, a Spanish Jesuit, and it was he who suggested they go to Spain, to St. Teresa's own country, and establish their monastery there.

It seems strange that M. Adelaide would look to Spain as the home of her Carmel when the Church there was suffering under an anticlerical government, but again the words of Scripture were to be fulfilled, "He who trusts in the Lord will not be confounded" (Rom. 10:11). When M. Adelaide was in Savannah she met a devout lady, Carmen

Barrasa, wife of the Spanish Vice-consul and niece of Saturnino Fernandez de Castro, Bishop of León. This kind lady had written to her uncle about the hardships that M. Adelaide had endured and of her poor daughters still in Guatemala. The bishop's answer was quick and positive; he would be most happy to accept them in his diocese. When M. Adelaide heard this good news, she did not hesitate a moment — she was always eager to imitate St. Teresa and what could be better than to do so in Spain itself. Together with her seven professed sisters and four novices, M. Adelaide left New York on May 18, 1881, aboard the *Ferdinand de Lesseps.* To ensure their safe arrival in Spain her brother, together with some of her generous friends, traveled with the sisters. The ship docked at Cádiz on June 5, and the Carmelite provincial of Andalusia, Fr. Ferdinand of the Immaculate Conception, received them most hospitably and presented them to Cardinal Lluch y Garriga, Archbishop of Seville, a Discalced Carmelite himself. On June 10, they were in Madrid where the Bishop of León was awaiting them. The bishop's greeting was warm and affectionate and he took the sisters on a tour of the various Teresian foundations: St. Joseph's in Avila on June 11, Valladolid on June 12, and Medina de Rioseco on June 13, It is easy to imagine the sentiments that M. Adelaide and her daughters experienced when they visited the cradle of the Teresian Carmel and sensed the living spirit of St. Teresa herself. She wrote: "Words could not express the emotions that stirred in our hearts; our silence spoke for itself." Since there were many monasteries in the city of León, the capital of the province, the bishop temporarily housed them in the Franciscan monastery of St. Clare in Villafrechos, a convent large enough for both communities.

Grateful as M. Adelaide and her daughters were for all that the bishop had done for them, nevertheless, they soon realized that they could not fully live the Teresian ideal of Carmel while living together with another non-Carmelite community. With evangelical liberty they explained to the bishop that they really needed a monastery of their own. The understanding bishop agreed to transfer them to Villalon, the second largest city in his diocese, but the house offered them was far from suitable for their manner of life. But Providence again came to her rescue. A very devout priest, Fr. Fermín Domínguez, Rector of the Seminary in Villalon and a native of Grajal de Campos, knew of an old Franciscan monastery founded in 1599 that had been abandoned at the time of the suppression of the religious orders. He told M. Adelaide that the monastery and church were in reasonably good condition, that it had a large vegetable garden and a good supply of water. Furthermore, it was situated on the outskirts of the village, a very quiet place with beautiful vistas.

At her first sight of the monastic ruins at Grajal de Campos, M. Adelaide knew this was to be her home. She bought the land and immediately set about having it restored. While the renovation was in progress she moved her community into a private home and there they lived according to the strict Carmelite observance until their new monastery would be ready. M. Adelaide herself designed and supervised the restorations and finally on December 18, 1882, the foundation was dedicated to Jesus Crucified, M. Adelaide's favorite devotion, and the eleven wandering Carmelites entered their permanent home. They were now able to dedicate themselves in peace to the Teresian rule: a life of prayer and intimacy with Christ for the good of the Church.

Now that her sisters were living their Teresian way of life at Grajal de Campos, M. Adelaide dedicated her efforts to the spiritual formation of her community. To do this more effectively, she wrote a small but fascinating book, *Instrucciones para Novicias* (*Instructions for Carmelite Novices*), which soon became the handbook used in other convents in Spain. But her own example was far more effective than her writings or instructions. M. Adelaide became for her daughters the best model of Teresian spirituality as lived in daily religious observance. Her struggles, worries, and sufferings together with the effects of her past illnesses brought about a fast deterioration in her health. Her eyes developed cataracts and she traveled to Madrid for an operation but with little success. While in Madrid she visited the Queen of Spain, the Royal Family, and the Papal Nuncio, Cardinal Rampolla. M. Adelaide returned to her community convinced that death was near but, nevertheless, she faithfully continued her strict following of the rule. When the Sister Infirmarian tried to prepare some special meals for her she would refuse saying, "My daughter, remember that in my formula of profession, I promised to observe the rule and the constitutions without any mitigation until death."

M. Adelaide's daughters loved her dearly and despite her poor health, imminent death, and over her many objections, the devoted community persisted in re-electing her Prioress. There was no one who could take the place of M. Adelaide. On April 11, 1893, she became dangerously ill and received the last sacraments of the Church with great fervor. When her last hour had come she feebly attempted to bless her sisters, but unable to do so, the chaplain took her arm and she made the sign of the cross over those who had shared persecution, exile, and poverty with her for the sake of God. She said, "Love, and be humble," then added, "It is all. Good-bye." M. Adelaide died on April 15. This American nun at the time of her death was in her seventy-fifth year, her fiftieth as a Carmelite nun, her eighteenth as an exile from Guatemala, her tenth since she arrived at her beloved foundation at Grajal de Campos. M. Adelaide's funeral was attended by townspeople and by many who had known her and had admired her for her saintly life.

Shortly after her death, there were many reports of favors having been granted and even "miracles" having been attributed to her intercession. Moved by such popular love and respect for M. Adelaide, a tribual was appointed, September 24, 1923, to initiate the lengthy process that precedes beatification. The acts of this process were submitted to the Sacred Congregation of Rites in Rome in August, 1927.

PRAYER
(Private use only)

O Jesus, my beloved Redeemer, You are the glory of the angels, the joy of the eternal Father, and the salvation of the world. My soul contemplates You upon the cross: Your head, crowned with thorns, looks toward earth with loving kindness; Your arms are extended to embrace sinners and draw them to Yourself; and Your side is opened with a lance so that the just may enter the refuge of Your Sacred Heart. Through the intercession of Your Blessed Mother, who, standing by Your cross, shared in Your sufferings, grant to me, Lord, the favor of seeing elevated to Your altar Sister Adelaide of St. Teresa, who during her lifetime was so devoted to the mystery of Your crucifixion. Amen.

FOR FURTHER READING

A. F. Valerson, O.C.D., *Mother Adelaide of St. Theresa* (Oklahoma City: Prompt Publishing Co., 1928).

CHAPTER 16

SERVANT OF GOD MOTHER MARIA MADDALENA BENTIVOGLIO, O.S.C.
Foundress of the Poor Clares (O.S.C.) in the United States.

16

With Light Step and Unstumbling Feet

MOTHER MARIA MADDALENA BENTIVOGLIO, O.S.C. (1834-1905)

Pius J. Barth, O.F.M.

BRINGING THE CONTEMPLATIVE life style of the Poor Clares of the Primitive Observance to the United States in 1875 was the heroic vocation of Countess Anna Maria Bentivoglio, born at Rome in the Castle of San Angelo on July 29, 1834, as the twelfth of the sixteen children of Count Dominic Bentivoglio and Angela Sandri. Although always a pious child in a devout family, her struggle toward sanctity as a Poor Clare began on October 4, 1865, as Sr. Maria Maddalena of the Sacred Heart of Jesus in the Monastery of San Lorenzo in Panisperna at Rome, where for ten years, despite her energetic independent spirit, she suffered many crosses and humiliations of both poverty and obedience. Her great desire for perfection is exemplified in the encouragement she received from her spiritual director to transfer to the more austere observance in the monastery of San Damiano in Assisi. But Divine Providence had other plans for her.

Italy was at this time experiencing its unification; the Papal States were threatened and religious communities were being extinguished as the revolution made progress. Thus it was that in 1875 the quiet heroism of Sr. Maddalena changed into an active challenge in bringing her holy way of life to a country which, in the words of Pope Pius IX who encouraged her, was more concerned with contemplating dollar bills than in the contemplative life. With the personal blessing of Pope Pius IX, and with the approbation of the Minister General of the Friars Minor, Sr. Maddalena and her blood sister, Sr. Costanza, also a Poor Clare, were transferred from the Urbanist Rule (a modified rule approved by Pope Urban IV) as practiced in the San Lorenzo monastery, to that of the primitive observance of San Damiano, and received the mission to found a cloister of strict observance in America similar to the one in Assisi. The Minister General then named Sr. Maddalena abbess and Sr. Costanza vicaress. The two sisters left their monastery and on September 27, 1875, they forever broke their ties with family and fatherland in order to bring to the United States a transfusion of grace and holiness.

Embarking on her mission to America this daughter of nobility followed the exhortation of St. Clare to Blessed Agnes of Prague: "Hasten on with swift pace and light step and unstumbling feet, so that your footsteps raise no dust as you move swiftly and joyfully, eagerly and carefully along the path of happiness. Trust in no one, yield to no one who wants to deter you from this goal or obstruct your path to prevent you from fulfilling your vows to the Most High in that way of perfection to which the Spirit of the Lord has called you." Fulfilling this exhortation would not be easy for one whose spirit was bent on preserving the charism of the primitive contemplative observance that she so wanted for herself at San Damiano. The expanding building programs of the United States' hierarchy and the social and vast educational activities of the American religious orders tried to lure her from her contemplative objective, but she remained adamant in pursuing the Poor Clare vocation as a heritage and a promise to future generations.

While this portrait is not intended as a strictly chronological account of M. Maddalena's activity, it might help if we chart events as they occurred. In 1874, M. Ignatius Hayes of the Third Order of St. Francis in Belle Prairie, Minnesota, traveled to Rome seeking priests and religious to help in her school apostolate. Not meeting with much success she visited the Poor Clare monastery of San Lorenzo, and learning that it was experiencing difficulties with the Italian government, she begged Pope Pius IX to allow the two Bentivoglio sisters, Maddalena and Costanza, to found a "power house of prayer" in Minnesota. It was M. Ignatius' hope that her community in Belle Prairie, which observed a form of enclosure, could fuse with the life style of the Poor Clares.

When the Bentivoglio sisters arrived in New York on October 12, 1875, accompanied by their spiritual director, Fr. Paolino of Castellaro, O.F.M., they sadly learned that he was now opposed to their plans of going to Minnesota and told them they should remain in New York. In the meantime he referred the Minnesota project to the Minister General in Rome, and because of the Minister General's silence, it was thought that he may have agreed with the director's opinion. The invitation to Minnesota was actually to an apostolate whose emphasis was on teaching and ministry. But this was not for M. Maddalena. Her courageous heart had as its objective the founding of a convent of contemplatives observing strict papal enclosure according to the rule of St. Francis and St. Clare.

Yielding to the director's opinion, M. Maddalena and Sr. Costanza stayed in New York and thought perhaps the archdiocese would make an ideal place for a Poor Clare foundation, but when they approached Cardinal McCloskey about establishing such a foundation, they were refused. M. Maddalena wrote about her contact with the Cardinal: "Oh sorrow of sorrows, to hear from his own lips that he would not receive us because our form of life was against the spirit of the country." With the humility, patience, and charity of a saint she accepted this rebuff, but she knew that the American Church was in need of the contemplative life's spirit to moderate its overly active ministry. Rejected by a leader of the Church and not knowing God's will for her, she wrote to her younger sister, Matilda, "What a life, my God, after twelve years of enclosure and quiet! The worst is this uncertainty."

While in New York, M. Maddalena came into contact with two active, and at times controversial, priests, Fr. Issac Hecker, founder of the Paulists, and Monsignor McGlynn, Pastor of St. Stephen's church. Both gave her encouragement and housing when they were needed, but Msgr. Mc-Glynn, unfortunately, subsequently left the Church in a dispute with his bishop and began to speak out against the Church. Years later, when M. Maddalena was in Omaha, which was to be her first permanent foundation, she heard that the former Msgr. McGlynn was in the city and scheduled to speak. Recalling her meetings with him, M. Maddalena sent him a note. The auditorium was crowded, but after he had read M. Maddalena's note he cancelled his tirade against the Church and refunded everyone's money. He must have appreciated M. Maddalena's mission since he permitted her note to so influence him. Perhaps her prayers played some part in his later reconciliation with the Church.

M. Maddalena had been told that the East offered the best opportunities for religious foundations, but that was not to be; the deep South and the Midwest proved more hospitable to the Poor Clare vocation. Unwanted in New York, and relying on the only supports she had, prayer and faith, she decided to seek approval for a foundation in Philadelphia or Cincinnati.

The two sisters arrived in Philadelphia and Archbishop Wood received them most benevolently and on August 10, 1876, gave them the keys to a house on Walnut Street to use as their residence. M. Maddalena felt great joy in her heart, and the Minister General in Rome was satisfied with the arrangement and kindly sent them money to help them along. But when she formally requested permission to establish a foundation in the Philadelphia archdiocese, she sadly learned that Archbishop Wood had been dissuaded by Cardinal McCloskey from offering them a permanent foundation. The archbishop also informed them that Fr. Paolino was no longer their director, and that they would have to leave the diocese.

In courageous simplicity and without letters of recommendation, penniless as Franciscans should be yet full of hope, the two sisters, following the suggestion of the Religious of the Sacred Heart with whom M. Maddalena had studied in Rome, decided to go to the "Rome of America" as Cincinnati was then called. But the result was the same. The Poor Clare vocation was not understood by the American Church. The bishops sought to recruit these cultured ladies as teachers, nurses, social workers, and catechists, but these ministries were not part of the vocation of a Poor Clare, and hence M. Maddalena again clung to her firm resolve. To this date Cincinnati remains the only city where M. Maddalena was refused and which did not later change its mind and welcome a Poor Clare foundation.

M. Maddalena and Sr. Costanza once more became pilgrims for Christ. They prayed to their heavenly Father and they knew He would not desert them. Their unsuccessful attempt to make a foundation in Philadelphia appeared in a news item that attracted the attention of a Franciscan tertiary in New Orleans. Archbishop Perché heard about M. Maddalena and her sister and invited them to come to New Orleans. They arrived on March 11, 1877, and it was from New Orleans that they received their first postulant, Ann Moran, and the sisters thought they finally found a permanent home.

At this time (1877), Fr. Gregory Janknecht, the Provincial of the German Franciscan Province of the Holy Cross, was visiting the friaries of the Commissariat he had established in Mid-America and preparing the way for their establishment as the independent Province of the Sacred Heart. Before he sailed for the United States, M. Maddalena and her small community had been placed under his jurisdiction by the Minister General; and so Fr. Gregory visited the Poor Clare monastery in New Orleans. Though it was a model Poor Clare convent of austere living and praying, it did not meet his expectations. Fr. Gregory felt the sisters and postulants should be situated closer to a Franciscan friary so that they could have a regular chaplain; he thought the house on Flood Street too small and the humid climate of New Orleans unsuited to the heavy habits the sisters wore. He reflected, perhaps Cleveland or St. Louis would be preferable since the friars were well established there and could easily offer the sisters spiritual direction.

Fr. Gregory had been in touch with Bishop Gilmour of Cleveland about a foundation of Poor Clares in his diocese, but left the details to another Franciscan, Fr. Kilian Schlocsser, to work out. About a year before Fr. Gregory's coming to the United States he visited Holland and promised the Poor Clare Colettines at Harreveld to seek a suitable convent for them in the United States. Thus it happened that seeing the need for M. Maddalena's group to be close to Franciscan priests for their spiritual direction he thought by sending the New Orleans community to Cleveland he could fuse both groups into one monastery. Unfortunately, he never took into consideration the differences in language and dress, constitutions and customs. These may have appeared minimal to him, but to the sisters these were to prove insurmountable obstacles. On July 30, 1877, he directed M. Maddalena's community to move to Cleveland.

M. Maddalena's memoirs are silent about this period in her life. The move to Cleveland was a great disappointment to the many benefactors in New Orleans, and to Archbishop Perché as well. In Cleveland, her obedience was to be sorely tested because she was still convinced that her mission was to found a convent like that of San Damiano in Assisi. While Frs. Janknecht and Schloesser, together with Bishop Gilmour, meant well, nevertheless, two diverse life styles, that of the Colettines and that of the Bentivoglio observance could not fuse into one.

The New Orleans community was the first to arrive in Cleveland — the convent was a converted cigar factory — and then, on December 15, 1877, the Dutch and German speaking sisters of the Colettine Poor Clares arrived. The community was established as a Colettine community and a German sister was appointed abbess, and M. Maddalena's group was expected to embrace the Colettine Constitutions. No one can realize the interior suffering that M. Maddalena experienced as she tried to conform to the Colettine way of life — she felt she was betraying the original mission entrusted to her by the Holy Father and the Minister General. Because it was impossible to integrate the rule and constitutions of the primitive observance with those of the Colettine reform, and because of the cultural and language difficulties brought about by their diverse Italian and German backgrounds, M. Maddalena realized that to preserve her peace and vocation she would have to leave Cleveland and seek to establish her own monastery.

In her suffering, M. Maddalena had written to the Minister

General, who consoled her with the thought that this humiliation would occasion a substantial growth in holiness on her part, and at the same time offered her and her sister a chance to return to Europe. But M. Maddalena was strong in spirit and still had hopes to accomplish her mission. In patience, generosity, and constancy, she and her sisters faced the reality before them.

After five months in the Colettine monastery, M. Maddalena and her group were pilgrims once more. They departed with a generous heart and bequeathed their few earthly belongings to the foundation in Cleveland, and headed for New Orleans where they knew they would be welcomed. Through all this M. Maddalena grew in patience and strength of soul realizing that her will must always conform to God's will and that in God's own good time her special mission to the United States would be accomplished.

While in New Orleans, they received an invitation to establish a foundation in Omaha. After many delays and disappointments, rejections and refusals, it pleased Divine Providence to permit a Poor Clare monastery of the strict observance to be founded in Omaha. Bishop James O'Connor received the sisters into his territory with friendly spirit and the Creighton family became the sisters' generous benefactors. While their monastery was under construction, a tornado and windstorm destroyed what already had been built (Aug. 1878); but after another four years of planning and the continuing kindness and generosity of the Creighton family, everything worked towards a favorable beginning. The Poor Clares were established in Omaha in 1882. What seemed impossible in 1875, and disappointing in Minnesota, New York, Philadelphia, New Orleans, and Cleveland, finally reached fruition in the Midwest on the banks of the Missouri River.

God's providence permitted everything to fall into place. The Omaha foundation took hold and some sisters came from Marseilles; several postulants were admitted and two sisters transferred from an active religious community. Omaha was thriving and by June, 1885, a new monastery was under way in New Orleans. This new monastery needed M. Maddalena's presence, and with the Minister General's permission she left Omaha with a few sisters for New Orleans. Since she did not await Bishop O'Connor's approval for her temporary absence, he was very displeased and felt his authority had been defied. In her humble way, M. Maddalena begged his pardon for this lack of deference. Later on she received permission to return to New Orleans and make it a permanent foundation with its first abbess, Sr. Mary Francis Moran, the first postulant M. Maddalena had accepted from that wonderful city.

Other unfortunate matters caused M. Maddalena additional trials, even banishment for a time from the monastery she had founded. Several extern sisters, one of whom had been dismissed, brought humiliating accusations which besmirched M. Maddalena's good reputation. This happened in Omaha in 1888, when M. Maddalena and her sister, Costanza, were shamefully denounced by an emotionally unstable sister, as guilty of irregular personal conduct, alcoholic intemperance, financial mismanagement and acting without due deference to the bishop. M. Maddalena was tried like gold in the furnace and proved innocent of the charges brought against her. Her composure and trust in God led to her complete vindication, and on January 12, 1889, Bishop O'Connor was officially notified by the Sacred Congregation of the Propaganda in Rome that the accusations brought against M. Maddalena were without justification.

During her life M. Maddalena often met frustration, but she never boiled over into anger and aggression; for, she always practiced inner mortification and outward self-control. Meeting refusal and suffering, denials and calumnies, she hastened swiftly with light step and unstumbling feet, not allowing her footsteps to raise dust that might obscure her vision or alienate others. In a short time she accomplished much because she was single-minded and her eyes were fixed on the light of Christ as her heart was attuned into his Sacred Heart.

In the same year that she suffered the calumnies within her community, Katharine Drexel, of Philadelphia, came to Omaha. As a child Katharine remembered the farewell dinner given in 1876 by her family for M. Maddalena and her sister after receiving Archbishop Wood's refusal to permit a Poor Clare foundation in Philadelphia. Katharine, daughter of a wealthy family, was thinking of founding a religious congregation to help Native Americans and Blacks. M. Maddalena had so impressed Katharine that she now desired to be educated in the religious life by M. Maddalena and the Poor Clares in Omaha. But the contemplative life is very different from the active religious life; it has its own emphases and life style, and since M. Maddalena knew that she could not train someone in a tradition in which she herself had not lived, she declined Miss Drexel's request.

M. Maddalena's third and last foundation was to be in Evansville, Indiana. Bishop Chatard, of Indianapolis, then called the Diocese of Vincennes, had recommended to M. Maddalena the young Elizabeth Reitman as a postulant. Elizabeth's father was a wealthy lumber dealer in Evansville. When Miss Reitman was professed as Sr. Mary St. Clare in April, 1893, she stated before taking her vows that she would like any inheritance that may come to her in the future to be used for a new foundation in Evansville, as a mark of "filial piety." After Mr. Reitman's death the foundation in Evansville was approved.

M. Maddalena, now in her sixty-third year, and somewhat weak from illness, set out (May, 1897), with three sisters to establish the new foundation. In the beginning the sisters suffered acute poverty, but this they accepted with great patience. For a time they lived only on bread and water. M. Maddalena's sister, Sr. Costanza, remained in Omaha;

and when she died in 1902, it was with great self-control that M. Maddalena announced the news to her community requesting everyone to raise their arms and recite the traditional Stations of the Blessed Sacrament for the deceased Costanza.

M. Maddalena kept faith with Christ, St. Francis, and St. Clare during her life, and now it was time for her to imitate them in passing from earth to glory. One of the sisters present at M. Maddalena's death recalled that on August 18, 1905, only the crucifix mattered since it showed forth a beautiful light as M. Maddalena lay dying. At her request, she was placed on a straw mat on the bare floor of her cell. Some twenty-three sisters came in and knelt near their dying Mother who requested that she be "allowed to go home" — she was convinced that if the sisters prayed for her health, their prayers would be answered. M. Charitas assured her that they would no longer pray for that intention, and during the recitation of the Litany of St. Francis, M. Maddalena, at 3:30 p.m., amid the tears of her daughters, closed her eyes in death.

A biographer of M. Maddalena, Marie Alice Zarrella, wrote: "The portrait of Maddalena as it emerges from the letters and testimonies of others is that of a prayerful woman, trusting entirely to the Will of God, always conscious of the importance of fidelity even in small things. Often she seemed lost in prayer. Yet she was an observant and compassionate woman with concern about the wants and needs not only of her own community of Poor Clares but of any one who called on her assistance."

Following her death, there were numerous reports of cures and petitions granted through M. Maddalena's intercession. On May 30, 1928, Bishop Joseph Chartrand of Indianapolis initiated the process of investigating M. Maddalena's life and reported miraculous happenings. At the exhumation of her body in April, 1932, the body was found still intact and her garments in a good state of preservation. In 1969 the

PORTRAITS IN AMERICAN SANCTITY

Congregation of Rites permitted the official introduction of her cause. The Vice Postulator of M. Maddalena's cause is the Very Rev. Pius J. Barth, O.F.M. The address of the Evansville monastery is: Monastery of St. Clare, 509 South Kentucky Avenue, Evansville, Indiana 47714.

PRAYER
(Private use only)

O Jesus, You deigned to elevate our hearts by the example of Your servant Mother Mary Magdalen; graciously grant us the favor we ask You through her intercession. Teach us her steadfast devotedness to You, her unquestioning trust in Your Providence, her heroic endurance in trials, and the supernatural simplicity of all her ways. For Your greater glory, for the exaltation of Your Holy Church and for the salvation of souls, hear our prayer and show us the power of her intercession. You Who live and reign world without end. Amen.

O Sacred Heart of Jesus, glorify Your faithful servant Mother Mary Magdalen by granting my request. Glory be to the Father, and to the Son, and to the Holy Spirit, as it was in the beginning, is now, and ever shall be, world without end. Amen.

FOR FURTHER READING

Mary Alice Zarrella, *I Will . . . God's Will: A Biography of Mother Mary Magdalena Bentivoglio, O.S.C., Foundress of the Poor Clares in the United States* (Evansville, Ind.: Poor Clare Monastery Press, 1975).

CHAPTER 17

SERVANT OF GOD MOTHER MARIANNE OF MOLOKAI
Foundress of the
Franciscan Sisters' Mission in Hawaii and Missonary to the Lepers.

17

Missionary and Nurse to the Lepers of Hawaii
MOTHER MARIANNE COPE, O.S.F. (1838-1918)

Sr. Mary Laurence Hanley, O.S.F.

THE SPIRIT OF Mother Marianne, the valiant woman who spent thirty years at Kalaupapa, Molokai, in caring for lepers, continues to inspire Franciscans and other peoples throughout the world.

The story of her personality "is one of indomitable bravery, notable fidelity to duty, and high religious heroism," wrote a successor to her position of authority in Hawaii. Admiringly, Sr. M. Sebastian Hensler, pointed out in her historical account of the heroic charity of the pioneer Franciscan community in Hawaii led by M. Marianne that, true to the example of the founder of the order, Saint Francis, their service to the most disadvantaged and disregarded of peoples exemplified the true spirit of their order begun so many years ago: "We find a religious order of women, the Sisters of St. Francis at their Motherhouse, the Convent of St. Anthony in Syracuse, New York, taking cognizance of the fact of Franciscan history that in its very beginning, at the dawn of the thirteenth century, their Seraphic Father and Founder, St. Francis of Assisi, had included in his surpassingly high ideals of service to his Lord that of actual personal service to lepers. To find a group of the gentler sex vowed to the service of the Master, Who is 'the same yesterday, today and forever,' willing, nay eager, to imitate Him and His devout disciple, the Poverello of Assisi, in this truly heroic task is surely significant. . . ."

The story of the leader of the "gentler sex" whose insight into Franciscan charism was remarkable is basically one of a saintly woman who instead of doing things "her way" looked for God's way. "Redouble your prayers," she would write, "so we may receive light from above to know the Holy Will of God," and then, realizing that the expectations might not be in accord with her own desires, added realistically: "and strength to put it into execution."

M. Marianne was born in Heppenheim in Western Germany on January 23, 1838, and was named after her mother Barbara Koob. (Variant spellings of the surname are Kob, Kopp, and now officially, Cope). She was the fifth child of her father's second marriage, her parents' third daughter, and the last child to be born in Germany.

Peter Koob, her father, was not a young man when the Koobs came to the United States in 1840. He was fifty-three years of age and it is unlikely that a man of his age and situation was seeking adventure. No doubt, being a practical man, he sought a better standard of living for himself and his family. In Utica, New York, where the Koobs settled, Peter became a laborer and was quick to purchase land on which to build a home. The family joined St. Joseph's parish, and it is probable that all the children attended the parish school. It is known that Barbara attended it for five years.

Although Barbara was not the oldest child in chronological age in the family, by the time she was sixteen, she was the oldest living at home with her parents and two younger sisters and a brother. Both these circumstances as well as a spirit of generosity and devotion gave her much responsibility. Her wish to enter religious life began at an early age, possibly when she was fifteen, but the question of entering a convent remained unsettled until she was twenty-four. Her wages, gained from work at a nearby factory, and her helpful hands were needed at home. Responsibility to her family kept her in Utica until one month after her father's death in July, 1862.

Barbara Koob entered the Sisters of the Third Franciscan Order at Syracuse, New York, in August, 1862, when it was a young and struggling community of only fourteen members. The community was an independent branch of a larger foundation established in 1855 by Saint John Neumann. Its members had settled in Syracuse and Utica in 1860 at the request of the Franciscan fathers, who were working with German immigrants in those cities. Although the move to central New York had the approbation of Bishop Neumann, his successor separated the group from the Philadelphia foundation because he anticipated legal difficulties, and made arrangements to have them accepted in the local diocese.

Considering its small size, it is rather an amazing fact that in addition to its teaching work, the founding group established two of the first hospitals in central New York State within the first ten years of its existence.

Sister Marianne, as she was known in religious life, served within the community most of these ten years as a teacher and principal-superior of schools. As a member of the community's governing boards, she also participated in activities leading to the establishment of the two hospitals. In June, 1870, she was appointed superior-administrator of the first hospital of Syracuse which opened in 1869, and she retained this position for seven years. In 1877, she was elected the second Provincial Mother of the Syracuse community, and it was in 1883 during her second term of office, that she accepted the call to Hawaii. By 1882 the community had grown to eighty professed sisters.

She had been prepared for the call both in mind and spirit. Hers was a characteristic response from the woman who served the neediest of her neighbors because in them she saw the suffering Christ: "I am not afraid of any disease; hence it would be my greatest delight even to minister to the abandoned 'lepers.' "

On April 15, 1873, a prominent legislator of the Kingdom of Hawaii wrote an unusual appeal in a local newspaper, the *Nuhou*: "If a noble Christian priest, preacher or sister should be inspired to go and sacrifice a life to console these poor wretches, that should be a royal soul to shine forever on a throne reared by human love."

The "poor wretches" to whom Walter M. Gibson referred were leprosy patients who were exiled at the settlement on Molokai, without the consolation of a missionary to live among them. His appeal was heard. Bishop Louis Maigret, a kind man, who at that time was Vicar Apostolic of the Catholic Church in Hawaii, immediately considered the matter with his priests, members of the Sacred Hearts community, and in May of the same year the lepers had their first resident missionary, Fr. Damien DeVeuster. The heroic Damien has deservedly achieved world-wide admiration for his sacrifice and seems well on his way to achieving official recognition as a saint by the Roman Catholic Church.

Ten years later the same politician who had sounded the appeal for heroic souls to come forth for the consolation of the outcasts at the leper colony was the Premier of the kingdom and also the president of its Board of Health. As the power behind the throne, Walter M. Gibson was more concerned than ever about this pressing problem in the small monarchy in the Pacific — what was to be done about the nursing care of the sick poor, especially for those patients afflicted with the dread disease of leprosy. The sickness had increased to epidemic proportions, and a system of hospital nursing care had to be set up for their benefit. It was evident to King Kalakaua and Queen Kapiolani, as well as to their eminent advisor, that the only persons who would accept the work would be those noble souls willing to make the ultimate sacrifice by risking their lives daily in close association with the lepers; and the idea grew among them that such a rare dedication might be obtained by an appeal to religious congregations which had already demonstrated supreme devotion to the sick.

Thus, it happened that in 1883, the newly appointed Vicar Apostolic in Hawaii, Bishop Hermann Koeckemann, was requested to invite sisters to come to the aid of the sick of the kingdom and to offer them in advance the profound obligation and recognition of the King and Queen, the gratitude of the government, and the blessings of the Hawaiian people.

The bishop in response hastened to dispatch Fr. Leonor Fouesnel on the mission, and the King gave the departing emissary a royal commission to assist him in his search. The priest agent experienced what Gibson later referred to as "arduous" and "baffling endeavors," during which he petitioned more than fifty religious communities before receiving the words of hope that brought him to the Convent of St. Anthony in Syracuse, New York.

The interview with the Franciscan sisters was a sequel to a written communication from M. Marianne in response to his letter of petition. Acting upon her word of encouragement, the emissary from Hawaii traveled to Syracuse. There, the interest of M. Marianne was kindled by a discussion of the plight of the lepers, and in an assembly of sisters many volunteers came forth. Aware that the approval of higher authority and the community counselors at a formal meeting was needed as yet, M. Marianne made clear her own thoughts in a letter to Fr. Leonor, who was assured enough of the success of his mission as to begin the return journey to Hawaii. She wrote: "We look for him every day [namely, for Fr. Lesen, the Provincial Minister of the Order, who was visiting in Rome] and I hope his good heart will approve my desire to accept the work in the name of the great St. Francis. . . ."

The request had been made by Fr. Leonor for twelve sisters, but only six could be spared from the community in Syracuse. The United States at the time was missionary territory itself, and the members of the early group in America had to be carefully allotted among the teaching and nursing apostolates to which they were already committed. Despite her heartfelt wish to be one of the members of the mission to work with the lepers of Hawaii, at the time that she left for this new field of work, it was her intention to see the sisters settled and then to return to her position of leadership in Syracuse.

The arrival of the small group of Franciscans in Honolulu on November 8, 1883, was heralded by the bells of the Roman Catholic Cathedral of Our Lady of Peace, and by a joyous welcome at least in the hearts of most of the inhabitants of the city. Gibson later suggested that mere praise for such a sacrifice as that made by pioneer groups of sisters to Hawaii was "out of place." But, he added, "since they had won the hearts of the sufferers for whom they cared, in return they should be revered in the people's memories and that the people should never forget the coming of this American mission of charity and 'Landing of the Sisters' Day."

By January, 1884, the sisters had begun their work at the Branch Hospital for lepers which was located on the Honolulu waterfront in an isolated spot about a mile east of the town. The convent that had been built for them was on the hospital grounds. In the several scattered hospital buildings, conditions were deplorable, patients numbering 200 lepers at the time. A petition for improvements was made immediately to the government by M. Marianne, who at the same time set out to better matters as much as possible. Results of a practical and spiritual nature were accomplished. No task was too menial for the small group of sisters, and with their scrubbing, cleaning, and just plain caring, they gave the patients an uplift in morale beyond measuring.

With the division of their number during the same month in order to fulfill the mission of setting up the first general hospital on the island of Maui, there was no possibility for M. Marianne to extend her work at that time to the leper colony of Molokai.

As demands and problems mounted; as the confidence of authorities, patients, and sisters in her grew apace; as word came that Fr. Damien had become a leper, it became apparent that she could not abandon the mission in those crucial times to return to Syracuse.

The formal dedication of the Kapiolani Home for healthy children of leprous parents took place on Monday, November 9, 1885, the day after the second anniversary of the arrival of the Franciscan sisters in Hawaii.

The greatest interest seemed to be taken in the events of the day by natives who witnessed the numerous carriages with "ladies and gentlemen" drawn along the road from the Immigration Depot to the new Home. Among those taking the greatest interest in the spectacle was a company of neatly dressed leper children who occupied seats under a temporary awning erected in the yard of the Home. The Royal Hawaiian Band occupied the town side of the structure.

Hardly anything was visible to arouse an unpleasant thought unless one took a closer look at the assembled youngsters. The Home was certainly not opening for them. It was too late for them, because they had already contracted the horrible disease. But, just perhaps, it was not too late for others.

More than one year before that time, in July, 1884, during her visit to the leper settlement on Molokai, Queen Kapiolani had been addressed publicly by two patients there, a man and a woman, who questioned her on the reason that healthy children had been allowed to remain in the colony and become patients through contagion. The man had held up in his arms a little girl and urged the Queen to allow some good to come to the child and others like her through the visit. Possibly it was after the time of this visit that Doctor E. Arning, who was present at the time of the appeals, discussed with M. Marianne the theory that if infants of leprous patients could be taken from the latter, they might be shielded from the disease. We do know that the horrors witnessed at Molokai by Doctor Arning aroused the pity of M. Marianne, and she brought the matter to the attention of Mr. Gibson, along with her request that the government allow the sisters to be the ones to do something about it.

When the idea of a Home for the unfortunate children was suggested, it at once engaged the interest of Queen Kapiolani. Soon Gibson proposed to the legislature the advisability of a refuge to be called "Kapiolani Home." The community-at-large was appealed to for funds, and by these means, as well as by government funds, the Board of Health was able to construct the necessary building.

Although four more sisters had arrived in April, 1885, to help with the work of the mission, Gibson thought their number still too few to extend their work. Yet, in the end, it was found necessary to build the Home within the hospital enclosure in Honolulu because only with the aid of the sisters could such a home be maintained.

Many years later another Kapiolani Home was built on a better site with a more adequate staff of Franciscan sisters. This establishment served the needs of the separated children until 1938.

In November, 1888, the transfer of the sisters to Molokai from Honolulu began. A change of government leaders in

1887 had quickly brought about a change of policies concerning the control of lepers. The new Board of Health ruled that all patients must be sent to the Molokai leper settlement. The fate of the sisters was decided at the time that the leaders of the new Board of Health obliquely asked M. Marianne for aid by inquiring if she knew anyone of the same character as those in her own community who would manage a home for women and girls at the settlement. She herself was anxious to go, feeling that it had been agreed upon from the first that some of the sisters would serve the lepers at Molokai. Fr. Damien too had been waiting for many years for them to come.

On November 14, 1888, M. Marianne arrived at the leprosarium on Molokai with two other sisters, Sr. M. Leopoldina Burns and Sr. M. Vincent McCormick. They took charge of the C. R. Bishop Home for leprous women and girls. On the day of their arrival Fr. Damien called to welcome them. The coming of the sisters made the ailing priest forget his sufferings, reported an eye-witness, and he, who had hardly recovered from a fever, "seemed to revive."

M. Marianne began this period of her life quietly and unheralded, and her sentiments written soon afterwards reveal that she thought it unlikely that she could ever return to Syracuse. Six months later, on May 6, 1889, she wrote resignedly to M. Bernardina, the Foundress of the Syracuse community: "Will I ever see those I love again? God's will be done."

Later in that same month M. Marianne sent for Sr. Crescentia and Sr. Irene from the Receiving Station for lepers at Honolulu. Fr. Damien had died (April 15, 1889), but not before she had given him her promise that she would see to the care of his boys at the Home he had established for them at the settlement. (This institution was later named Baldwin Home, after its chief benefactor.)

The sisters had charge of Baldwin Home until 1895, when four Brothers of the Sacred Heart community came. At that time the leadership was turned over by the government to "Brother" Joseph Dutton, a layman from America who had first assisted Fr. Damien and then M. Marianne. This change freed the sisters for other work in the Islands' apostolate.

On Friday, August 9, 1918, at the C. R. Bishop Home in Kalaupapa, Molokai, M. Marianne died. She devoted nearly thirty years of her life caring for women and girls at the Home, in addition to five years served earlier at the Branch Hospital in Honolulu from November 8, 1883 to November 13, 1888. Her age at death was eighty years, six months, and seventeen days.

M. Marianne had become such an inspiring part of Hawaii's life that the *Honolulu Sunday Advertiser* wrote a mournful editorial two days after her death:

"Throughout the islands the memory of Mother Marianne is revered, particularly among the Hawaiians, in whose cause she has shown such martyr-like devotion.

"Those who have met the sweet, delicate little woman, whose face was almost spirituelle, have always been impressed with her intellectual qualities, for she was a woman of splendid accomplishments, and had fine executive ability. She impressed everyone as a real 'mother' to those who stood so sorely in need of mothering."

In 1974 the Syracuse sisterhood began preliminary research for the cause of the beatification and canonization of Mother Marianne, under the direction of a temporary Postulator in Rome. By 1976 the preliminaries for establishing an official cause were completed at the Sacred Congregation for the Causes of Saints and an official Postulator was named to represent the Franciscan community. On August 9, 1980, the Bishop of Honolulu, John J. Scanlan, established an official Historical Commission for the study of the cause of the Servant of God, Mother Marianne of Molokai. The Directress of the cause in the U. S. is Sr. Mary Laurence Hanley, O.S.F., Cause of Mother Marianne, 1024 Court Street, Syracuse, New York 13208.

PRAYER
(Private use only)

Lord Jesus, You gave us Your commandment of love of God and of neighbor, and identified Yourself in a special way with the most needy of Your brethren; hear our prayer.

Faithful to Your teaching, Mother Marianne Cope, loved and served her neighbor, especially the most desolate outcast, giving herself generously and heroically for the victims of leprosy. She alleviated their physical and spiritual sufferings, thus helping them to accept their afflictions with resignation, as a pledge of God's love and their eternal happiness.

Through her merits and intercession, grant us the favor which we confidently ask of You so that she may be raised to the altars of the Church, and that the People of God, following the inspiration of her life and apostolate, may practice fraternal charity, according to Your word and example. Amen.

FOR FURTHER READING

Sr. Mary Laurence Hanley and O. A. Bushnell, *A Song of Pilgrimage and Exile: The Life and Spirit of Mother Marianne of Molokai* (Chicago: Franciscan Herald Press, 1982).

CHAPTER 18

SERVANT OF GOD MOTHER MARY THERESA DUDZIK, O.S.F.
Foundress of the Franciscan Sisters of Chicago

18

With Charity Towards All

MOTHER MARY THERESA DUDZIK, O.S.F. (1860-1918)

Joseph N. Tylenda, S.J.

THE TINY AND OBSCURE village of Plocicz in Western Poland dates from the sixteenth century. It was always small in size; so small that it was without its own church but belonged to the parish of Kamien, just a few miles away, where the villagers had to go to attend Mass and services. It was in this little-known hamlet that Josephine Dudzik, the future Foundress of the Franciscan Sisters of Bl. Kunegunda, now known as Franciscan Sisters of Chicago (since 1970), was born on August 30, 1860. Josephine was the third of several children born to John Dudzik and Agnes Polaszczyk, and together with her sisters and brother she grew up on her father's small but successful farm and attended the village's unpretentious school. When she had completed her elementary studies, but unable to pursue

251

higher academic courses in Kamien because such courses were denied to Poles by order of the Prussian government that had annexed Western Poland in 1793, Josephine did what was second best. She matriculated in a vocational school in Kamien, operated by the Sisters of St. Elizabeth, and there acquired great skill in various forms of needle-work, but especially in the designing and sewing of women's dresses. What she had learned at Kamien was of great use to her not only in Plocicz where she had established herself as a much sought-after seamstress, but was to be one of her sources of income when she accepted the poor and needy from the streets of Chicago into her small and modest home.

Josephine grew up at the time when Bismarck was the iron-handed Chancellor of the Prussian nation. Bismarck's intention was to de-Polonize western Poland by forcing them to learn the German language and by preventing them from social and economic advancement. This Bismarck tried to accomplish by keeping the Poles from attaining higher academic degrees. He also intended to diminish the strength of the Catholic Church in Western Poland and thus he chose to foster the formation of a Prussian National Church which would have been Protestant. In 1874 he ordered the arrest and imprisonment of Archbishop Ledochowski of Gniezno and Poznan for not yielding to this program of "civilizing" Poland. Such was the outcry of the Catholic world against the German Chancellor that he eventually capitulated and released the archbishop. In a defiant measure against Bismarck, Pius IX named the Polish archbishop, while still in prison, a cardinal of the Roman Church and termed him "that brave defender of the faith." No matter how energetically the Germans had attempted to implement their "civilizing mission" in Poland, most of the Poles refused to be Germanized. It is not surprising then that countless Poles in the late nineteenth century came to the United States in search of freedom.

Josephine's uncle, Joseph, on her father's side, rather than being compelled to serve in the Prussian army, left Poland for the United States sometime prior to 1866 and settled in the northwest section of Chicago where there was a growing Polish community. Josephine's older sister Rosalie left for Chicago in 1872, when she was seventeen, to help her Uncle Joseph's wife who was housekeeper at St. Stanislaus Kostka rectory. Then her sister Marian followed in 1873 at the youthful age of fifteen. The family in Chicago frequently wrote home trying to induce Josephine's father to sell the farm and join them in this land of the free. They described their new home as a place where no one ever suffered because of nationality. He was told there was enough work in Chicago for all newcomers, and best of all they had a church whose priests spoke Polish and lived in a district where they could preserve their mother tongue.

Emigration is never appealing at first — no one relishes the idea of leaving one's country and the cozy farm that had been home for so many happy years. But since the children thought it good to go to the United States and because young Joseph, now approaching eighteen, preferred not to be coerced into serving in the army of a nation that had occupied their homeland for almost a hundred years, the father, now fifty-eight years of age, bravely made the decision to emigrate to Chicago. In early 1881, Josephine's father sold the farm; and the family, i.e., parents, Josephine, young Joseph and sisters Frances and Katherine, left their beloved Poland never to see it again.

When the Dudziks arrived in Chicago, sometime towards the end of May, 1881, Rosalie was waiting for them with her husband as was Uncle Joseph and his family. The Dudziks had a smooth and easy introduction to Chicago, unlike most immigrants. Rosalie's husband had arranged for a house for them and there were jobs waiting for young Joseph and Frances in the rectory. Without wasting time Josephine established herself as a successful seamstress while Katherine, the youngest, still had to finish her schooling.

It was not long after her arrival that Josephine's serious-
ness and piety came to the notice not only of the priests of
St. Stanislaus but also to the many young ladies in the parish.
Josephine was elected an officer in several parish confra-
ternities and became co-foundress of the Archconfraternity
of the Immaculate Heart of Mary. When the Third Order of
St. Francis was organized in the parish, Josephine was named
Mistress of Novices.

Besides her increasing work in designing and sewing
dresses, she took care of the altar linens, a task she attended
to for sixteen years. She would never refuse to do anything
for God or the Church.

Josephine was the eldest of the children at home and it
was her dressmaking that helped support the family — her
clients were many and wealthy. In December, 1883, her
eighteen-year-old sister Frances received the reluctant permission of her parents to enter the novitiate of the School
Sisters of Notre Dame in Milwaukee. Josephine was truly
happy to see Frances enter the convent, and if there were
any sorrow in her heart it was only because she herself
could not imitate her younger sister's action. Her parents
had need of her. Frances was professed and received the
name Sr. Leovina and lived a full life, dying in 1931. Not
long after Frances' departure and even before her parents'
hearts had a chance to heal, Kate, the youngest in the family,
wished to enter the convent of the Sisters of the Incarnate
Word. Josephine's parents would not go against God's will,
but it was with sadness that they saw Kate become a postulant. When Kate moved (1885) to San Antonio for her
novitiate, the family was heart-broken. Within a year after
her arrival in Texas and just after she had made her profession, receiving the name Sr. Barbara, she met with a tragic
accident (November, 1886) as she made her way to minister
to the sick. Josephine's parents were inconsolable. Josephine
was now the only daughter left at home, and though she

felt God drawing her, she was still unaware to what He was calling her.

The economic success that the citizens of Chicago had once known began to pass; the number of the unemployed grew larger and the soup kitchen lines became longer. Josephine's heart went out to these unfortunates — her charity was such that she was spiritually drawn to those without work and clothes, without shoes and hope. When her father died in May, 1889, she could no longer refrain from extending a loving and helping hand to Chicago's destitutes. One by one she brought them into her spacious home and began to care for them. In her later years she wrote: "For a number of years I had been contemplating ways and means by which I could provide comfort and lodging to poor girls, widows, and to the sick who were unable to work. I had sheltered too many of them in the limited quarters of my home. As a result, my mother often objected, because she was exposed to many inconveniences. . . ." Josephine's house was crammed; she had given up her own bed to sleep on the floor. She saw the sacrifices that her aging mother endured, but what could she do when charity impelled her to serve humanity. "I felt the misery and sufferings of others, and it seemed to me that I could not love Jesus or expect heaven if I were concerned only about myself and my mother, suffered nothing and lived a life of ease."

Josephine had now been taking care of homeless women for four years, and one day while at prayer the surprising idea came to her to buy or rent a home near the parish church and gather around her a few tertiaries from the parish who would be willing to live in common, pray, and work for the poor and the homeless. She took her plan to Fr. Vincent Barzynski, her pastor and spiritual guide, who readily agreed but also insisted that the project be established within the framework of religious life. With such good news in her heart Josephine confided her plans to her best friend, Rose Wisinski, who thought well of the idea and promised to join the group. When Josephine's proposal was brought before the tertiaries during their October, 1893, meeting it was accepted with joy; but Rose suggested that it might be better to pray over the matter for another year.

A year is a long time to wait for one whose house is overflowing with destitute ladies and when the economic situation in Chicago was not improving. The number of the needy increased day by day; parish and school halls together with church vestibules were opened as shelters for the homeless. When the year finally did come to an end Josephine again brought the matter before the tertiaries, and to her great happiness seven volunteered to join her work. The pastor met with the eight ladies and instructed them in what to expect in the future; and since they needed a home for their "convent" Josephine graciously offered the already crowded Dudzik residence as temporary quarters. Thus, on December 8, 1894, the Franciscan Sisters of Blessed Kunegunda (as they were first known) came into existence and on December 23, Josephine was elected superior of the group. Living in the Dudzik home was uncomfortable for it had to serve two purposes; it was not only a convent for the group, but it was also the shelter for several women. To support their project they engaged in sewing, taking in laundry and doing housework — their earnings went into a common fund to be used to build a home for the aged.

Within months after their founding, discontent made its ugly way into the community and soon only three of the original seven were left. It was suggested to Josephine that the reasonable thing to do was to abandon her project, but Josephine only worked the harder. She hunted for land where she could one day build her home for the aged and infirm and finally discovered in October, 1895, twelve lots, at a reasonable price, in isolated Avondale, several miles from St. Stanislaus parish. She made a down payment of $1,000; but when it came time to meet the mortgage payments she was penniless, and very much against her natural disposition she went begging from house to house. The result of her begging netted her $780.

But God's work was not to be curtailed. In April, 1897, the decision was made to begin planning the new home in Avondale. Construction began in September and on March 23, 1898, Josephine, who was now known as Sr. Theresa, led the members of her community and her charges to the newly completed St. Joseph's Home. That night she thanked God "for all the graces You have poured on us, but especially for leading us into this wilderness out of Babylon (Chicago)."

The early months at St. Joseph's were indeed difficult. Their funds were almost exhausted and Sr. Theresa had the impossible task of continuing to supply food for some two dozen people. Even though the Home did not have enough money to care for those who dwelled there, the parishes in Chicago continued to send homeless persons to Avondale. Sr. Theresa's constant worry was how would she be able to feed such a crowd. When the purse did become empty she was not ashamed to spend a day or two begging so that her poor could have a meal. As the number of the elderly increased so also did vocations to her community, and she was thankful to God for the extra hands to help carry on the community's work. She planted a vegetable garden and bought two cows to supply milk for the Home. By September the financial strain was much less for they were now living off the produce provided by their own garden. But there was another strain that tugged at her heart. The Home was located some distance from the nearest church with the uncomfortable result that the sisters were able to go to Mass but once a week, on Sundays. It was only on rare occasions that Mass was celebrated in their own chapel.

Since the members of the community were all Franciscan tertiaries they were looking forward to October 4, the feast of St. Francis of Assisi. It had been arranged that Fr.

Barzynski was to come and celebrate Mass for them, but to their surprise another priest had come. After Mass they learned that Fr. Barzynski would visit them that afternoon and they eagerly awaited his arrival. When Father did arrive and when he began to speak to the sisters there was nothing that he could have said that would have been more foreign to their expectations. Without any introduction and without preliminary preparation, Father announced that from that moment onward Sr. Theresa was no longer superior of the group but in her place he was appointing Sr. Anna. Sr. Anna was Rose Wisinski, Sr. Theresa's close friend. By a single statement and in the matter of a second Sr. Theresa was removed from office. She was no longer superior of the community she had founded four years previously. The reasons for such an abrupt removal were never made known and the docile and humble Sr. Theresa never requested to know them. She remained obedient to her spiritual director and said that she felt a heavy weight being removed from her heart.

Now that she was relieved of matters of government, Sr. Theresa took on the task of milking the cows and doing various household chores. In losing Sr. Theresa as superior the community was to go through years of trial, for Sr. Anna was without the qualities essential to a good leader. But as long as Sr. Theresa was at Avondale the religious spirit continued in the community. At times despondency seemed to overwhelm her. The thought of leaving the community passed through her mind: she had surrendered all her family's savings and property to help purchase the Home, and this is how it all ends — she was still young, only thirty-eight, and very much capable of supporting herself and her mother in the world. But she never permitted her discouragement to take control and rather than yield to such cowardly thoughts she gained encouragement from knowing that she could take her problems to Jesus and depend entirely on Him. She greatly valued the religious life and she would fight for the survival of her community.

On December 8, 1898, the fourth anniversary of their foundation, the four sisters were finally admitted to the postulancy. Fr. Barzynski died the following May (1899), and Fr. Spetz succeeded in caring for the spiritual needs of the community. Under his care they began their novitiate training on May 21. He blessed the new habits before Mass and the four new novices, now garbed as Franciscan sisters for the first time, took as religious names those they had previously taken when they were tertiaries. That same day four candidates received the postulant's veil.

The financial worries of the Home were far from over. It was towards the end of May that the sisters learned that the orphanage connected with St. Stanislaus parish in Chicago had to be closed and that all the orphans, about 130 of them, were to be sent to St. Joseph's Home in Avondale. The Home was without space and without money; without equipment and without help! How could only a few sisters care for the elderly and all these orphans? But the sisters knew that they could not refuse. They remodeled the attic, the fourth floor of the Home, and made it ready for twenty-four girls ranging from 12-14 years. There was no way that they could possibly accommodate the many boys without building an orphanage. Without funds but with great confidence in God the sisters undertook its construction, and by the end of December (1899) the boys were transferred from Chicago to Avondale. As the century ended St. Joseph's had about one hundred and fifty hungry mouths that needed to be fed daily.

The number of candidates to the community began to increase and Sr. Theresa was put in charge of their training. By 1900 there were fourteen of them. Besides instructing these candidates she had responsibility for the elderly, had charge of the laundry and saw to the mending and distribution of clothes. Added to this, Sr. Anna, the Superior, had not been in good health for some time, and it fell upon Sr.

Theresa to discharge many of the burdensome duties of the superior.

When their novitiate year was over the four novices pronounced their first vows in the congregation on June 3, 1900. Sr. Theresa was elated; this is what she had been waiting for. That same day eight postulants were received into the novitiate and Sr. Theresa was appointed to care for their spiritual formation, a task she scrupulously performed for the next nine years; for, she well realized that the future of any religious congregation depended on the thorough religious formation of its members.

God so blessed the congregation with a wonderful increase of vocations that the sisters decided to erect their third building at Avondale — this was for postulants and novices. When they moved into their new quarters in January, 1905, the novices numbered twenty-three. There were about seventy members in the entire congregation and they were involved in orphanages, hospitals and parochial schools. Since Sr. Anna had been suffering from ill health for the past several years she had been unable to meet the demands of the office of superior, and so Fr. Spetz suggested (October, 1905) that a new administration be appointed. As superior he chose the twenty-nine year old Sr. Vincent and made Sr. Theresa her assistant. Sr. Theresa's health now began to fail, and though she insisted on attending to her daily chores many were the days when she had to be led back to her room for much needed rest. In 1907 she underwent two operations and nowhere did she leave any indication as to the nature of her illness. She wrote in her memoirs: "I cannot remember many incidents for the year 1907, because I was too weak." The following year was a better year for her. Not only did her health return to a certain degree, but joy was brought to her heart when a retired priest was appointed permanent chaplain at Avondale. They were now able to have daily Mass and receive Communion as often as it was permitted.

In time Fr. Spetz came to realize that Sr. Vincent was much too young to be superior; she was inexperienced and the older sisters were not happy in obeying someone so much younger. To save the congregation and return it to its proper path he judged that Sr. Theresa alone was capable of doing the job. On New Year's Day, 1909, before he began his homily at Mass, Father made the announcement that henceforth Sr. Theresa was superior. Sr. Theresa had always been obedient to her director and once again she accepted the burden of office as the divine will. A General Chapter had been planned for 1910, and Sr. Theresa spent the months of her second term as superior in preparation for the chapter. The community's Constitution had to be studied, revised, and submitted to the delegates for final approval. During these tedious months there was a growing antipathy against her and her understanding of the religious life. It would seem that it was a question of strict observance versus a less strict observance, and her conception of the religious life unfortunately merited her hatred and suffering.

It was on August 12, 1910, that the delegates to the First General Chapter met and on that day the hostility that had grown up against Sr. Theresa during the previous months made itself manifest in the election of the ailing Sr. Anna as first Mother General of the Congregation. Sr. Anna had been incapable of leading the congregation when she was first appointed superior and was even less capable now because her health had become worse. If we were to regard this event merely from a human point of view we would have to say that this was Sr. Theresa's defeat; but if we were to consider it from Sr. Theresa's point of view, we would have to say with her that nothing happens without the will of God. When the new appointments were made by the Chapter, Sr. Theresa was not among them. Her remaining years in the convent were to be spent taking care of the garden, and when the cool weather set in she assisted in the laundry and sewing room.

Misunderstandings arose within the congregation and M. Anna unfortunately was unable to handle them. There was nothing that Sr. Theresa could do but watch and pray for successful resolutions. She spent six years working in the garden and greenhouse and while her hands were pulling weeds, tending blooms or spreading fertilizer, her heart was praying for perseverance and the future stability of her congregation. In later years the sisters, who as postulants were assigned to work with Sr. Theresa in the greenhouse, unanimously attested that she would never permit them to overwork, and always feared that they might catch cold; it was she who insisted on pushing the heavy wheelbarrow full of dirt or dung. These six years were hidden and painful years, but they were prayerful and fruitful years; perhaps she made greater spiritual advancement during this period than she had in all her previous years.

In 1916, Sr. Theresa's health began to decline and she became progressively worse. This was also the year of the Second General Chapter, and much to her surprise she was elected a delegate. Fourteen delegates met in January of that year, and their first duty was the election of a new Mother General. M. Anna was now bed-ridden with no hope of recovery. On the first three ballots Sr. Theresa received one-third of the votes, the remaining votes were divided between two other candidates. On the fourth ballot Sr. Aloysa was elected Mother General.

Since M. Anna had been confined to bed, Sr. Theresa visited her as often as she was able. They had been friends ever since Josephine Dudzik had come to Chicago in 1881, and after thirty-five years they were still the best of friends. Her visits brought much consolation to M. Anna who died on January 28, 1917. Sr. Theresa was deeply saddened by this loss and when M. Anna's body was taken from the chapel of the motherhouse to the church for her funeral, and while most sisters rode in cars, the frail Sr. Theresa insisted on walking behind the hearse all the way to the church even though the day was bitterly cold. It seems Josephine Dudzik wanted to have a last walk and final talk with her friend Rose Wisinski.

Sr. Theresa's health began to deteriorate; her attacks became more frequent and her pain intensified. She grew weaker by the day and in March, 1918, she collapsed which necessitated her being taken to the hospital. After a month's stay she returned to her beloved Avondale but now mostly confined to her room and bed. Throughout the months of her illness, she never complained; she never gave thought to herself — her only concern was, as always, her congregation. Sr. Theresa followed M. Anna to eternity by dying in the early morning of Friday, September 20, 1918. She was fifty-eight years old and had spent twenty-three years in religion. She was buried on Monday, September 23, after a very simple funeral in St. Adalbert's cemetery, Niles, Illinois. The simplicity of her funeral was the perfect mirror of the simplicity of her life.

It was only after her death that the Franciscan Sisters of Blessed Kunegunda (known since 1970 as Franciscan Sisters of Chicago) came to appreciate that Sr. Theresa, though she had never been Mother General, nevertheless, was their true Foundress and that the spirit that had given life to their congregation had been given it by her. Remembering her intimacy with God both the congregation and those who had come to know Sr. Theresa during her life began to seek her intercession with God for favors needed. Sr. Theresa's intercessory power has not ended and thus it was decided to initiate the process that might one day number her among the Church's saints. In October, 1972, her body was moved from her resting place in St. Adalbert's cemetery and solemnly transferred to the chapel of the motherhouse in Lemont, Illinois. On September 8, 1979, Cardinal Cody, Archbishop of Chicago, formally opened the diocesan process for the beatification of the Servant of God, Mother Mary Theresa Dudzik, O.S.F.

To promote M. Theresa's cause, the Sisters maintain the League of the Servant of God Mother Mary Theresa, 1220 Main St., Lemont, Ill., 60439.

PRAYER
(Private use only)

O God of infinite love and mercy, Who inflamed the humble heart of Mother Mary Theresa with the virtues of love and mercy, which flow abundantly from the Sacred Heart of Your Son and from the Immaculate Heart of His Blessed Mother, grant, we beseech You, that Mother Mary Theresa may become our constant intercessor before Your Divine Throne. Grant, O Lord, that the virtues of charity and mercy, which Mother Mary Theresa exercised on this earth toward the needy, abandoned and suffering, may also be obtained for us from You. Through Christ Your Son, our Lord.

O Mother Immaculate, whose honor was promoted by Mother Mary Theresa, we implore you, that through her intercession before your Divine Son, we may be granted the favor we humbly request. Amen.

FOR FURTHER READING

Henry M. Malak, *Theresa of Chicago* (translated by Ann K. Dudzik [Lemont, Ill.: League of the Servant of God Mother Mary Theresa, 1975]).

CHAPTER 19

SERVANT OF GOD FATHER STEPHEN ECKERT, O.F.M.Cap.
Friend and Apostle of the Blacks

19

Minister to Urban Blacks

FATHER STEPHEN ECKERT, O.F.M.Cap. (1869-1923)

Michael Crosby, O.F.M.Cap.

IN THE COURTYARD between St. Anthony Hospital and St. Benedict the Moor parish in Milwaukee, at the entrance to the junction of I-43 and I-94 stands a larger than life-size statue of a Capuchin Franciscan. As the cars speed by, the bearded, crew-cut friar with a football player's build looks across the street to the Court House. But few people know who that statue represents. It is not because of ill-will. It is just that what once was considered greatness and heroism in one historical set of circumstances and attitudes has, in another context, proved itself to have been limited and even incomplete. Just the engraving on the monument of Stephen Eckert, which was erected in 1958, twenty-five years after his death, attests to one of the ways changing times bring about changes — even in terminology: "Apostle and Champion of the Colored Race."

When he died in 1923, Stephen Eckert had struggled to empower the black community of Milwaukee that lived around St. Benedict's in the best way he knew. Now the black community has moved north, displaced by an industrial zone; and today it might be said Stephen's approach smacked of paternalism. Yet, for that time, it was innovative, challenging and far-reaching.

Stephen Eckert ministered in the midst of almost insurmountable obstacles coming from his own Capuchin province as well as from hostilities engrained in a white-dominated Church and society. But what he did in the ten years between 1913-1923, and what was done in the decades following, still call for new apostles and champions of human rights for people of all racial persuasions.

The following story of his life might give inspiration to those who will carry on his dreams.

John Eckert was born April 28, 1869, of German immigrant parents in Ontario, Canada. The fifth of nine children, he lived with his family in an English-speaking, Irish Catholic community which was surrounded in good part by German Protestants. Later in life, especially when he ministered among New York's Irish, Stephen would brag that he came from Dublin (Ontario), even though the closest town was St. Columban's.

At a time when nationalism was strong, the fact that John and Kunigunda Eckert remained Catholic was quite singular among many immigrants of that time who "fell away from their faith." That faith was tested each Sunday when they took the children six miles for Mass at St. Columban's. But since the area had few priests, Sundays usually found the family going to the homes of various neighbors to participate in a regular program of devotions. First the Mass prayers were said in common, followed by the readings.

The people would then listen to an instruction from *Goffine's Handbook* and a reading of a chapter from the Bible. On rare occasions, the neighbors would come to the Eckert's home to participate in Mass. It would be celebrated in the room that always remained equipped with an altar. The celebrant would be one of the travelling missionary priests of the Diocese of London.

Many biographers of people such as John (Stephen) Eckert might wax eloquently about the holiness of their parents. In Stephen's case, however, he himself regarded them as model Catholic parents. Shortly before his death he indicated that he wanted to perpetuate their memory by writing their lives' story. In the words of another brother who was able to write about them, "they were sturdy pioneers who had but one desire in life — to get a home for themselves and their family. They were hard-working people and frugal, so that they could provide for us."

Their hard-working and frugal characteristics seemed to have rubbed off on John in later years as a Capuchin. However, before that, he would reflect all the normal tendencies of any farm boy growing up in a pioneering environment. His sturdy build lent itself to rough sports, especially football, which he thoroughly enjoyed. It also came in handy on the farm as well as in situations such as that which happened when he was preparing for confirmation.

It happened that there were several in the class who were being ridiculed and abused by a group of boys. More than once John himself was the brunt of their treatment. He tried not to let it bother him, but after a while he had had enough. On the way home from class with a few companions, they met about a dozen fellow classmates who were ready for a fight. John sprang to the offensive; with fists flying he did not stop until the gang had been properly humiliated. Afterward he became a hero to his friends, and a respected classmate to the others who never molested him again.

Without playing psychologist, this incident might indicate

some of the psychic drives that seemed to have motivated his future Capuchin ministry: a desire to champion the cause of weaker people who were exploited by others' power; a kind of underlying unpretentiousness which could have moments of brilliance; a need or a desire to do the heroic in spite of adversity, rejection, and great obstacles.

John first became personally acquainted with the Capuchins during his school years at St. Jerome's, a school for men interested in the priesthood which was run by the Resurrectionists at Berlin (now Kitchener), Ontario. During his first semester of philosophy there, two Capuchin Franciscans gave a mission at the local parish church. The following summer (1890), he asked to spend a few days at their headquarters in Detroit that he might investigate the life of these bearded, brown-robed and sandaled followers of St. Francis. He had determined that a decision to make a possible lifetime commitment in a religious order demanded more than first impressions. While visiting St. Bonaventure's in Detroit, he discovered that the Capuchin Franciscans' effort to combine the contemplative and active dimensions of the gospel in the context of austerity and community appealed to him.

So, after returning to school at Berlin, he applied for admission to the Order. He was invited to spend a short period of probation before entering the novitiate. However, after his arrival, the first reaction of the novices toward the new postulant was far from favorable. Since most of them had come from a closed, highly regimented seminary high school, John's spontaneity and sense of independence, security, and freedom, coupled with his love of sports, appeared to them as too worldly. In spite of his sincerity and candor, his cheerfulness and co-operativeness toward the novices, many doubted whether he was fit for the Capuchin life.

One of his brothers, who looked back on those days, noted that their doubt was so strong that, when John received permission to go on an errand the day before his investiture retreat, the novices predicted he would never return. To their surprise he did return, made his retreat, and was invested on May 21, 1891, with the Capuchin habit and given the name Stephen.

The Capuchins viewed the novitiate as a time of testing for possible full membership. While John submitted to the regular discipline and reacted to it like the other novices, other unintended trials seemed to affect him even more than those deliberately imposed by the system. Sports as a form of leisure were not then viewed as part of the Capuchin identity. To abandon all activity in athletics was especially difficult. Furthermore, the German language was used throughout the province. While his parents' mother tongue was German, Stephen's first language was English. The fact that courses were conducted in German made it doubly difficult for his average intelligence to comprehend.

Consequently, Stephen never excelled in studies; no great academic achievements came his way after the novitiate. Instead, when he arrived in Milwaukee for theology in 1892, what his peers noticed was not his academic prowess but a change in his personality. One of them later wrote:

"When he came to Milwaukee from the novitiate, we could hardly recognize our Frater Stephen, so great was the change. He was very serene, always cheerful, yet he would never break the silence. He was a fresh-air addict, employing the few moments of free time to walk up and down the cloister garden absorbed in something, prayer or study. He often made visits to the Blessed Sacrament. . . . The only conversation we had was at table when dispensed from silence, and then we talked on classes, books, studies. His hobby at the time was 'public speaking' and he never tired of expounding its necessity, often deploring the lack of training for it in those days. His attitude showed plainly that it was his great desire to become a missionary. He was certainly a model, though often criticized mildly for his so-called eccentricity in rigidly observing silence."

When he was ordained to the priesthood on July 2, 1896, Stephen was twenty-seven years old. While his desire was to spend his Capuchin priesthood as a missionary, it would be another sixteen years before that dream would be realized.

From August 31, 1896, until 1911 he spent almost all of his time in and around New York City. While engaged primarily in parish ministry, this time also afforded Stephen some experiences which started specifying his particular kind of missionary activity with American Blacks.

While he worked at Sacred Heart parish in Yonkers (1897-1905), he tried to enable people to develop their own gifts. Stephen gave retreats to lay people, even mini-retreats to first communicants; this was before such practices were common. In a special way, he began to develop a desire to work among American Blacks, particularly after a visit to the Philadelphia motherhouse of the Sisters of the Blessed Sacrament who were recognized at that time as devoted to the Indian and Negro missions. It was this experience that made him determined one day to become a missionary, not in some far-off land, but in his own country.

Despite this dream, his approach to missionary work among Blacks was as impractical then as his ministry to the people of New York was a source of inspiration and emulation. He envisioned himself as a kind of roving evangelist in the South, converting all kinds of people to the Roman Catholic Church. It would not be until much later, when a visiting bishop from Sierra Leone in Africa would show Stephen the value of a more organized, centralized approach, that he began to shed some of his grandiose, free-wheeling ideas.

In 1906 Stephen sensed he would soon be headed South. The Capuchin provincial superiors had written several bishops in the South indicating the province's interest in opening a mission. Stephen checked with others about logistics of the tentative mission and even urged a group of nuns that "some of you should come too, to instruct the Negro children." However, no clear response was forthcoming from the bishops. Furthermore, higher superiors in Rome then decided the time was inopportune. So the project was abandoned. A disappointed Stephen was assigned in summer 1906 to Our Lady of the Angels in Harlem, then strongly Italian and Slavic.

Even though he was clearly disappointed and frustrated he had also developed a much deeper sense of abandonment which saw such human factors as part of God's overall plan. As he wrote to a friend soon after arriving at Harlem:

"Nothing surprised me more than to hear the word that my mission field should be in New York City for a time. The word came to me thus: 'You desire missionary work; our largest field is Harlem, so go in virtue of holy obedience.' The Lord in His goodness deigned to show me the truth of this the very first day I was here, when being called in haste to a dying person I found several families neglectful of their Christian duties, and one person not of our Faith who professed to become a Catholic, and since then I have found many on visits through the parish, which is very extensive. It is a great consolation to me to be where I had no desire to be, since, this, I trust, will make all my work more pleasing to God, though the thought often pervades me, why should I not be where there is a great scarcity of friends, while in the city of New York they are in abundance; but such is the will of God, and He must have sent me for something in particular; the reason why perhaps I will learn only when time has passed away."

Time did not pass slowly before Stephen was reassigned to St. John's in New York. The superiors needed someone who could speak English well to minister in the parish which was rapidly losing its character as a German parish staffed by German-speaking Capuchins.

This assignment in the heart of midtown Manhattan (1907-1909) offered Stephen the chance to broaden his apostolate beyond traditional parish ministry. One door that opened led him to St. Zita's Home for Friendless Women, a shelter for prostitutes and other undesirables the city had committed to institutions. Another door found him getting very involved — too involved some thought — in the St. Vincent de Paul Society. In one instance, at least, his desire to serve the needy indicated his tendency to impetuostiy, especially in that very desire.

Stephen had developed an approach to his ministry that was geared to reach adults through children. At all three parishes in New York where he was stationed, he taught in the schools, visited homes and public schools and walked the streets rounding up youngsters for instructions. He learned about their home conditions and became aware of their religious and physical needs. Thus it was that on one of his walks in the neighborhood he happened to see a number of boys in ragged clothing and bare feet. He rounded them up and brought them into the meeting of the St. Vincent de Paul Society being held at that time. He made an eloquent appeal for help, citing the boys as concrete examples of poverty, but after a few questions from the men it was discovered that the boys were not poverty-stricken at all. It was vacation time and they were saving their shoes and good clothes for more "appropriate places." Needless to say Stephen was the butt of a few jokes around St. John's the following days, all of which he took in good stride.

It was during this period that Stephen was led to his first direct ministry among Blacks. Quite a few Blacks had settled into the parish around the turn of the century. Stephen used his "to adults through the children" approach with slow but promising results. His efforts grew to the degree that he made plans to buy an old Protestant church for the use of the new converts who didn't seem to be totally welcome in the Irish congregation. But again, his plans were frustrated by those of his superiors; they reassigned him to Our Lady of the Angels.

During the subsequent years in Harlem (1909-1913), Stephen added to his parish duties the role of preaching parish missions in various parts of the United States and Canada. As early as his days in theology Stephen had worked to improve his preaching. His voluminous notes and long hours of practice seemed to make up for his deliberate, methodical style. The current techniques that the Capuchin preachers used in giving missions, Stephen applied to Our Lady of the Angels for one of its missions. Writing of its successes and failures, he noted in a letter which revealed his prejudices:

"Within one month over a thousand families were visited by us. Our work was more than rewarded, for it brought back to the Sacraments many who had been away for years. This result was due mainly to the house visitation and to prayer. Only about half a dozen families were found who absolutely refused conversion. The German-Hungarians in general were found to be rather hopeless, being engrossed in the cares of this world. They seem to come to this country with no other thoughts than to make money."

The approach of some German-Hungarians to dealing with "the cares of this world" was in their promotion of socialism. True to his fighting spirit and love of challenge, Stephen made great efforts to get invited to their closed meetings that he might listen and debate the current issues. He would show where he could support their goals and where he, as a Catholic, had to differ. He explained one of these encounters:

"I addressed the assembly briefly, showing that not all the miseries of life came from capitalism, and that much of the injustices of the capitalists is due to bad government, inasmuch as many men are in office who work for self-aggrandizement instead of the welfare of the people. Hence the importance of electing good men into office. I made an appeal to the Socialists to work in harmony with the Church for the betterment of social conditions on sound principles; and above all not to lower themselves so as to place themselves among brute creation by denying the immortality of the soul and the existence of a personal God."

The final year, 1913, at St. John's would be memorable for Stephen. First, his father, who seems to have made the deepest impression on his spirituality, died. "I really hope that I may leave this world with the same strong faith and love of God," Stephen noted at the time. "He died as he had often prayed, without being ill, wishing to be a burden to no one. I hope I may die as he did." The second memorable event came contained in a little slip of paper from his superior which Stephen received in early July. He was being transferred to St. Benedict the Moor "Mission for the Colored."

St. Benedict the Moor Mission had been established in a row of three two-story houses in Milwaukee's "colored district," in June, 1909. At first varoius priests ministered there, along with the School Sisters of Notre Dame. In time the diocesan authorities recognized the need to place the Mission on a more secure basis; and to insure this, St. Benedict's was turned over to the Capuchins on January 22, 1911. They, in turn, placed the Mission under the ministry of St. Francis Parish, not far away. Soon growing numbers forced a move to a group of houses which would serve as a chapel, a social center, and meeting hall. A large building was purchased for a school. In September, 1912, under the School Sisters of Notre Dame the school was established. It had nine pupils.

Stephen took over the first resident pastorate on July 13, 1913. When he began Milwaukee census statistics showed 84 Catholics among a total of 2,000 black residents.

Capitalizing on the methods he had used successfully in New York, Stephen began door-to-door visits of homes. Within a month hundreds of families had been visited. His offer to teach convert classes and to have the people participate in Mass soon made it necessary to have two Masses on Sundays. His persuasion to have parents send their children to the school bore fruit as well. By September, 1913, almost forty children were enrolled. Boarding students were also accepted when he found two brothers in destitute circumstances. "More good can be done in one year in a boarding school," he used to say, "than in five years by a day school."

In later years he opened a club room and an employment agency for girls and women, as well as a boarding house to help them safeguard "their virtue." He also opened a day nursery where working mothers could leave their children in responsible and caring hands.

As the Mission increased its services and ministry, so did the need for money to run it. Not waiting for needs to be met by money falling from heaven, Stephen had various schemes and resources which covered the gamut of traditional fund raisers. But in addition he had several unique approaches. One was his own personal prayer. In commenting on this, a fellow Capuchin noted: "I never met a more deeply spiritual man or one who tried harder to hide his virtues. Oftentimes when I visited the church at nightfall I would detect him alone in the church going around the stations. How rapt in God he was at such times! He was a silent sermon to me."

Besides turning to God in prayer at times of need, Stephen also insisted that the students do the same. He would say, "Our work must begin, continue, and end with God through prayer"; and to make sure the students supported the work, he inaugurated "storm novenas" which would be held regularly and at a moment's notice, depending on the need.

Prayer would not be the only way he would appeal to have his needs met. He employed various forms of begging. He would visit "Commission Row," the local wholesale food distribution center for the city. The vendors said they could not refuse him food for the children when they feared that the "light from his eyes" would cut through any defenses or excuses they might try to offer.

Another source of revenue came from his preaching of retreats, missions, and Forty Hours devotions. At these times he would try not only to gather funds, but he used the occasions to remind Whites of their Christian obligation to be open to the Blacks. He believed there really was not a "colored problem" but a white problem. Often he would say, "We must convert the white man to the colored cause before we can do anything for the colored."

An example of this twofold approach of getting financial help for the Mission while addressing white prejudice as well is evidenced in a letter he wrote in 1916 requesting permission to preach at all Masses:

"Convinced that it is the duty of the white man, who brought freedom to the colored, to help him spiritually and materially until he can take proper care of himself, and that no truer help can be given him than by opening a school, in which the children, at least of parents of good will, can be properly trained, we appeal to the charity of the faithful through their good priest, that we may be able in the near future to have a building constructed to extend true help to a greater number of colored children and with yet greater success." Having noted the States from which the boarders came, he continued:

"We intend to extend our appeal to all the dioceses from which we have children and which as yet have made no provision for colored children, so that people of each diocese can share in the good and help bear the burden which will be very light if the respective parishes contribute but a little.

"No charity is greater, for no people have been more neglected. His Grace, Most Rev. S. G. Messmer, writes: 'I most heartily endorse this appeal in behalf of a most excellent work.' While our Province is willing to meet the expenses of running the Institution, it is not in a financial condition at the present time to raise sufficient money to meet the necessary outlay involved in having an adequate building constructed. . . .

"In case you have debts to meet and fear the loss of the collection, you may rest assured that charity extended to the downtrodden Negro child is twice blessed and thus will enrich you and your people and make them all the more generous."

By 1920 such appeals had been able to realize a sizable building fund. Believing the Mission would be better off stressing the boarding school and wanting to get it to be self-sufficient in food and other basic necessities, Stephen began looking for a more rural setting. When he learned that Holy Rosary Academy near Corliss (Sturtevant, Wisconsin) was to be put on the market, he negotiated a one-year agreement with the owners, the Dominican Sisters of nearby Racine. The Racine Dominicans would be in charge of the newly-located boarding school. It would begin September, 1920, with Stephen as director. Since St. Benedict's was more than twenty-five miles away, this decision necessitated a new leader there: Fr. Philip Steffes was named director to replace Stephen.

The school year would not pass by before it became increasingly clear to almost all but Stephen that his "back to the land" dream would never work. For financial reasons Corliss had to be abandoned the following April. Although Stephen tried every tactic in getting money and seeking more time from his superiors, it was decided he should return the boarding school to Milwaukee.

With the aborted attempt at Corliss, some voices began to surface in open criticism of Stephen's approach. Much criticism arose from peoples' submerged racist hostilities and attitudes. Nevertheless, Stephen's enthusiasm affected his objectivity and administrative decisions, making him vulnerable to sincere but reactionary people.

It was decided that Fr. Philip would remain as director

when the boarding school returned to Milwaukee. Stephen, the founder, would become the fund raiser. This decision was a humiliation to the man who had built the Mission from nothing but a dream. The superiors had decided to leave the directorship in the hands of a man many years his junior, with little or no experience, who would now depend on Stephen to raise money to keep it going.

Despite the anomaly and his admitted disappointment Stephen had by now developed a deeper perspective on life which flowed from his prayer and understanding of God's action in him. He determined to be faithful to his assignment and sank into his preaching by using his voice and pen.

He found time to write pamphlets, especially geared to converts such as had enlivened St. Benedict's and the parishes in New York where he had developed unique approaches to evangelization. One, *What Everyone Should Know* sold over 100,000 copies. He wrote an article in *Our Sunday Visitor* appealing for personnel and got some volunteers — as well as a reprimand from his superior for not getting the usual, necessary permission to seek publication for such an article. But the form of preaching, which took up most of his time, was that devoted to missions, retreats and Forty Hours.

In January, 1923, the superiors decided to expand St. Benedict's, due largely to the continued growth made possible by the money Stephen had raised. Soon after the decision to build, Stephen headed for Annunciation church in St. Paul, Minnesota, to preach at Forty Hours. There he met the pastor of St. Patrick's church in Britt, Iowa, who asked him to preach a triduum there which started January 21.

When he finished, the night of January 23, Stephen was perspiring; but there were many confessions to hear in the cold confessional. By the time he returned to the rectory he had the chills and severe pain in his side. Not paying much attention to his condition, Stephen visited local pastors to obtain future preaching engagements. But after three days of such visits, his condition became worse. He visited a doctor who told him to remain in Britt, but Stephen wanted to get back to Milwaukee.

By the time he got home, his condition had so deteriorated that he was put into a hospital. After several days, pneumonia set in. Although this caused him much pain, those who visited him commented on his prayerfulness and sense of peace, as well as his concern for others. Once he remarked to Fr. Philip not to visit him so often because the Mission might suffer. To those who showed their concern for him and his future, he would slough it off saying, "So much attention given to me and Christ had none."

When he was told that his condition was poor and that death seemed inevitable he merely responded, "I am ready for anything." He carried this spirit of resignation to his last breath, the morning of February 16, 1923. He was not quite fifty-four years old.

Stephen Eckert was buried in the Capuchins' plot in Calvary Cemetery, Wauwatosa. But, after the faithful began to attribute favors and blessings to his intercession, serious discussion began about the possibility of beginning the process of beatification. It was also believed his body being buried at the Mission might be a source of inspiration to others. As a result, the body was exhumed and reburied on the Mission grounds on the twenty-fifth anniversary of his death, February 16, 1948.

The diocesan process was completed on June 25, 1959, and the documents were sent to Rome where Fr. Stephen Eckert's cause is now under consideration.

PRAYER
(Private use only)

Eternal Father, Who are in heaven, I offer You all the Masses which are being celebrated today throughout the world to obtain the great favor of the Public Veneration of Father Stephen. O Jesus, hasten to glorify Yourself in Your humble servant. Amen.

FOR FURTHER READING
Berchmans Bittle, O.F.M.Cap., *A Herald of the Great King: Stephen Eckert, O.F.M.Cap.* (Milwaukee: St. Benedict the Moor Mission, 1933).

CHAPTER 20

SERVANT OF GOD FATHER LUKAS ETLIN, O.S.B.
Lover of the Holy Eucharist and Benefactor of the Needy

20

Apostle of the Eucharist
FATHER LUKAS ETLIN, O.S.B. (1864-1927)

Louis Meyer, O.S.B.

"LIFE IS SHORT! Let us put all the divine love we can into every moment of it!" These words, uttered by the Benedictine monk, Fr. Lukas Etlin, when he was sixty years old, serve as the key to the understanding of his entire life. Love for the Holy Eucharist was the impelling force behind his many fruitful labors that included the globe-encircling *Caritas* program at the end of World War I, and it was his ardent love for the Eucharist that inspired him to publish a magazine to spread devotion to the Blessed Sacrament. Highlights of this remarkable life reveal how ordinary tasks performed with extraordinary fervor lead to a growth in holiness. At the time of Fr. Lukas' death, Bishop Gilfillan of St. Joseph, Missouri, noted: "He was the most wonderful combination of the active and contemplative life which has ever come under my observation."

Sarnen, the capital of Canton Obwalden, snuggles peacefully in the southern foothills of the Swiss Alps and its snowcapped peaks for centuries have been the much cherished heritage of the canton's loyal Catholic families, some of whom number St. Nicholas de Flue among their ancestors. It was here on February 28, 1864, that Alois Etlin and his wife Barbara (nee Amstalden) welcomed the gift of a second son and in baptism gave him the name Augustine Alfred.

In the playful company of his older brother, William, and younger sister, Maria, Alfred grew to be a healthy though, at times, a mischievous lad. When he had completed his elementary studies at the Benedictine *Realschule* at Sarnen, he enrolled (1880) in the college of the Benedictine Abbey at Engelberg. He was always joyous and he sometimes played jokes; but he was, nevertheless, beloved by classmates and professors alike. As the years passed Alfred became more serious. His contemporaries attest to his reverence and attention during Mass and visits to the Blessed Sacrament, and his zeal in attending meetings of the Sodality of the Blessed Virgin Mary. Young Alfred's artistic talents were discovered by the Benedictine art professor who saw that they were properly developed through drawing and in executing scenery for the college's theatrical productions. His natural bent for drama was given its outlet when he successfully took on the comic roles in the various school plays. Crayon sketches of the heads of Leonardo da Vinci's apostles, done at Engelberg and still extant, give eloquent testimony to Alfred's natural talent.

But this wonderful gift was to bring about a struggle in his life. When the time came for him to leave school he seriously sought "to discern the will of God" (Eph. 5:17). The monastic life-style of the Benedictines both at Sarnen and at Engelberg had greatly appealed to him;

but there was another attraction that had obsessed him, i.e., the career of an artist. Alfred rationalized that he could actually accomplish both — he could realize the spiritual longing in his life by creating future ecclesiastical works for God's glory. For a long time he reflected on which path to follow — to be a monk, or to be an artist — and in his indecision he confided his case to Mary, the holy Mother of God. "Speak, Lord, thy servant is listening" (1 Sam. 3:10) was his favorite aspiration then as it was in later years. Finally, in the presence of the Blessed Sacrament in Our Lady's Sodality chapel at Engelberg both light and courage were given him.

Under divine guidance Alfred chose to sacrifice an artist's fame in order to present himself as a candidate for the Benedictine way of life and the priesthood. His parents were indeed saddened when they learned of their son's desire to leave Switzerland and enter the newly-established monastery of Conception Abbey in northwest Missouri, a foundation of the Engelberg Abbey. Alfred remained firm in his decision, and finally his parents gave their blessing as he and his classmate, Caspar Lussi (the later Fr. Peter Lussi), left for America on September 9, 1886. In a letter to his parents he wrote: "My love for you will never grow cold. . . in the monastery it will be ennobled. It will manifest itself in ways more beneficial to you than my attaining earthly distinctions. . . .Pray. . .that I may be equal to my vocation and fulfil it wholly and entirely."

After a year's novitiate Alfred, the young aspirant, was admitted to monastic profession on November 13, 1887. It was on this occasion that he received the name Lukas, making St. Luke, evangelist and artist, his new heavenly patron. For the next three years Lukas continued to develop in "the school of the Lord's service" dividing his time between prayer, work, and study as spelled out in the Benedictine Rule. As a young monk he perceived that the love of God and that of neighbor formed the very essence of the monastic Rule. In ever greater degree this teaching of St. Benedict permeated every aspect of Lukas' monastic life and in his characteristic thoroughness he noted how frequently and how forcefully Benedict speaks out against mediocrity. The holy founder would have his monks "run — hasten — exercise zeal with most reverent love — bear others' infirmities with utmost patience — never desist — encourage one another," and many other such exhortations.

With four companions Lukas completed his course in theology at Conception Abbey in 1891, and was ordained to the priesthood on August 15 of that same year, the feast of the Assumption of the Blessed Virgin Mary. In the response to the request made by the Benedictine Sisters of Perpetual Adoration at Clyde, Missouri, whose monastery was but two miles from the abbey, Fr. Lukas celebrated his first Mass in their chapel on August 20. In March, 1892, he was appointed chaplain to this community of sisters — an assignment he fulfilled for thirty-five years, until his death.

While involved in his duties of daily Mass at the convent and giving conferences to the sisters, Fr. Lukas also supervised the restoration of the murals in the Abbey Church which had suffered severe damage in a tornado, June 21, 1893. The large mural of the Immaculate Conception that adorns the apse of the Abbey-Basilica and several murals on its side walls had been previously painted by Fr. Lukas. And just as he helped the abbey community with his artistic and architectural knowledge, he also aided the sisters in expanding their monastery. But throughout these labors, the spiritual growth of the sisters in the Clyde community had priority.

The liturgical movement in the United States was at this time still in its infancy and many of the clergy doubted its ultimate significance, but not so Fr. Lukas. Though he was never in the forefront of the movement, he sponsored the use of the Daily Missal long before it was promoted in parishes and communities. He knew that those who used the prayers of the Mass would be instructed in the truths of the faith and learn to appreciate the mysteries of Redemption and the inner joys of religion most effectively through the Eucharistic liturgy. He gradually replaced the sisters' "special devotions" during Mass by their union with the celebrant "to pray the Mass" rather than "to pray at Mass." "It is the Mass that matters" might well have been of his coining. He endlessly stressed: "Co-offer with Christ and the priest! Unite with the prayers at the altar." And in his desire to render the liturgical celebration of Mass with utmost dignity and devotion, he arranged for Fr. Gregory Huegle, a fellow Benedictine from Conception Abbey and a recognized promoter of the Solesmes method of singing Gregorian Chant, to instruct the sisters.

Fr. Lukas was always an ecclesial person — he lived with and for the Church. His well-worn four-volume set of *The Monastic Breviary* gives manifest proof of his love for the official prayers of the Church, so richly centered in the celebration of the Eucharist, and the very heart of monastic prayer-life. With evident joy on his face he welcomed Advent, the beginning of a new liturgical year, as another gift of time to enter deeply into the unfolding of the works of Redemptive Love. This joyous spirit naturally found its way into his weekly conferences and in his special sermons. As the liturgical season progressed and as the feasts of the year occurred, Fr. Lukas imparted a deeper understanding of and love for the mysteries of salvation.

It was during the relatively carefree period of his novitiate that Fr. Lukas laid the foundation for that intimate union with our Lord in the Holy Eucharist which became the very source and summit of his life and labors. With the permission of the Director of Novices, he would at night spend two hours before the Blessed Sacrament, and if he should have any free time during the day he was to be found near the altar. He persevered in this custom, and later on as chaplain he continued to follow the deep impulse of his heart and at night he would often kneel for hours in the sacristy looking through the open door into the sanctuary. Fr. Lukas' personal zeal for adoration of the Holy Eucharist constituted a most impressive sermon of faith, reverence, and love. For him this "mystery of faith" was the "mystery of love." "Behold the tabernacle of God with man" meant that the Sacred Host in the ciborium, or in the monstrance, was the sacramental presence of Christ Jesus. "Gaze at the Sacred Host! Make the words 'through Him, with Him, and in Him' the breath of your life" he counseled. The adorer's prayer is then no longer finite but becomes infinite in value because it is the Second Person of the Blessed Trinity rendering all honor and glory to the eternal Father, in union with the Holy Spirit.

As a means of sharing the fruit of their contemplative life, the sisters, under the guidance of Fr. Lukas, began to publish the magazine *Tabernacle and Purgatory*. The first issue appeared in May, 1905, and it clearly gave the sisters' objective: "that the knowledge of the Most Holy Eucharist be increased, and the love toward It be enkindled more and more in the hearts of the faithful . . . our little booklet should therefore increase the esteem for Holy Mass, encourage a frequent reception of Holy Communion, and awaken and strengthen a lively faith in the Real Presence of Our Lord in the Holy Eucharist." The subscribers to *Tabernacle and Purgatory* numbered thousands. Its articles instructed its readers in true devotion to the Sacred Heart emphasizing the fact that this devotion is actually inseparable from devotion to the Blessed Sacrament. Theological articles made it clear that Christ's divine heart symbolized His unbounded charity that was made manifest in the mysteries of His life — the Incarnation, Paschal mysteries, institution of the Holy Eucharist, His eternal priesthood and intercession at the throne of the Father. Veneration of the Blessed Virgin Mary, of the angels and saints, and the offering of suffrages for the departed, especially during Mass, were also featured in its pages.

In his office Fr. Lukas kept a near life-sized painting of the Madonna by the German artist, Baroness von Oer, standing on the floor near his desk. Ever since his youth he had a tender devotion to our Lady who "prepared, fashioned, nourished, and bore our Redeemer." Countless were the times that he prayed a Latin "Hail Mary" before this image as he integrated his union with our Lady into his daily schedule of activity. Before planning each issue of *Tabernacle and Purgatory,* he was accustomed to kneel with an associate editor before this image and say three "Hail Marys"; and while working at his desk he would frequently glance at the painting and whisper, "O dearest, sweetest, purest Virgin Mary, I love you." When the issue did appear, he would place it near our Lady as he did letters that required special discernment. On her feasts he spent hours before this image, conscious of her presence, often with rosary in his hand. He was frequently seen with this rosary — either walking beside the chapel or in a secluded pine grove near the convent. His perennial advice to priests who sought his counsel was: "Cultivate a personal love for Jesus in the Holy Eucharist and a tender love for the Virgin Mother of God, and you will never defect."

As a consequence of World War I abject poverty prevailed in many parts of Central Europe. Fr. Lukas could not help but think of the millions unable to feed themselves and their children, of the scattered religious communities, the monasteries, convents and seminaries destroyed by the war. In his deep concern and love of his neighbor he wrote an editorial in the June, 1920, issue of *Tabernacle and Purgatory* initiating an appeal for money to be sent to Europe to benefit the hungry children and the homeless religious. The response to this appeal was much more than he had expected, and within months after his request he sent nearly $25,000 to Europe. But Fr. Lukas recognized an even greater need, and in the May, 1921, issue he requested donations for scholarships for seminarians of the many impoverished dioceses of Europe. This urgent plea to help adopt future priests touched the kind hearts of thousands of Americans who readily made sacrifices for these needy students. These funds, now known as *Caritas,* were channeled through bishops and superiors of religious communities and were used to clothe and support the seminarians while in their studies as well as help bring relief to those religious dying of malnutrition. Between the years 1920-1927, when Fr. Luke directed the program, over $2,000,000 had been collected and distributed in 30 countries, a part of which helped finance some 2800 seminarians in their priestly studies. The funds were used, for example, to support the seminarians at the *Germanicum* in Rome, the seminary for the German and Hungarian theological students, as well as for the Benedictine College of Sant' Anselmo also in Rome. Among the beneficiaries of these funds three became cardinals, five archbishops, twenty bishops, twelve Benedictine abbots, etc. Records of all the alms received, disbursed and acknowledged was part of Fr. Lukas' thorough handling of this "sacred trust." The records are faithfully preserved to this day.

Trips to Europe, offered by bishops whose seminaries and seminarians had been helped through these funds were all declined by Fr. Lukas. He would not claim credit for this splendid work but attributed its success to God's blessing and the generosity and goodness of American Catholics. He rejected all honors except the faculty of endowing a specified number of rosaries with special indulgences. Fr. Lukas was successful in this appeal primarily because he drew compassionate love for the suffering from his close union with Christ in the Holy Eucharist. The appeals which touched hearts were inspirations he received kneeling before the altar. He would hurry to his desk even before eating breakfast to put "some sparks on paper," he said, "before they cooled" in his mind. In this spirit he identified with the poor by discouraging the purchase of anything new for his personal use. His wardrobe consisted of only necessary clothing and thus he rejoiced in following the Benedictine Rule.

The experience of God's presence within him preserved Fr. Lukas from what others would have found a frenetic activity of a five-fold chaplaincy: spiritual conferences to the sisters, teaching religion to the girls in St. Joseph's Academy, supervising the erection of buildings, editing *Tabernacle and Purgatory,* and finally directing the world-wide *Caritas* program for seven years. The secret of his peace was: "Let no person, circumstance, nor thing, deprive you of your precious treasure: union with God through love." When he had been misjudged, and those who knew the true circumstances would urge him to make a clarification, he would reply: "If I need to be defended God will defend me."

The rigidity that Fr. Lukas had as a young man mellowed with his years. Still, his own love of silence, reverence and zeal for prayer, his unmitigated self-giving to Church and community made him expect the same sacrifice from others as well. No sacrifice was too great for him when it came to promoting devotion to the Blessed Sacrament. These words of his are indelibly engraven in many a heart: "At the hour of death our greatest regret will be that we have not realized our Great Treasure: Jesus with us in the Holy Eucharist."

Fr. Lukas apparently had a premonition of his impending, though totally unexpected, call to eternity. After having concluded his regular catechetical instruction to the girls at St. Joseph's Academy in Clyde on December 16, 1927, he astonished each of them by saying: "We ought to be ready to die at any time. If it is time for us to die, we should not even ask for a day longer. Even if one were to die in an auto accident he ought to accept it as the holy will of God." He then left the classroom, but suddenly returned to impart his blessing to his students.

Now, Fr. Lukas had made arrangements with a friend who acted as his chauffeur, to go that day to St. Joseph, Missouri, to reclaim two ornate sanctuary lamps that had been gold-plated. But before he left on this errand, he felt urged to complete the work for mailing a dozen letters that he had written in answer to requests for aid under the *Caritas* program. During his instructions to the Academy pupils, the typed list of Mass intentions, scholarship papers, and drafts, with the letters he had written during the night, were folded and the envelopes sealed. He always wished to affix the varied commemorative stamps. This done, he left his room and descended the stairs, but immediately turned around, retraced his steps and looked kindly and piercingly at the sister who served as his secretary, and said: "Divine Love be with you!" This was Fr. Lukas' final verbal message.

That afternoon about 5:15 p.m., as he and his driver were returning home and as they were approaching Stanberry, about fourteen miles from the convent, a car suddenly darted on to the highway from a concealed road and collided with them. Fr. Lukas, clutching a rosary in his hands, was heard to say, "O Jesus, Jesus!" and was instantly thrown from the front seat of the car on to the pavement. The pastor of Stanberry came to anoint him, but since Fr. Lukas had sustained a fatal blow on the right temple, he was already with God. On December 16, 1927, Fr. Lukas fulfilled the offering he had often voiced in his conferences: "Life for Life, love for Love, blood for Blood, and one day death for Death!" Hidden in his spectacle case a final message was found written that same day on a tiny slip of paper: "He has loved me and delivered Himself for me, and I must love Him and sacrifice myself for Him."

Fr. Lukas' funeral services were held on December 19, in the Abbey Church — the church he had helped decorate —

and his body was taken to Clyde and now rests in a simple grave in the shadow of the Adoration Chapel, the great shrine which he had built to honor Christ in the Blessed Sacrament.

When the news of Fr. Lukas' tragic death reached the outside world, letters of sympathy and condolence began to pour in from all parts of the world. The letter of Fr. Lukas' own bishop, the Most Rev. Francis Gilfillan, Bishop of St. Joseph, Missouri, is typical of them:

"The loss of our dear saint would indeed be irreparable if we did not feel that he is today looking down from heaven and blessing the work he has done so faithfully and with such divine enthusiasm.

"So true a priest he was, and so devoted to the interests of his Beloved Master, that it was impossible to spend five minutes in his company without being improved by it, and without coming away with the impression: Here, surely, is a man of God.

"It is a remarkable thing, too — for one who did everything in his power to conceal his own merits — the wide and genuine sorrow his death has caused. It seems to me to be an evidence that our Lord wants to make it known that this man was His true servant. . . ."

From the time of Fr. Lukas' death to the present day many persons have asked his intercession with God in various needs and have reported that their prayers have been answered. Because petitions for the beatification of Fr. Lukas had been received from the hierarchy, priests, religious, and faithful in many countries, the ordinary diocesan informative process was formally opened on August 13, 1960, under Bishop John P. Cody, then Bishop of Kansas City-St. Joseph. At the present time prayers continue to be offered to discern the will of God with regard to the beatification of his servant, Fr. Lukas Etlin, O.S.B.

The address of the Vice Postulator for the Cause of Fr. Lukas is: Rev. Louis Meyer, O.S.B., Conception Abbey, Conception, Missouri, 64433.

PRAYER
(Private use only)

O God, You favored Your servant, Father Lukas Etlin, with a deep love for Your Son in the Mystery of the Holy Eucharist, for the Virgin Mother of Jesus, for the angels and the saints, and with apostolic charity for all. Grant us to live always in Your grace through his intercession. Deepen our faith and love in the Holy Eucharist, so that we are inspired to be of service to Your people everywhere. Listen in particular to our special needs . . . so that manifesting Your good pleasure in Father Lukas Etlin, You may be pleased to bring about his beatification to the advantage of Your Church. We ask this through Christ our Lord. Amen.

FOR FURTHER READING

Edward Malone, O.S.B., *Father Lukas Etlin, O.S.B.: Apostle of the Eucharist* (Clyde, Missouri: Benedictine Convent of Perpetual Adoration, 1961).

CHAPTER 21

SERVANT OF GOD SISTER MIRIAM TERESA DEMJANOVICH, S.C.
Model and Instructor of Religious Sisters

21

Unto Greater Perfection

SISTER MIRIAM TERESA DEMJANOVICH, S.C. (1901-1927)

Sr. M. Zita Geis, S.C.

TERESA DEMJANOVICH was born in Bayonne, New Jersey, on March 26, 1901, the youngest of seven children. Her parents, Alexander and Johanna Suchy Demjanovich, came from Bardejov (Bartfeld), a picturesque town on the southern slopes of the Carpathian mountains, then part of the Austro-Hungarian Empire. A few months after their marriage they emigrated to the United States (1884), and first resided in New York, but only for a short time, before settling in Bayonne.

Teresa's family belonged to the Byzantine Ruthenian Rite — a Greek Catholic rite named after the province of Ruthenia in Eastern Europe. Teresa's early background

299

was thus a happy union of East and West; her cultural and religious roots were Greek Catholic but her years in Bayonne were heavily influenced by Roman Catholicism. Her elementary and secondary education were completed in the Bayonne public schools and her college training was at the College of St. Elizabeth, conducted by the Sisters of Charity of St. Elizabeth, one of the six branches of the community founded by St. Elizabeth Ann Seton.

Teresa was a true comtemplative, though her activities were those of a gifted and very busy person. In her daily life she was keenly aware of the influence of the Holy Spirit upon her and she consciously experienced God — even from her childhood years — but she never realized that these were extraordinary gifts until she entered the novitiate and began to learn about the spiritual life.

In 1905, not yet five years old, Teresa began her elementary education in the local public school. Despite her age she was soon at the head of her class and successfully maintained this standing throughout her grammar school years. She was everyone's favorite; her gray-blue eyes and blond hair added to the sweetness of her expression and her high-pitched voice accented the childishness of her speech. During these years she acquired a great love for reading which only increased with time. Later on she would reproach herself for any overindulgence in this regard. Her scholastic success never lessened her high spirits for play. After school, and on holidays as well, she enjoyed playing baseball with Charles, a brother closest to her in age. Like all children they had their moments of merriment as well as their squabbles especially when the game did not go according to Teresa's liking. They were inseparable; they went to school together and returned home together. They often read from the same book, one waiting for the other to finish before turning the page. Within the family circle, each child had his or her specific duty, and it was characteristic of Teresa never to betray her preferences, but do whatever had to be done and do it with a joyful enthusiasm.

Teresa's religious education first began within the family. Before her she had the wonderful example of parents, brothers, and sisters. Her parents ruled the home with love and good example rather than through fear. Morning and evening prayers daily, grace before and after meals, and the Angelus were never omitted. Besides Sunday Mass, devotions during the week were an added spiritual refreshment. Obedience and respect seemed to come to the children naturally. They constantly saw the self-sacrifice of their parents who deprived themselves, even of necessities, in order to offer their children comfort and happiness.

Teresa began her high school studies at the Bayonne Public High School in February, 1913, when she was not quite twelve years old. She would have preferred a Catholic school but, at that time, there was none in Bayonne. But her religious instruction was not wanting. The pastor of the Ruthenian Greek Catholic Church, to which the family belonged, held religious classes every day after school and Teresa was faithful in attending. Her four years in high school were happy years and she graduated in January, 1917, as salutatorian of her class. It was time to look to the future.

Teresa never had a doubt about her vocation. She always wanted to live for God and to give herself to Him wholly and for ever. But when and how was she to accomplish this? Characteristically, she kept this secret to herself. Her mother had been ill for some time and it was clear that she would not improve. Being aware of her mother's condition Teresa faced the problem before her sensibly and honestly and took over her mother's duties around the house. Exteriorly her life was that of Martha, but interiorly Teresa was living the life of Mary. God was calling her to an ever closer union with Himself; He was preparing her in silence, prayer, and work for some future mission. Then, on November 27, 1918, Teresa's beloved mother died. With her usual selflessness, she did her best to support her father, sisters, and brothers in their affliction. Several years later she wrote: "I shed a few tears when my mother died, because those I loved were so very much afflicted, all the while wondering what kind of stone-hearted being I was not to be able to feel that it was *my* mother, and that she was dead. Only twelve months later did tears come to relieve that oppression, and then I wept for hours, with such torrents of tears as I have never experienced."

After her mother's death, Teresa continued in her role as housekeeper. The winter and spring months passed, and when summer arrived her father conferred with his older children about Teresa's future. They all agreed that she should continue her education since this was what their mother had wanted. What did Teresa think of this idea? She was not all that enthusiastic since it was her silent desire to enter the Carmelite Order. College would mean four more years of study and four years could be an eternity for someone who longed for the cloister. But at the same time she knew that God had given her talents which she could, perhaps, best use in the classroom. Above all, Teresa did not want to do her own will; ever since childhood she had schooled herself in doing the will of others rather than her own. In everything she only sought to do God's will. When the family decided that college was the only sensible path for her, she quietly acquiesced and prepared to go to the College of St. Elizabeth in Convent Station, New Jersey.

Late in September, 1919, Teresa began her college career. This was a new and totally different life, and adjustment was somewhat difficult after two and a half years of keeping house for her family. Some time passed before she became accustomed to the spacious campus and her new companions, all care-free freshmen. She ranked as an "A" student in her class work and was always ready to have fun during the hours of recreation. But at the same time she was serious and zealous in performing her devotional exercises. From her first days at St. Elizabeth's she manifested herself as one who appreciated the spiritual over the material. She did not need the religious training that the average student required, for she was alrealy adept in prayer and had long put into practice the spiritual maxims of her patroness, St. Teresa of Avila, the great reformer of Carmel.

Teresa's prayer always was "to be ignored by all." This prayer was granted her in so far as she succeeded in concealing many of her marvelous graces, but there were whispers among the students that heaven was a stronger reality to her than earth. A student once came to visit her and found her so absorbed in prayer that she had to call her several times before she answered. She noticed Teresa's face, slightly raised and radiantly happy, and asked "What is the matter, Teresa?" Teresa, on this occasion, was unable to conceal her supernatural graces but exacted promises of silence from her visitor. Daily she made visits to the Blessed Sacrament, but these did not make her conspicuous since the other students came and went while Teresa remained in prayer. Christ in the tabernacle spoke to her soul and held it captive, oblivious of all else. Teresa's four years in college were profitable; academically she graduated with a "summa cum laude" and spiritually she achieved intimate union with her Lord.

Upon graduating from college in 1923, Teresa taught Latin and English at St. Aloysius Academy in Jersey City. The summer of 1924 was free and she spent her time caring for the family home and giving herself to prayer. Her other diversions were reading and music. When September came she had no teaching position and was uncertain as to what she should do, though her soul still longed for a life of complete sacrifice and Carmel appeared to be the only place where her desires could be satisfied. This state of perplexity remained until December 8, when a sudden change came over her. She now felt the assurance that

God wanted her to enter the Sisters of Charity at Convent Station in whose college she had studied. So eager was she to enter religious life and so certain that this was what God was asking of her, she desired to do it before Christmas, but it was considered better to wait until February 2.

Just three days before she was to go to the convent her father died, January 30, 1925. He had been ill with pneumonia; and the same love and care she had shown her mother during her illness, she now manifested in caring for her father. Teresa remained with him day and night, doing all in her power to save him, but without success. Her father's death and the family's grief were a further test to her. Should she not now stay at home, at least until the burden of sorrow had lessened? She felt she should disregard this natural inclination and was determined to go to the convent the very afternoon of her father's funeral, which was held on February 2. This she certainly would have done, if she had not received word from the motherhouse to postpone her entrance until the 11th.

On February 11, she had her last meal with her two brothers and two sisters, and then left by train for Convent Station. In the convent Teresa found herself alone with God. She was very happy and was prepared to meet whatever future might bring for the sake of Him whom she loved so ardently. She might have trembled had she known the sacrifices that were to be asked of her generous soul.

From the early days of her postulancy she stood out from the rest for her eagerness to practice the rule and customs of the institute. She performed her spiritual exercises and duties with exactness and care. She lived the routine life of a postulant cheerfully and looked forward to the day when she would receive the habit of the Sisters of Charity. On May 17, 1925, the day when Thérèse of the Child Jesus, the Little Flower, was canonized in Rome, Teresa Demjanovich received her habit and the religious name of Miriam Teresa as she had requested. She chose Miriam in honor of the Blessed Mother, and Teresa in remembrance of her patroness St. Teresa of Avila and St. Thérèse of Lisieux on whose canonization day she was first garbed as a religious.

As a novice Sr. Miriam Teresa continued to grow in perfection. She conformed exactly to common life, and if there was anything for which she was conspicuous it was her usual fidelity to little things. In September, though still a novice, she began to teach in the Academy carrying a full schedule of classes, besides performing her regular duties in the novitiate.

When she entered the novitiate her sole desire was to lose herself in the community, to do whatever she was told, never to seek personal recognition and thus conform herself more and more to Jesus. At the same time she realized that she could not pass through the novitiate without having an influence upon the lives of her companions, and she was determined that this influence should be a strengthening one. She knew that her every thought, word, and deed was to have its effect not only on the members of her community but even on the members of the whole Church as well. Thus, she determined to be as perfect a religious as possible.

Besides this quiet life "hidden with Christ in God," she was to have another way of doing good for souls. God made use of her to instruct others in the way to holiness. In June, 1926, her spiritual director, knowing that she enjoyed extraordinary insights into the religious life and possessed experiential knowledge of the science of the saints, conceived the idea that she should write conferences and instructions for her fellow novices. He knew that Sr. Miriam Teresa's written word would best describe the working of grace within her soul and, furthermore, he thought these conferences would contribute to the appreciation of her merits after her death. Having discussed this idea with the superior, he commanded her to write such a conference — the subject matter was up to her — and send it to him while he was away during the summer. Her first conference she entitled "Where Thy Treasure Is There Is Thy Heart." He found the conference very acceptable and ordered her to write one a week for the coming year. In writing these conferences she received assistance from no one, and no one but her superior knew what she was doing.

When her spiritual director returned in September he began to use Sr. Miriam Teresa's conferences as his own instructions to the novices. As they had usually done with his conferences, these too were multigraphed and distributed to the sisters in the other convents, the true authorship being closely guarded.

Towards the very end of November, Sr. Miriam Teresa became quite ill with a sore throat and a week later, when her condition became worse, she was admitted (December 9) to St. Joseph's Hospital in Paterson. Her case was diagnosed as tonsilitis and hypertension, but because of her weakened condition she was not operated on until the 20th. She returned home but when it was time for the spring semester to begin, it was obvious that she was unable to go back into the classroom and her superior decided she should return to the hospital. On January 24, 1927, Sr. Miriam Teresa left her convent for St. Elizabeth's Hospital; she was suffering from exhaustion, shortness of breath and occasional pains in the heart. She celebrated her twenty-sixth birthday (March 26) in the hospital and on the following day was seized with intense pain. It was believed to be acute appendicitis but on the following day when she felt much better the operation was not deemed advisable. Thus her condition fluctuated — one day better, the next somewhat weak.

Her brother, Father Charles, who had been ordained just a few days before her graduation from college in 1923, was her most frequent visitor. There was no one, except perhaps her spiritual director, who understood her better. While others hoped for her recovery, Fr. Charles knew she would never leave the hospital, and he thought of the one happiness that her soul still longed for on earth, so he took it upon himself to request of the superior if his sister, now in danger of death, would be able to pronounce her vows in religion while still in the hospital. He obtained this permission and on April 2, her spiritual director went to her bedside with the comforting news that she was permitted to make her profession as a Sister of Charity. Sr. Miriam Teresa was greatly overjoyed, and within her heart she knew that this was but the fulfillment of a premonition she had for almost a year that she was not to pronounce her vows with the others of her group.

In early May, Sr. Miriam Teresa suffered another severe attack of appendicitis, and on Friday, May 6, she was operated on. It seemed to have been a success, but the next day an unexpected and unfavorable reaction occurred. She suffered intensely and steadily grew weaker. By Sunday morning her condition was critical and all hope of recovery had passed. The sisters and her family received word that she was dying; but before they were able to come to her, death had come and she went to her God without the presence of those whom she so loved on earth. Fr. Charles was the first to arrive, but he was ten minutes too late. Speaking of her death, her spiritual director said, "She died of divine love. The operation was the occasion, I believe, but not the cause of her death."

The news of Sr. Miriam Teresa's death reached the motherhouse at 10:30 a.m., and it was a great shock to her novice-companions for everyone was confident that she would get better after the operation. That afternoon, during their period of adoration before the Blessed Sacrament, the stillness of the chapel was periodically broken by subdued sobs. A strange and inexplicable atmosphere pervaded the convent and though no one spoke of it openly, everyone felt that a saint had left them forever. On Monday, her body was brought to the convent and the sisters looked upon a wasted form and a thin face with its lines of long-endured suffering. The funeral was celebrated on Wednesday, May 11, by Monsignor Thomas H. McLaughlin, later to become Bishop of Paterson; and the burial was in the sisters' peaceful cemetery at the foot of the hill. To the eyes of the world this was the end, but in reality it was only the beginning.

Sr. Miriam Teresa's spiritual director had once told her that her conferences were making him famous and that his day of humiliation was sure to come when he would have to acknowledge that he was not their author. Immediately after Sr. Miriam Teresa's funeral, he posted this notice on the sisters' bulletin board, "The conferences which I have been giving to the Sisters were written by Sister Miriam Teresa."

That evening, after the funeral, Monsignor McLaughlin felt the need to record his convictions about Sr. Miriam Teresa. He wrote of his several meetings with her:

"The impression made on me, although each of these occasions was short duration, was most singular, awakening pious admiration and awe. She scarcely spoke but there was something inexpressible about her which made me feel that I was in the presence of one apart. . . .

"There are certain other mysterious things which I feel I should set down while fresh in my memory. Never a complaint to my knowledge, nor criticism, nor anything approaching it, came from her lips during her illness. . . . She was cheerful and happy, with an unusual happiness. I know that she was misunderstood, from the things I have heard, not from her brother, but from others. . . .

"When her brother asked me. . .to conduct the services, I do not know what came to me to say it should be the *Missa Dilexisti.* Today, the moment her Spiritual Director. . .met me, he said, 'Monsignor, the Mass should be *pro Virgine et Martyre.* Her life did not contain a willfull venial sin. She made the vow of greater perfection, the vow never to gratify any of her senses. Though no one knew it, in many cases not even herself, her conferences which I ordered her to write have been used in many convents in this country, and even in Rome. She has been set for the salvation of many, particularly of this Community.'

"The meeting with her Spiritual Director and his recital of the depths of her sanctity, heroic virtue, and the inward life of Sister Miriam Teresa inspired me with renewed enthusiasm for the work that God called me to perform, and I made every effort to offer up a perfect Oblation on the occasion of the funeral. My prayer is that the departed one may in conformity with the divine will intercede for me and for those entrusted to my care; that if it be the Will of God, her life and virtues may become known, that they may be a source of edification to her sisters in religion; and also effect the harmonious interaction of the different rites of the Church, particularly here in America."

Two days after the funeral, it was Friday, the day for the spiritual director's usual conference to the novices. On this special day he opened his conference saying:

"Sisters, you have lost a companion who is a saint. It frequently happens when a religious dies that people say, 'She was a saint.' I do not mean that, I mean that you have lost one who will, perhaps, be canonized some day. You knew her; you lived with her, and how privileged you are! But you could not appreciate her. I wanted to tell you many times to profit by her example, but, of course, that was out of the question. I hinted though. You recall the day I told you that if the Little Flower herself lived with you in the novitiate, you might not like her, that her constant fidelity to the least details of the Rule would annoy you. That is what happened to many of you with reference to Sr. Miriam Teresa. Her life was a reproach to some and that was not agreeable. It is now too late to profit by her presence in your midst, but, at least, you can profit by all you remember, and all that you will learn about her in the future.

"I know the secrets of her life, and I know that she lived entirely for God from the time she arrived at the age of reason. She never offended God by a deliberate venial sin. You need not read the lives of the saints in order to find an example to follow. You have seen a saint in action. Thank God that you lived with her. You will be grateful for this grace the rest of your lives."

The conferences that Sr. Miriam Teresa had written were collected after her death and published in 1928 under the title *Greater Perfection*; and over the years they have been translated into Dutch, French, Spanish, Italian, and Chinese.

The ordinary informative process investigating Sr. Miriam Teresa's cause for beatification was begun by Bishop McLaughlin in December, 1945. In May, 1979, her remains were transferred from the cemetery to a vault in the Holy Family Chapel at the Convent of St. Elizabeth; and on June 19, 1980 the cause of the Servant of God was formally introduced in Rome. For further information on Sr. Miriam Teresa, contact: Sister Miriam Teresa League Headquarters, Convent Station, New Jersey, 07961.

PRAYER
(Private use only)

Most Holy and Blessed Trinity, whom Sister Miriam Teresa loved so ardently, grant that we, like her, may become ever more conscious of Your Divine Presence within our souls. We implore You, to show signs that Your humble servant enjoys glory with You in heaven, and to hasten the day when we may render her a public tribute of her veneration and love. Amen.

FOR FURTHER READING

Greater Perfection: Conferences of Sister Miriam Teresa, edited by Charles C. Demjanovich (New York: P. J. Kenedy, 1928); A Sister of Charity, *Sister Miriam Teresa (1901-1927)* (New York: Benziger, 1936); Theodore Maynard, *The Better Part* (New York: Macmillan, 1952).

CHAPTER 22

SERVANT OF GOD FATHER THOMAS AUGUSTINE JUDGE, C.M.
Vincentian Founder of the
Missionary Servants (priests and brothers) of the Most Holy Trinity
and of the Missionary Servants (sisters) of the Most Blessed Trinity

22

America's Pioneer in the Lay Apostolate

FATHER THOMAS AUGUSTINE JUDGE, C.M. (1868-1933)

David F. O'Connor, S.T.

FATHER JUDGE, was a dedicated missionary — a man of faith and action. He disturbed the religiously complacent with his thoughts and plans concerning what more could be done for the Church and souls. So great was his zeal, his prayerfulness, his self-sacrifice and holiness, that by word and deed he constantly spurred others on to a similar life. His avowed purpose was to make every Catholic a missionary. But he taught that this vocation from the Holy Spirit could be fulfilled only under the guidance of the Church and that personal holiness should accompany apostolic activity. Fr. Judge encouraged frequent reception of the sacraments, devotion to the Holy Spirit, and a concern for the spiritual and corporal needs of one's neighbor. Possessing a burning love for God and an extraordinary generosity, he appealed to these qualities in others and asked them to render a personal service to God. His childlike trust in Divine Providence and obedience to the will of God was coupled with a mature determination to do all possible to lead people to Jesus. His simplicity and detachment attracted countless people closer to God.

The evident holiness of the man did not make him a cold severe rigorist, nor an intellectual given to hair splitting. His was an attractive, magnetic personality exuding and breathing a charming amiability, a humble kindliness, a delightful simplicity, and affectionate interest in everyone. He was approachable and inspired confidence. To all his spiritual sons and daughters he was simply: Father.

He pioneered the lay apostolate in the United States with a great foresight which paralleled the insistent call of the Roman Pontiffs to organize apostolic lay people in every parish of the world. He desired to help form an enlightened and dedicated laity who not only knew their faith and lived it, but would be zealous to share it with others. From this work with the lay apostolate there also developed two religious missionary congregations which continue to grow and prosper and thereby multiply and extend the work of this zealous priest.

Thomas A. Judge was born in South Boston, Massachusetts, on August 23, 1868. His parents were Thomas Judge (+ 1887) and Mary Danahey (+ 1912), immigrants from Ireland. He was the second son and fifth of their eight children. His parents provided an ideal Catholic home for their children. Thomas' mother was accustomed to attend daily morning Mass and his father led the family rosary every evening. They instilled in their children a great love for the Catholic faith and a warm reverence for the priesthood.

God blessed the family by eventually calling three of the children to the religious life, Thomas and two of his younger sisters. Alice Gertrude entered the Daughters of Charity in 1899 as Sr. Alice, Ann Veronica married Mr. Daniel Ledwidge and bore him five children. When she was a widow and her children were grown, she entered the Congregation founded by her brother and became Sr. M. Gerard, M.S.B.T. in 1924.

Since there were no parochial schools for the Judge children to attend, Thomas was enrolled in the John A. Andrew Public School in September, 1876. He proved to be a normal, healthy boy and a good son.

As Thomas grew in knowledge and love of his faith and matured into a young man, he gave thought to the possibility of a priestly vocation. However, on May 3, 1887, his father suddenly and unexpectedly died. Thomas found it necessary to help support his family by working at various jobs during the day and finishing his high school education by attending night classes. This seemed to express God's will for him and he temporarily put aside all thought of entering a seminary. Within a few years the family was subsisting prudently under the wise direction of his mother. His brother and two of his sisters were also employed and the family was provided with some stability and security.

In the spring of 1889, the priests of the Congregation of the Mission conducted a parish mission at St. Augustine's, his parish, and Thomas sought their counsel. With their encouragement and the blessing of his mother and family, he decided to enter the apostolic school of the Congregation of the Mission. Thomas entered the school at St. Vincent's Seminary, Germantown, Pennsylvania, on January 25, 1890. He was then twenty-one years old, a mature, hard-working young man who quickly became impressed by the life of the recently beatified John Gabriel Perboyre. Thomas developed a life-long devotion to this son of St. Vincent de Paul martyred in China and desired to follow him as a missionary to pagan lands.

Thomas entered the novitiate at Germantown on January 24, 1893, and professed his four vows of poverty, chastity, obedience and stability in the work of the Congregation on the feast of the Conversion of St. Paul, January 25, 1895. He studied philosophy and theology at St. Vincent's Seminary, Germantown, between 1894 and 1899. At this time he became a daily communicant with the permission of his director, a practice that was not common in those days and one that was open to criticism.

In 1898 his health had been gravely weakened by tuberculosis. When Thomas was ordained a priest by Archbishop Ryan in the chapel of St. Charles Seminary, Overbrook, on Pentecost Sunday, May 27, 1899, it was generally believed that he would soon die.

Immediately after ordination Fr. Judge was sent home to his family to recuperate or die. To the suprise of all he began to recover to such a degree that at the end of the summer he could be given very limited duties. For the next few years he passed his time in St. Vincent's Church, Germantown, and St. Joseph's Church, Emmitsburg, Maryland. At St. Vincent's parish, he first became aware of the many people whom the priests were unable to reach through their daily pastoral ministrations.

In the summer of 1903, his health had improved sufficiently so that he could be assigned full time to the Mission Band resident there at St. Vincent's. An outstanding preacher and confessor, he inspired people to do more for Christ. The Mission Band preached missions in Maryland, Pennsylvania, New York, and New Jersey. He found many people responding to a call to live a holier life. Some sought him out as a spiritual director and confessor. Despite the rigors of the life, he gave his time for rest and recreation to directing them and to seeking out the poor and the needy.

Fr. Judge's constant exhortations to frequent, even daily,

Communion and his preoccupation with the spiritual needs of individuals did not go uncriticized. This helped occasion his transfer to St. John the Baptist Church, Brooklyn, New York, in 1909. Here he became more convinced of the necessity of a spiritualized laity and their apostolic labors among the thousands not being reached by the Church.

On his parochial visits in this single parish of a city of millions, he saw many growing lax in their faith, immigrant Catholics being seduced by proselytism, children going uninstructed in the fundamentals of their inherited faith, and many people living in invalid marriages. He appealed to the generosity of good, zealous, mature Catholic laywomen. He told them of the good that would go undone, the people that would never be reached unless they did it. He sent them out two by two and guided them, directed them, inspired them. This small group which gathered in Perboyre Chapel in April, 1909, became the nucleus of a lay organization that would call itself the "Missionary Cenacle." He encouraged them to: "Be good, do good, and be a power for good."

In August, 1910, Fr. Judge was assigned to the Mission Band at St. Vincent's Mission House, Springfield, Massachusetts. His preaching activities brought him into many parishes in Massachusetts, Vermont, Rhode Island, Connecticut, New York, Pennsylvania, Maryland, and Ohio. Generous people sought him out for direction after he appealed to them in sermons and in the confessional to interest themselves in the spiritual needs of their neighbors. Teachers, office workers, lawyers, nurses, clerks and laborers became mission-minded and apostolic. Fr. Judge instructed them that they had a true vocation which was founded on a practical devotion to the Holy Spirit. The response was tremendous.

Unable to remain among them for more than a few weeks, he took to encouraging them by letters which he wrote at the sacrifice of rest and recreation. He encouraged those already doing an apostolic work to befriend and assist those beginning such a work. A comradeship was developed among them and they were united under their common spiritual director, Fr. Judge. Groups of them developed in various cities and towns. They received the commendations of prelates and pastors. The Missionary Cenacle of Brooklyn assumed the duty of fostering a family spirit among the members. In 1912 some of the members, who were predominantly women, desired to dedicate themselves completely to this type of activity. They chose a house in Baltimore and began living a common life. By 1915, there were hundreds of members in the Missionary Cenacle.

In the summer of 1915, Fr. Judge was made superior of St. Mary's Mission House in Opelika, Alabama. The area given to the priests of the Congregation of the Mission comprised 5,300 square miles with 210,000 people, 120 of whom were Catholics. He was encouraged by the former superior to start a school but was unable to obtain any sisters.

Violence, bigotry and opposition met the work of the priests everywhere they turned. As a last resort he appealed to some of the generous Missionary Cenacle members to come South. In 1916, a small group of men and women came to Alabama. When cruel prejudice stifled the work in Opelika, they moved to another area of the mission territory and opened a school in Phenix City, Alabama. Despite the Ku Klux Klan and threats of violence, the school met with some success. Some of the lay people had decided to remain and give their lives to the apostolate and more came to offer help.

St. Patrick's School at Phenix City met with a good response. The "Catholic ladies," as they were called, were living a community life and accomplishing much good. During an epidemic of influenza in 1918, they nursed the sick and the dying and won the favor of the townspeople.

Fr. Judge encouraged and directed them in their apostolic work.

The men were living and working on a nearby plantation owned by a Catholic. The Bishop of Mobile, the Most Rev. Edward P. Allen, gave the group permission to incorporate civilly so that other property could be bought. This property became known as Holy Trinity, Alabama, and a school was erected later called St. Joseph's School. The concept of forming a religious missionary congregation was now firmly established in the minds of many of the lay people living under Fr. Judge's direction. On November 22, 1920, the Very Rev. Patrick McHale, C.M., an assistant to the Superior General of the Congregation of the Mission, wrote Fr. Judge that he was given permission to work exclusively with the growing apostolic organization, remaining directly responsible to his Superior General in France.

The lay apostolate was Fr. Judge's primary interest throughout his priestly life. He desired to inspire every Catholic to be a missionary. However, when the lay associates in the Missionary Cenacle developed their own distinctive customs, practices, and spirit, and some began to live a community life with the intention of becoming religious, Fr. Judge saw this as the working of the Holy Spirit.

Without ever disrupting the original purpose of this lay apostolic group, there developed out of this activity two nascent religious missionary congregations, one for women and the other for men. These in turn had the intention of continuing to foster the lay apostolate as well as directly undertaking missionary activities in the abandoned areas of the United States and preserving the faith. However, it was never the initial intention of Fr. Judge to found the religious congregations. When things developed in that direction, he complied with what he believed to be the will of God. Yet, he never ceased to be a member of the Congregation of the Mission and loyal son of St. Vincent de Paul.

On January 22, 1921, Bishop Allen gave approbation to the inauguration of the institutes under the name of the Missionary Servants of the Most Blessed Trinity. St. Joseph's School at Holy Trinity, Alabama, became exclusively a seminary in 1926. A few priests came from other parts of the country to assist Fr. Judge. A residence was purchased near Catholic University of America, Washington, D.C., to provide seminarians with the opportunity for higher studies. Fr. Judge viewed all this as the work of the Providence of God.

Fr. Judge kept ecclesiastical authorities informed of his activities and corresponded with the Apostolic Delegates to the United States, the Most Rev. Giovanni Bonzano, and the Most Rev. Pietro Fumasoni-Biondi, when prudence demanded it. He was befriended by Cardinal Dougherty, Archbishop of Philadelphia, and the Most Rev. George J. Caruana, Bishop of Puerto Rico and Apostolic Delegate of the Antilles.

On December 18, 1928, the new Bishop of Mobile, the Most Rev. Thomas J. Toolen, sought the permission of the Sacred Congregation of Religious to canonically establish the priests and brothers as a religious community. This was granted on March 20, 1929. On April 29, 1929, the Missionary Servants of the Most Holy Trinity were officially erected by the bishop.

Under the patronage of Cardinal Dougherty, the sisters received canonical recognition on February 20, 1932, as the Missionary Servants of the Most Blessed Trinity and Mother Boniface Keasey became the first Custodian General and is considered to be the Co-Founder of the sisters' community.

Both institutes began to expand. The burdens of administration and the spiritual formation of the infant communities fell on Fr. Judge's shoulders. He traveled about to the various localities where the congregations were laboring and always reminded them to give primacy to the spiritual despite the pressing financial and material burdens confronting them. His holy life and example, his inspiring conferences and exhortations helped develop a missionary spirit of the highest order.

On August 14, 1933, Fr. Judge returned from a missionary visit to Puerto Rico. His health the previous two years had brought him endless days and nights of suffering. It helped bring about the final spiritualization of a holy life. His weakened condition made him a mere shadow of himself. The doctors insisted he curtail his labors and enter the hospital. After a brief visit with his spiritual sons and daughters, he offered his last Mass at Holy Trinity Missionary Cenacle, Silver Spring, Maryland, and entered the old Providence Hospital, Washington, D.C., on August 27, 1933. During the next three months he suffered silently and patiently, apologizing to all for being a burden to them. When visitors questioned him about his illness he would turn the conversation away from himself and speak of the things of God or the great missionray work still to be done for people. Confinement to bed was an added cross to this zealous priest. His health worsened and he found it impossible to concentrate on his customary long prayers: "I have made a contract with God. All I have to say is: Jesus! I cannot pray as I would like, for I am sick — but Jesus understands."

Physically spent, his alert mind considered further work to be done for the poor and the abandoned. On November 7, on the feast of one of his patrons, Blessed John Gabriel Perboyre, he dictated what proved to be his final letter to his spiritual children, urging them to increase their love of God and devotion to the saints.

On the morning of November 23, 1933, he awoke, smiled and blessed the day as was his custom. Early in the afternoon he took a little something to eat and blessed his medicine. Now a mere shell of a man and completely worn out by his years of uninterrupted missionary labors and poor health, he asked to rest. Several minutes afterwards at 3:00 in the afternoon, without pain or struggle, he peacefully died as a priest raised his hand in absolution. He was sixty-five years old.

On the following day, Friday, his body was transferred to Philadelphia to Blessed Trinity Missionary Cenacle, the motherhouse of his spiritual daughters. The rosary was recited continually for the next six days while a constant procession of visitors filed by the coffin. On the sixth day the body of Fr. Judge was taken to St. Vincent's Seminary, Germantown, where the priests of the Congregation of the Mission recited the Office of the Dead. The Requiem was celebrated by priest members of the Congregation which he founded in the presence of Cardinal Dougherty, bishops and prelates. The final procession was to Holy Sepulchre Cemetery in Philadelphia, where he was buried in a simple grave surrounded by his spiritual daughters who had preceded him in death.

Since that day many years ago, the fame and reputation of Fr. Judge have continued to grow and become widespread. His two religious congregations have grown and received Pontifical recognition from the Holy See in 1958. His concept of the lay apostolate and frequent Communion have now become commonly accepted. The wisdom and foresight of this holy priest have proved to be far in advance of his time.

He was a brilliant preacher and conversationalist, but it was the rock bed of his faith and holiness which moved others and left on them a permanent mark. His ideals were those of a man of faith. He aimed at nothing short of converting the world and used every available means to win souls and make the holy more holy and zealous.

Fr. Judge was a prolific writer and preacher. His love of the faith, his knowledge of Holy Scripture, and his zeal for the spread of the Good News are clearly evident in his sermons and writings. He had a great love for the Church and a fervent filial devotion to the Holy Father. He also had a profound love of the Trinity, especially the Holy Spirit. His two missionary congregations were named in honor of the Triune God and he named institutions and religious houses with Trinitarian symbolism. He preached, "I never can pray any greater blessing than for you to teach some child of the Trinity. Greater and more wonderful is the act of him who traces this cross upon a little child and teaches its use than he who takes a kingdom with many battles . . ."

As the years of his life multiplied, the faith of Fr. Judge became more profound and deepened, especially as it was tested by trials, tribulations and sacrificial demands. He always taught obedience to the Church and respect for ecclesiastical authority. He wanted the Missionary Cenacle spirit to be the Catholic spirit. His love for the Church, for the faith, was exemplified in thirty-five years of exhausting missionary labors, the fostering of the lay apostolate and the establishment of two religious missionary congregations. At the end of his life he had worn himself out in the service of God and Church.

The ordinary diocesan process to investigate the Servant of God was opened in the Archdioceses of Washington and Philadelphia in 1963 to comply with the canonical norms which require such a process to be opened within thirty years of the death of the Servant of God. It was also intended to record the life and virtue of Fr. Judge through the testimony of living witnesses. This was accomplished. The official record is preserved in the files of the Archdiocese of Washington pending further developments in the process. The address of the Postulator of Fr. Judge's cause is: Rev. David F. O'Connor, S.T., Holy Trinity Mission, 9001 New Hampshire Avenue, Silver Spring, Maryland, 20903.

FOR FURTHER READING

Joachim V. Benson, S.T., *Father Judge, Man on Fire* (Holy Trinity, Alabama: Cenacle Press, 1973).

CHAPTER 23

SERVANT OF GOD MOTHER KATHARINE DREXEL, S.B.S.
Foundress of the
Sisters of the Blessed Sacrament for Indians and Colored People

23

A Woman of Vision and Courage
MOTHER KATHARINE DREXEL, S.B.S. (1858-1955)

Josephine E. Burdwell

KATHARINE DREXEL, Foundress of the Sisters of the Blessed Sacrament for Indians and Colored People, was a woman of vision and courage far ahead of her time. When she was born, four years before President Lincoln issued his Emancipation Proclamation, 4,000,000 Blacks were in slavery and some 300,000 Native Americans were living in poverty and virtual bondage. Between the years 1778-1868 the United States had made 394 treaties with the different Indian Nations the persual of which presents a flagrant repetition of broken promises. These were the downtrodden races of Americans that Katharine Drexel, sensing sorrow, shame and injustice, pledged her life and wealth to assist and make free.

Katharine, the second of three daughters of Francis A.

Drexel, the wealthy and internationally-known banker of Philadelphia, was born on November 26, 1858. Her mother, Hannah Langstroth, a Baptist Quaker, was seriously ill at the time of the birth and died five weeks later. Katharine's sister, Elizabeth, was older by three years. Sixteen months after her mother's regretted passing her father married Emma Bouvier who, in effect, became the only mother the girls had ever known; and in 1863, her sister, Louise, was added to their number.

Katharine's childhood was happy and carefree, surrounded by the deep affection of relatives and family and by the comforts that wealth could supply. She possessed a lively wit, an eager intelligence, an unassuming simplicity. The winters were spent in their city home on Walnut Street where her mother, a woman of deep faith and strong love of God, fitted out an oratory as a place of prayer for her family. The summers, on the other hand, were spent in the relaxed atmosphere of a farm outside Philadelphia.

Three times a week, Mrs. Drexel, assisted by her daughters, dispensed food and clothing, medicine and rent money to those in need. Being an efficient business woman she likewise engaged an assistant to follow up on the cases that came to her door and to search out others who were in want. By the Christian example of their parents the Drexel daughters learned that wealth was entrusted to them by God to aid those who were far less fortunate, it was to be shared and not hidden away. Katharine long remembered this lesson and practiced it all her life.

When Katharine was twelve her father purchased a new country home for the family, located in Torresdale, a suburb of Philadelphia, and it was named after St. Michael. A statue of the archangel was carved over its entrance and a stained glass window in the house depicted the same, hence it was only natural for the girls to choose Michael as their guardian. As the daughters grew through their teens and adolescence they were taught to assume responsibility, each being placed in charge of some specific duty at St. Michael's. Elizabeth directed the kitchen and stable, Katharine oversaw the housekeeping and sewing, while Louise supervised the farm, garden, and dogs.

Privately tutored from childhood, Katharine was further educated by pleasant travel with her parents through many parts of the United States and Europe, all of which were carefully and vividly recounted in the journals and letters her teacher, Miss Cassidy, requested her to write. These journals reveal Katharine as an engaging diarist, delightfully describing cities visited and places seen. They also disclose her natural spontaneity, her careful and logical thinking, and her charming sense of humor. Katharine loved life greatly but beneath her exterior manifestation of gaiety and love of entertainment there was another Katharine who tried to exercise herself in personal discipline and the practice of virtue. In addition to her journals she kept another set of notebooks but these were for her eyes alone. Here she recorded almost in accountant-like fashion her efforts towards acquiring virtue and eradicating faults, listing the number of times she was successful in gaining self-control or how many times she refrained from taking delicacies at meals. It is in these smaller notebooks that Katharine discloses her growth in prayer and her earnest desire for a close union with Christ. At the time of her First Communion (June, 1870), she was not yet in the habit of recording her inmost thoughts and feelings, but fifty years after the event she recalled that day: "I remember my First Communion and . . . Jesus made me shed my tears because of His greatness in stooping to me." Ever since she was twelve Katharine felt drawn to Christ in the Blessed Sacrament and that attraction grew as she herself grew in holiness.

In 1872, when Katharine was fourteen, Fr. James O'Connor became pastor of St. Dominic's, the parish in which St. Michael's was located. He became a visitor to the Drexel home and came to know Katharine quite well so that she chose him as her spiritual director. Four years later he was consecrated bishop and appointed Vicar Apostolic of Nebraska, but throughout the years he exercised a worthy influence on her spiritual growth; and though he had been transferred to Omaha he, nevertheless, continued to guide her by means of letters and infrequent visits.

Katharine's years of education had finally come to an end and in January, 1879, the banker's daughter made her debut in society and continued her enrichment through broad reading and travel. But a shadow began to loom over the happy household in the worsening illness of Mrs. Drexel who, it was learned, had cancer. After weeks of enduring severe pain this devoted mother died on January 29, 1883. The family's grief was intense and to alleviate some of the loneliness in the house Mr. Drexel took his three daughters on a trip to the Northwest and then abroad. But sorrow again struck the family when the father died on February 14, 1885. A few months before his death he made provision for his daughters, and to insure that they would not become victims of fortune hunters he drafted a carefully detailed will. At his death the family estate had the approximate value of $15,500,000; and according to the will one tenth of that amount was to be disbursed immediately among twenty-nine charitable institutions (churches, asylums, homes, hospitals, colleges, etc.) which he himself had listed. The remaining $14,000,000 was put into a Trust Estate with each of the daughters receiving an equal share of the annual income. If the daughters were to die without issue then the entire amount was to be distributed among the twenty-nine organizations listed as beneficiaries. During her lifetime Katharine, because her two sisters had predeceased her, had the use of the income not only for the works of her congregation but also for her other foundations as well. However, at her death in 1955, the father's entire estate was distributed to the charities he had designated in 1885; and the community which she herself had founded was not included among them. While alive she disbursed her income to others, and as for her congregation she expected it to rely on Divine Providence for its continued existence.

In imitation of their parents' charity each of the Drexel daughters chose a field for her own special benefactions. They not only felt an obligation but also an earnest desire to share the wealth their father had acquired to alleviate others' distress and spread faith in the redeeming Lord. Katharine first became interested in Native Americans when Bishop Martin Marty of Northern Minnesota and Fr. Joseph Stephan, Director of the Bureau of Catholic Indian Missions, shortly after Mr. Drexel's death, approached Katharine to help them build, staff, and maintain schools among the Indians as a means of preserving and spreading the Catholic faith. They spoke of the poverty their people experienced, of the government's discontinuance of certain programs, and the project whereby the government would assist in the support and board of students if schools and housing were provided. Thus Katharine began her lifetime flow of money and effort for these earliest of Americans. She built schools, churches, and convents, and in many cases donated salaries or subsistence for teachers. By 1907 she and her sisters, not counting other donations to universities and hospitals, had given more than $1,500,000 to the Bureau of Catholic Indian Missions.

In 1886 Katharine and her sisters, still unmarried, made another lengthy tour of Europe. It was during this trip that Katharine had a memorable visit with Pope Leo XIII. For some time she had been distressed about the lack of priests among the Indians. By herself she was able to provide buildings for schools and their maintenance and there were sisters who were willing to teach, but there were not enough priests to serve these Native Americans. Even Bishop O'Connor, knowing that Katharine was about to go to Europe, asked her to try to induce some European priests to come and work among the American Indians, but in this she was unsuccessful. So she decided to take the matter to the Pope. She relates the event in these words: "Kneeling at his feet, my girlish fancy thought that surely God's vicar would not refuse me. So I pleaded missionary priests for Bishop O'Connor's Indians. To my astonishment, His Holiness responded, 'Why not, my child, yourself become a missionary?' In reply I said, 'Because, Holy Father, sisters can be had for the missions but no priests.' " The Pontiff's prophetic words deeply touched her, even to tears, since she did not clearly understand what she was to do.

When the three sisters returned to America they set out for Omaha to learn the conditions in the Indian Territories and inspect the works they had financed. They saw docile children and grateful parents. They thrilled at the idea that they had a small part to play in this harvest of souls, but they also observed that there was still a grave need for more sisters even though several congregations were working among the Indians. In setting up her schools Katharine would first purchase the land, then erect plain but serviceable buildings and then deed them to the Catholic Indian Bureau. She was always of the belief that education was the primary means of helping the poor to help themselves, and within five years after her first involvement in Indian matters a line of schools enjoying her benefactions stretched from the great Northwest to the Mexican border. But while she was aiding the Indians, she was also becoming very much aware of the sad plight of the Blacks, especially in the South, and began to include them in her charitable gifts.

Since the time of her mother's death Katharine's desire to consecrate herself to Christ through vows in a contemplative community steadily grew stronger. Deep within she knew that life in the society to which she was born could never satisfy her longings nor give her any real happiness. Long and painstakingly she searched for her place in God's plan. During these years Bishop O'Connor was aware of her desire, but he believed that her vocation was to remain in society and express her love for Christ through her many charitable donations as she had been doing. But Katharine was of another opinion; she firmly held that God's will differed from that expressed by her spiritual director and on November 26, 1888, she wrote to him: "Are you afraid to give me to Jesus Christ? . . . It appears to me, Reverend Father, that I am not obliged to *submit* my judgment to yours, as I have been doing for two years, for I feel so sad in doing it because the world cannot give me peace, so restless because my heart is not rested in God."

These words convinced the bishop of Katharine's vocation and in his next letter he suggested possible congregations to which she might apply. But she made it clear that she was interested in a "missionary order for Indians and Colored People," and was about to investigate the Franciscans in Philadelphia. When he read her letter, it became clear to him that Katharine should found a community specifically dedicated to helping Native Americans and Blacks. This advice came as a surprise and she cringed at the thought of becoming a foundress, but she humbly followed this prompting as the will of God; and despite her anxiety and feelings of inadequacy she, at age thirty-one, entered the novitiate of the Sisters of Mercy of Pittsburgh on May 7, 1889. Wholeheartedly she entered into a life of prayer and study and humbly performed the many duties that are part of novitiate training. It was not until she had received the habit on November 7 of that year that it was made known that she intended to found a new religious community.

To Sr. Katharine's great sorrow, Bishop O'Connor died in May, 1890, and she wondered whether the plans they had made for the new congregation could possibly continue. But she found her answer in Archbishop Ryan of Philadelphia. The archbishop had known the Drexel family for many years, had met Sr. Katharine on many occasions, and was acquainted with her plans; so, returning from Bishop O'Connor's funeral, he visted her in Pittsburgh and made the offer, "If I share the burden with you, if I help you, can you go on?" His words were the encouragement she needed. But sadness once more entered her life for in September of that year her sister Elizabeth, married but eight months, suddenly died.

While Sr. Katherine was still completing her training in the novitiate, young women began to seek admission to the new foundation. These were admitted to the Mercy novitiate and began their formation. On February 12, 1891, dressed as a bride of Christ, Sr. Katharine pronounced her vows in the presence of Archbishop Ryan and chose "Sisters of the Blessed Sacrament" as the name of her new congregation. The addition "for Indians and Colored People" was the suggestion of the archbishop to give the community further identification.

Accompanied by Mother Inez, a Sister of Mercy, who was to act as Mistress of Novices for one year, Mother Katharine and her ten novices and three postulants left the Mercy convent in Pittsburgh (July, 1891) to take up residence in their temporary home — the Drexel country home known as St. Michael's now vacant after Elizabeth's death — until their motherhouse, in what was later to be known as Cornwells Heights, was completed. With great fervor and hope this young community set about its daily tasks of prayer, instruction, and study, all the while realizing that these were the foundation stones of a very important structure. By the end of 1891, the number of sisters had grown to twenty-eight.

The sisters moved into the new motherhouse, St. Elizabeth's, named in memory of M. Katharine's recently deceased sister, on December 3, 1892, even though it was not yet completely ready. Both M. Katharine and the sisters were eager to initiate their work in the active apostolate —

the mission schools in the West were clamoring for sisters —
but wisely the archbishop cautioned them to wait until
their minds and souls were properly prepared and developed
before undertaking apostolic works. Their own spiritual
reservoirs must first be full before they can share with
others.

In 1894 it was time to launch out. The first tearful departure was when a group of four, to be followed a week
later by five, left for St. Catherine's Indian School among
the Pueblo Indians in Santa Fe. The school which bore M.
Katharine's patroness' name was one of the many she had
built before she had become a religious; and since it now
had an acute need of teachers and administrators, it was to
this school that the pioneer Sisters of the Blessed Sacrament
had first gone. M. Katharine then turned towards the great
Navajo nation, the largest tribe of Native Americans. She
purchased a tract of land in 1896 and envisioned a boarding
school in the Arizona desert to which she could bring the
light of Christ. Some 25,000 Navajos lived in this magnificent but difficult land of red-rock mountains and canyons.
She secured Franciscan priests for the mission and agreed
to support them. They arrived in 1898 and worked zealously
to spread Christ's Good News. In 1902, St. Michael's
School, which M. Katharine arranged to have built, was
ready for occupancy, but the parents were reluctant to turn
over their children to these strange women from the East.
A mutual trust began to grow and soon the sisters had
forty-seven children under their care. A high school was
added and later more buildings so that a total of several
hundred could be accommodated. Besides being taught the
basics, the children were also taught to cherish and retain
their heritage and culture.

For some time M. Katharine had been nurturing in her
mind the establishment of a boarding school for the training of young black girls. She felt that by living with the
sisters in peaceful country surroundings the girls would im-

bibe a firm Catholic way of life while being, at the same
time, helped toward a teaching career or some other form
of employment. Education, as a rule, was closed to these
girls and the usual means of livelihood open to them was
domestic service. Once more, M. Katharine believed that
education was the best way of bringing freedom to those
who were not free. With this in view, the week after her
first group had departed for Santa Fe, she went to Virginia to purchase land. She bought a six-hundred acre plot
forty miles west of Richmond, arranged for the clearing of
trees, and for a quarry and brick kiln so that this great
structure, which now stands overlooking the James river,
could literally rise from the Virginia soil. In memory of
her father she named the school after St. Francis de Sales.

Even before she had begun her novitiate, M. Katharine
had been answering requests for funds to help Blacks and
did her best to respond to all requests that came to her. In
some cases she approached bishops offering to finance the
erection of schools and churches but always stipulating that
an entire aisle from front to back was to be reserved for
the Blacks, not just a few pews in the rear. To witness conditions for herself and to examine what her benefactions
had accomplished, she went in 1904 on an extended tour
of the South. She was profoundly saddened to see the destitute poverty of the Blacks, the inadequate provision for
education, and the deprivation of rights that should have
been theirs by reason of American citizenship. She knew
she had a mission to carry out, and her zeal to accomplish
it drove her relentlessly in spite of fatigue and opposition.

Besides visiting the institutions that she had been finan-
cing, she also visited her own missions and continued to
govern her fast-growing community which reached 104
members in 1904. The expenditure of her income and the
many duties entailed by her building projects did not keep
her from attending to the needs of her religious congregation. When at home in the motherhouse she always did her

share of manual work and never allowed any special concessions for herself. Rather, she led the way in her strict observance of poverty, personal discipline, and deep prayerfulness. So that others would not know, she often rose at night to keep vigil before the Blessed Sacrament. She was abstemious at meals and exercised a rigid form of frugality in the use of things, expecting her community to do likewise. Her reasoning was: "Whatever we can save can be used to help others."

Bishop Byrne of Nashville had made several insistent pleas for her to start a school in his city and staff it with her sisters. She had been warned of possible opposition, and so she purchased property and a temporary building through an intermediary. When it was discovered that M. Katharine was the true buyer a furor broke out among the citizenry, fanned to great heat by the press. But this dauntless lady responded with a gracious letter, then silence. It was her custom to answer scorn and rebuff with candor and serenity. The remodeled school opened and accepted more than a hundred Blacks. Eventually a new building was constructed for them, and some years later a second school was opened in the northern part of the city.

Other foundations were located in Macon, Atlanta, and Montgomery. Hearing that Columbus had 30,000 Blacks, none of them Catholic, induced her to establish a foundation there; and she likewise opened five schools in Harlem. The same pattern was followed in Cleveland, St. Louis, and Philadelphia. With the increase of missions her visitations consumed a good part of the year, yet she tirelessly went on.

M. Katharine had been in correspondence with Bishop Janssens of New Orleans who was worried about the loss of faith among Blacks. She sent him funds and built St. Katharine's church, but hesitated to send sisters to do work that was already being done by another congregation. But in 1913 the picture changed. In that year Southern University, the state operated school for Blacks in New Orleans moved to Baton Rouge leaving its building vacant. Hearing about this move M. Katharine knew that her dream for Catholic higher education for Blacks in New Orleans was about to be fulfilled. She purchased the vacated building and opened her new school in 1915 for students from grades seven to eleven. The response was so great that they had to begin afternoon and evening classes in typing and sewing, and later on initiated a Normal School course. It became obvious that the school would have to move in order to provide a more extensive program for the growing number of students. Following her usual procedure, M. Katharine built a new school, named it Xavier University, with its first class entering in 1932. For years it was the sole Catholic University in the United States for Blacks. The university has prospered over the years and its many graduates have taken their places in all fields of endeavor, well-equipped to contribute professional service and leadership.

The State of Louisiana claimed the service of more Sisters of the Blessed Sacrament than any other because of its heavy concentration of black Catholics. In dozens of areas, M. Katharine built rural schools and for each she engaged graduates from Xavier University, paying their salaries, and putting them under the supervision of the sisters in New Orleains or New Iberia.

M. Katharine's countless labors and accomplishments continued through the years. Her generous heart always responded to the pleas for sisters and for funds that arrived almost daily from various parts of the nation and even from parts of Africa. Her only sorrow was that she could not satisfy them all. She rejoiced at the news of many baptisms, the graduations and the accomplishments, small and large, of the peoples — Native Americans and Blacks — whose causes she had espoused. She knew she was running against time and this only increased her zeal. At the time of her death her sisters numbered nearly six hundred, working in sixty-eight centers in twenty-one states.

While M. Katharine, in her seventy-seventh year (1935), was making a visitation of her missions in the West she suffered a severe heart attack and several lesser ones. Brought back to the motherhouse, she was warned that unless she ceased her constant activity and relinquished her heavy responsibilities she would most probably suffer a stroke and either be paralyzed or die. Remarkable as she had always been, M. Katharine changed her manner of life and without objection quietly resided in a couple of rooms on the second floor of the motherhouse and periodically came to community assemblies in a wheel chair. In the 1937 General Chapter she was replaced as Superior General by Mother M. Mercedes, one of the first who had joined her in the Mercy novitiate in Pittsburgh.

M. Katharine now had the time and leisure to live the contemplative life that she had always desired since she had been a young woman. During these years of retirement she looked forward to visits from the sisters who were either en route to or returning from missions, interested in everything they had to tell her. Placing her hands on their heads in blessing she would say, "Remember, souls are saved through blood."

To everyone's surprise and joy M. Katharine lived among them for another twenty years remaining a model of prayer and an inspiration in the religious life. She spent most of her day and part of her night in prayerful union with God. Several times it was feared that her end was imminent, but she somehow rallied. Finally on March 3, 1955, in her ninety-seventh year, it pleased God the Father to take His daughter unto Himself.

No one can adequately praise this woman of God, this daughter of the Church, this pioneer missionary, who loved the Lord her God above all and her neighbor — especially the two races she tried to set free — for His sake. These, together with her spiritual daughters and countless others rise up to call her blessed. The Lord's spirit had not been given her in vain. Aware that she had been sent to fill a special need among God's people she had, with dedicated diligence and generosity, taken Christ's Good News to the poor and courageously espoused the cause of racial equality and justice.

For two days loving crowds passed by her bier in the motherhouse in a final gesture of affection and respect. After an early Mass on the third day, the cortege made its long way to the cathedral in downtown Philadelphia for the solemn funeral. More than 250 prelates, priests, and brothers filled the sanctuary, and the great church was filled with many having to stand outside. Afterwards her body was returned to the motherhouse and interred in a crypt prepared for her in the basement of the chapel directly under the altar.

Nine years after M. Katharine's death, John Cardinal Krol of Philadelphia announced the opening of the diocesan process leading to beatification. The acts of that process are now in Rome in the Sacred Congregation for the Causes of Saints. The Sisters of the Blessed Sacrament maintain the Mother Katharine Drexel Guild, 1663 Bristol Pike, Cornwells Heights, Pennsylvania, 19020.

PRAYER
(Private use only)

O God, who inspired Your valiant and faithful servant, Mary Katharine, with an ardent love of You and a zeal for souls, and who led her to devote herself and the Community she founded to the instruction and care of Your Negro and Indian children, grant, we humbly beseech You, that she may one day soon be raised to the honors of Your altar. Amen.

FOR FURTHER READING

Sr. Consuela Marie Duffy, S.B.S., *Katharine Drexel: A Biography* (Cornwells Heights, Penna.: Mother Katharine Drexel Guild, 1977).

CHAPTER 24

SERVANT OF GOD FATHER SOLANUS CASEY, O.F.M.Cap.
The Porter of St. Bonaventure's

24

Friend of the Poor and of the Sick

FATHER SOLANUS CASEY, O.F.M.Cap. (1870-1957)

Leo Wollenweber, O.F.M.Cap.

THE MIGHTY MISSISSIPPI cuts a path through mid-America and separates the East from West but at the same time it joins both halves together like a magnet attracting a constant flow of people. From one coast to the other they come bridging that river. This paradox finds its expression in the lives of many men and women.

One such American sought a quiet place in the cloister that he might be alone with God, only to find himself thrust into the limelight of popularity. His life began on the banks of that river in a simple log house near the town of Prescott, Wisconsin, on November 25, 1870. His Irish immigrant

347

parents named him Bernard Casey, after his father, but always called him affectionately "Barney." Today he is known by thousands simply as Fr. Solanus, the name he received when he joined the Capuchin Franciscans in 1897. Although he died relatively recently, on July 31, 1957, his fame now extends far beyond both banks of that great river and spans the vast land it waters. Why this fame? Who and what is he to America and to the world?

Like a prophet he bears a message for our time and our world, but his message is very simple; it is one that we might understand if we are earnest about our salvation. He lived a life concerned for God's people, suffering and laboring for the conversion of sinners, including himself. His message, always one of faith and trust in God, was to console and encourage. He promoted peace by a kindly insistence on our "right relationship to and dependence upon God and neighbor." His message seems more timely now than ever. Our times sorely need to find that right relationship and dependence, not only on God but upon our neighbor as well.

Bernard Francis Casey was the sixth of sixteen children born to Bernard James Casey and Ellen Elizabeth Murphy, who had emigrated from Ireland, driven westward by the poverty and famine of the mid 1800's. Ellen came in 1852 and Bernard in 1857. Both landed in Boston and met at a July 4th picnic about 1860. Married in Salem, Massachusetts on October 6, 1863, they first settled in Philadelphia where Bernard made shoes for the Union Army. After the Civil War, Bernard turned to farming, following Ellen's two brothers, Owen and Pat Murphy, who had already settled in Wisconsin.

The Caseys bought land next to the Murphys along the Mississippi. Their first home was a log house of two rooms, yet it seemed a mansion to their children. Five healthy children were born in that mansion among them Bernard, or "Barney."

From an early age Barney was taught obedience, diligence,

and piety mainly through the example of his parents. In later years he often voiced his thanks and appreciation for the example of his good parents. The Caseys reared their children in an atmosphere of honest work, prayer, and good example. Bernard Sr. was a rather stern father who would brook no nonsense, yet he also knew how to balance recreation with the farm chores. The children learned all the favorite Irish ballads; and when a visitor left an old violin behind, young Barney taught himself to play it. He was popular with the young people because he could provide music for the neighborhood barn dances. Outdoor activities were not all work either. The nearby waters provided swimming and fishing and the woods and hills were exciting hunting grounds. Barney grew up with a genuine love and appreciation for nature because it was such a real part of his childhood. Although he was not as rugged as his older brothers, he loved all sports, except boxing. The ten Casey boys had their own baseball team and they took on the neighborhood players with some distinction. Within this environment. Barney lived a normal average life. It also provided him with a sturdy resourceful character and the qualities of unselfishness and cheerful optimism.

Barney learned a wholesome piety from his mother who sought to make her home truly Catholic. The family rosary was a custom never to be omitted. Many lessons of charity and goodness were shown her children who realized later how much these virtues affected their own spiritualities.

In October, 1882, the family moved to a large 345 acre farm near Burkhardt, Wisconsin. Their parish church was now St. Patrick's in Hudson, about nine miles away, and it was there that Barney received his First Communion. About this time he began to think about becoming a priest. In a letter written to his brother years later, he recalled the deep impression he felt the first time he attended a Solemn High Mass. By this time, his older brother, Maurice, was a a student for the priesthood in the Milwaukee seminary.

Many Irish families expected to have one son a priest and Maurice seemed the chosen one, but young Barney secretly wondered if they might not have two priests in the family.

In 1887, Barney completed his elementary grades at the District School. Since crop failures for two successive years put quite a drain on the family finances, Barney was anxious to help his father by finding outside employment; so he found work in the thriving town of Stillwater, Minnesota, the center of a booming logging industry. First he worked as a hand on the logbooms, then as a part-time prison guard, and finally as one of Stillwater's first street car operators when the city installed the newfangled electric trolley cars.

Barney was quite enterprising; and when he heard that Appleton, Wisconsin, was installing an electric trolley, he went there confident that his experience would land him a job. After a short time, an even better opportunity appeared. Superior, Wisconsin, at that time a rival of Milwaukee, advertised for operators for their new electric car line. Barney moved to Superior in 1890, and found steady work, first as a conductor and then as a motorman. Before long he was training others on the job.

Superior was a place of opportunity in those days and since the family farm was not prospering, Barney persuaded the rest of the family to join him. By 1891, they sold the farm, and Bernard Casey Sr., with his sons, took up dairy farming near Superior. Not only was the new location fairly successful, but more importantly it provided the opportunity for higher education for all the Caseys.

In Superior, Barney met the well-known Franciscan, Fr. Eustace Vollmer, who became his spiritual director. He was aware of the many moral dangers surrounding a Christian in the bustling competitive world of his day and, becoming more earnest about his relationship with God, he joined the Third Order of St. Francis. Now that the family no longer needed his earning power he began to think seriously about the priesthood.

With the advice of Fr. Eustace and a recommendation from his pastor, Barney entered the Diocesan Seminary in Milwaukee. His brother Maurice had studied there but had given up when his health broke. Since Maurice had his difficulties, Barney wondered if he could make it. He was now twenty-one years old, and it would not be easy to begin studying again at High School level. But Barney's diligence paid off, for he soon won the esteem of his professors and companions. He even managed to earn part of his tuition by working as the students' barber.

After four years the faculty had its doubts about his academic qualifications. Many classes were in the German or Latin languages, a definite handicap for an Irishman. He was advised not to continue, but sensing the presence of a true vocation, the Rector recommended religious life to the young man.

In the spring of 1896 Barney came home, uncertain and unsettled. His spiritual director, Fr. Eustace, wisely encouraged him toward a religious vocation and suggested his own Franciscan Province of the Sacred Heart (St. Louis), as well as the Capuchin Franciscans whose headquarters were in Detroit.

Both Franciscan families gave him a favorable reply, and so he had to make a choice. To aid in his decision Barney asked his mother and sister to join him in the novena for the approaching feast of the Immaculate Conception. While praying after Holy Communion on December 8, 1896, he felt a clear urging from our Lady to "go to Detroit." "Detroit" meant the Capuchin Order was our Lady's choice for him. Interpreting this to be a God-given inspiration, he began preparing for his entrance into the Capuchin Order in spite of some reluctance. Years later, he wrote his brother that "he went half against his will" for the austere, bearded Capuchins did not really attract him.

Without waiting to spend Christmas with his family, he left home on December 21, 1896. It took three days to reach

Detroit by train, due in part to heavy snows. On Christmas eve, he finally arrived at St. Bonaventure Friary exhausted. He was shown to a small room and, left to rest a little, he stretched out on the hard bed and fell fast asleep. At midnight he suddenly awoke to sounds of Christmas carols. Jumping up he opened his door to find the friars, continuing a Capuchin tradition, waking the community with bells and song for the solemn feast. Now refreshed, he joined in the songs and sacred celebration.

During the next few days he became acquainted with Capuchin life. On January 13, 1897, after some anxious moments of indecision, he was invested as a novice, receiving the brown habit and the name Francis Solanus. From that time severe doubts about his vocation vanished. At the end of his novitiate he pronounced the vows of poverty, chastity, and obedience on July 21, 1898, in a spirit of great joy; and three years later he made those promises a lifetime commitment. He considered the call to the Franciscan way of life a special grace and privilege. For him, gratitude and appreciation for God's gift of a Capuchin vocation was the surest means for perseverance.

Frater Solanus, as he was now called, continued his studies at St. Francis Friary in Milwaukee under the direction of Fr. Anthony Rottensteiner. Director and fellow students recognized in the new friar a deep spirituality, sincere love of God, and a genuine humility. Although he applied himself strenuously, theological studies did not come easy to him. The classes were held in either German or Latin, and German in particular was a major obstacle. While he maintained passing marks, his professors again voiced reservation about his academic ability. Despite their concern, he refused to allow any discouragement to deter him from his goal of living his life as a Capuchin priest.

Approval for advancement towards the priesthood finally came from Fr. Rottensteiner who shortly before his death in February, 1903, declared, "We shall ordain Frater Solanus

— and as a priest he will be to the people like the Curé of Ars." On July 24, 1904, Archbishop Messmer of Milwaukee ordained Frater Solanus a priest of God. Sharing in this form of Christ's priesthood, however, was not to be received without condition. It was decided he would remain a "simplex priest," unable to hear confessions. Humbling as this was, Fr. Solanus accepted it as God's will and never sought to have it reversed. Eight years after he had left home, he returned to celebrate his First Solemn Mass with his family assisting; it was July 31, 1904.

Shortly after ordination Fr. Solanus was sent to Yonkers, N.Y., where the Capuchins staffed the busy Sacred Heart parish. When the superior learned that his new assistant was without faculties to hear confessions, he appointed him sacristan and director of the altarboys. It was not a very exciting apostolate, but it was an opportunity to foster an intense devotion to the Holy Eucharist; and there, near the Blessed Sacrament, he expressed his own love and gratitude for the gift of the Eucharist and prayed for his own needs and those of his family and friends, and especially the poor, so numerous in that large city.

Before long the superior gave him the job of porter or doorkeeper at the Friary Office. This was eventually to become his life-long work. However, other parochial duties also fell to him, especially the apostolate to the sick, to whom he became very dedicated. He was continually sought out by those suffering physical and mental pain. When people became ill the word went about that Fr. Solanus should come to their bedside and many began to attribute their healing to his prayers and blessing.

Fr. Solanus also developed a genuine missionary zeal that prompted a special interest in the non-Catholics of the area. On occasion, his parochial duties included visiting parishioners employed as servants in the homes of non-Catholics; and he tried to show his concern for the spiritual welfare of the employers as well as the servants. It was at this time that he became friends with the famous Anglican convert, Paul Francis Wattson, founder of the Society of the Atonement and advocate of Christian Unity. Fr. Solanus was present when Fr. Paul Francis received Catholic orders, and he preached for his friend's First Solemn Mass on July 3, 1910, in Graymoor, N.Y. Fr. Solanus kept a close interest in the young Society and its founder, and he maintained an active interest in ecumenism that was far ahead of his time.

After fourteen busy years in Yonkers, Fr. Solanus was transferred to the church of Our Lady of Sorrows in lower Manhattan and three years later to the parish of Our Lady of the Angels in Harlem. His labors, much the same as before, now began to attract greater notice. People reported that when Fr. Solanus promised to pray for them, things happened. But Solanus did not just pray for people and their needs; he urged them to be aware of the needs of others, especially in the Capuchin missions. To help them direct their efforts, he promoted a means of mission support, called the Seraphic Mass Association (SMA). The SMA had been founded by a Swiss laywoman about 1900 to support the missions of the Capuchins who, in thanks, remembered their generous benefactors in their Masses and prayers. When people reported astounding favors after Solanus' prayers, he would attribute them to their support of the SMA and their share in the grace of the Eucharist.

Another transfer came in 1924, this time to St. Bonaventure's in Detroit where his Capuchin life began twenty-eight years before. The Detroit Friary needed a porter, and so Fr. Solanus once again took up his duties at the door. In the busy office he was constantly sought for his counsel and advice by the troubled and the poor, and for his prayers and blessings by the sick. Every day people who had heard of the power of his prayers crowded the Friary Office content to wait an hour or more, just to speak to him. He seemed to have time for each person as though he were the only one waiting; he never hurried or cut anyone short. Sharing his faith and confidence in God with them, he was able to lead others to a stronger faith, hope, and charity.

When the great depression of 1929-1930 hit Detroit, Fr. Solanus' concern for the poor took on a concrete form. Many unemployed began to visit the Friary seeking food. Fr. Solanus would daily bring a big pot of steaming soup to the office and there, with the help of one of the brothers, dispense soup and bread to all who came in. When this operation grew out of hand, the Third Order Fraternity at the Friary took over. This great work of charity, known as the "Soup Kitchen," became famous in Detroit and still serves hundreds daily. Realizing the need of the poor to find their dignity once more, he drew on his influence and friendship with Detroit businessmen and city officials to obtain jobs for the many who sought his help. To a reporter who once interviewed him, he remarked: "I have two favorites, the poor and the sick."

His ministry to the sick and troubled continued unabated, even in the later years of his life when his superiors, desiring to give him a well-earned retirement, sent him in the spring of 1946 to the Friary of St. Felix in rural Indiana. There he continued to spend his time in prayer and the ministry to the sick and troubled until his own infirmities took their toll. Early in 1956 his chronic eczema worsened and began to spread, and his superior decided to consult a Detroit physician. He was hospitalized and soon seemed much improved, but as a precaution it was decided to leave him in Detroit. There on January 14, 1957, the friars celebrated the 60th anniversary of his Capuchin commitment. Assembled in the little chapel where he first pronounced his vows, they again witnessed his solemn dedication. Repeating those promises to which he had been faithful, he was so overcome with emotion that a confrere had to complete the formula for him. Like Paul it seemed he realized, "I have finished my course."

Throughout his long life, Fr. Solanus was intent on the conversion of self and neighbor. Since he could no longer be of direct service to people, his final sufferings would be offered for them. In the past he had encouraged others who suffered to reflect on the shortness of life and its pains and urged them to look forward to the joys to come. Now that the end of his own life was approaching, he would take no sedatives because he wanted to accept death consciously and willingly. During these last days his great pain was mixed with heavenly consolations. When asked one day, "Where does it hurt?" He replied, "I hurt all over, but thanks be to God," and again, "Would that it was ten thousand times worse that I might have something to offer God."

The night before he was to die, he told his Provincial, "Tomorrow will be a wonderful day." The next morning at eleven o'clock, July 31, 1957, while fully conscious, he peacefully offered himself to God with the words, "I give my soul to Jesus Christ." It was the very day and hour of his First Mass celebrated so many years ago. He was almost 87 years old.

The news of his death passed quickly through Detroit and thousands came to mourn. At the funeral the Father Provincial spoke more as a spiritual son than a superior, saying: "Father Solanus' life was so gloriously successful because he served God so faithfully, so earnestly, and so selflessly. He loved people for what he could do for them, and for God, through them." His body was laid to rest in the small cemetery beside St. Bonaventure's where he had labored so long for the people of Detroit. There his friends and acquaintances, old and new, came asking his help and intercession.

After his death reports concerning his virtuous life and works of charity began to increase. In May, 1960, a group of friends anxious to preserve his memory organized the Father Solanus Guild which today numbers over 10,000 members in the United States and many foreign countries.

In 1966, prompted by many appeals, the Capuchin superiors in Rome appointed a Vice Postulator, and since that time the work of documenting Fr. Solanus' life and work has gone forward. In January, 1977, the Archbishop of Detroit, John Cardinal Dearden, initiated the diocesan process investigating Fr. Solanus' life and these documents have since been sent to Rome and now await examination by the Sacred Congregation for the Causes of Saints. The Vice Postulator is Brother Leo Wollenweber, O.F.M.Cap., and the address of the Father Solanus Guild is 1780 Mt. Elliott Avenue, Detroit, Michigan, 48207.

PRAYER
(Private use only)

Father, I adore You. I give myself to You. May I be the person You want me to be and may Your will be done in my life today. Thank You for the gifts You gave Father Solanus. If it is Your will, glorify him on earth so that others will carry on his love for the poor, lonely and suffering of our world. Amen.

FOR FURTHER READING

James Patrick Derum, *The Porter of Saint Bonaventure's: The Life of Father Solanus Casey, Capuchin* (Detroit: Fidelity Press, 1969).

CHAPTER 25

SERVANT OF GOD MOTHER ALOYSIUS OF THE
BLESSED SACRAMENT, O.C.D.
Foundress of the Carmelite Monastery of Concord, New Hampshire

$\mathcal{L}et$ us be
souls of prayer
...and $\mathcal{G}od$ will do
the rest.

Mother Aloysius
of Concord Carmel

Strive for the greater honor
and glory of God in all things.

St. John of the Cross

In joyful rememberance
of
the Solemn Profession
in Carmel
of
Sister Louise Marie
de la Visitation
October 15, 1994
Carmel of Our Lady and St. Joseph
Concord, New Hampshire

25

Give All — And Ever

MOTHER ALOYSIUS OF THE BLESSED SACRAMENT, O.C.D. (1880-1961)

Adrian James Cooney, O.C.D.

ON FEBRUARY 18, 1880, A GIRL, the ninth child of Timothy and Mary Rowe Rogers, was born in the front room of their home in the small Massachusetts town of Billerica, some thirty miles west of Boston. Four days later, the baby was baptized and received the name Alice. Years before, Timothy, at the age of seventeen had left Dublin, Ireland. Eventually, he found work as the caretaker of the Bennet estate, and it was there that he met Mary Rowe who had a position in the stately mansion. Mary had come from Cork, then known as Queenstown, and she and Timothy were married in Boston.

361

They lived in North Billerica until Mr. Joshua Bennet built a home for them opposite his manor on the Boston Road. Joshua Bennet liked Timothy and Mary and showed this affection by making a gift of the newly-built house set on a couple of acres. It was an ideal home for the already large family. The Rogers were well received by their Protestant neighbors who came to know their goodness in sharing with others whatever they could, yet some thought they went too far in having a Black take lunch with them each day. Alice delighted in sitting next to him; and she went to school with his daughter, Amanda, who was one of her closest friends.

Another child was born to Timothy and Mary — she was named Frances but called Frannie. In all, there were eight girls and two boys; and it was a proud Timothy who drove his family in the square-box buggy to the Catholic church in North Billerica, three miles from their home. Timothy and Mary shared with their childern the deep faith that was the center of their own lives. Sunday Mass at St. Andrew's, once a Unitarian church, was the occasion of the week. Unlike the other children, Alice directed her attention toward the priest rather than reading the prayer book in her hands. The mystery of the Mass had already taken hold of her.

On weekends, Fr. J. Edward Emery, O.M.I., came to stay with the Rogers and he celebrated Sunday Mass in the church. Over the years Alice confided in him, and one day she told him of her desire to become a Carmelite nun. Knowing how closely united the family was, Fr. Emery said that it was impossible for any child to be separated from the others. As young as she was, Alice determined that she would enter the Boston monastery and follow that way of life that her Grandmother Rowe spoke about so often.

Alice distinguished herself in high school and graduated as the valedictorian of her class; shortly after that, in September of 1899, she entered Lowell State Normal School. Although she wanted to enter Carmel after her completion of the two-year course, Alice followed her director's advice and taught for three years, two in West Billerica and one in Ayer, a town far enough away to make it impossible for her to live at home. Alice deliberately sought this position, so that it would help make it easier for her to enter the Carmelite convent. While boarding with a Protestant family in Ayer, she busied herself sewing altar linens for her brother Frank who was soon to be ordained a priest; but the family with whom she lived thought she was getting her hope chest ready, much to Alice's amusement.

Finally, on September 12, 1904, Alice braced herself as she was about to leave her family. Tears welled up, and she said to her sister, "Oh, Frannie, if I can just get beyond the front gate, I will be all right!" Fr. Frank and her sister Elizabeth accompanied her, and they boarded the train in Billerica. Alice thought she was seeing her family for the last time; she was unaware that periodic visits were permitted at the monastery.

After four months as a postulant, Alice received the habit on January 25, 1905, and took the name Aloysius of the Blessed Sacrament in honor of the Jesuit saint who had a great devotion to the Eucharist. As Frannie accompanied Alice, dressed as a bride and carrying a candle, into the sanctuary, the veil caught fire and her father was quickly beside her to put out the flames. Later that day Alice, now Sr. Aloysius, said to Frannie, "I thought we were both going to burn up in the flames of love."

The Prioress, M. Augustine, guided the novices until the saintly M. Beatrix returned from the Philadelphia Carmel and took charge of them. In 1936 M. Beatrix confided that on meeting the novice Aloysius, "I knew that she was a saint."

On February 2, 1906, Sr. Aloysius made her final profession, and the entire Rogers family gathered at the monastery for the ceremony. As they went back to Billerica, Timothy and Mary were pleased. The ceremony was beautiful, despite moments of anxiety; but unknown to them, it marked the last time that Timothy would see his Carmelite daughter. Shortly after that happy day he was working in a field when he became ill; Mary rushed to his side and he died as she held him close to her.

It seemed but a short time before Mary followed her husband in death. Sr. Aloysius' grief was intense, yet she experienced new depths of gratitude that she and the other children had shared in that love and faith they had known from their earliest days. In reading the letters that she wrote and in reflecting on her life, it is evident that her parents had given her that spirit that informed her whole life.

In 1915, the nuns elected Sr. Aloysius to be Subprioress and in 1918 she was chosen as Prioress, making her, at thirty-eight, the youngest Prioress in the Boston Carmel's long history. For this, a dispensation from Rome was needed; at that time forty was the minimum age required by Canon Law for election as a major superior. After a term of three years, she served as a member of the Council until in 1924 she again became Prioress. That year was a difficult and sorrowing one; six of the nuns, one the oldest and another the youngest, died. Despite the many processions to the burial vaults, she showed trust in God's will.

At forty-five, she had much experience, and her joyful spirit impressed all who came in contact with her. The confidence in her leadership as Prioress is shown in her being elected to three consecutive terms, the last requiring a second rescript from Rome. After a total of fifteen years as superior of the Boston Carmel, M. Aloysius was happy when in 1933 the nuns elected Sr. Immaculata as Prioress.

In the autumn of 1934, M. Ignatius, the superior of the small Carmelite community in Seattle, Washington, asked if M. Aloysius would come help them both in the liturgy and community life. When M. Aloysius agreed to do so, it was decided that Sr. Margaret Mary should accompany her and remain with her during what was to be only a year's stay. The long journey by train across the country took four days and five nights, but Fr. Frank and her sister Elizabeth accompanied them.

M. Aloysius took on the role of Subprioress and Novice Mistress, and did all she could to help relieve M. Ignatius in her various problems. Some were easily resolved, such as the need to put in practice the ceremonial of 1927; others were of a more delicate nature. M. Ignatius suffered constantly from an unsuccessful spinal fusion and was grateful for the quiet way that M. Aloysius had in serving the community.

Great tact was needed in M. Aloysius' position. In all that she did, she showed, as one nun has described it, the obedience of a novice to M. Ignatius. Her example of generosity and happiness brought great peace to the community and all took care to seek her counsel. The stay was extended beyond a year; but after sixteen months she and Sr. Margaret Mary had to return to Boston.

When the time of departure came, the sisters knelt at the enclosure door and M. Aloysius said gently, "Sisters, see that God is loved in this house." Over twenty-five years later, one of the nuns in recalling this incident said, "Never have I seen grief so great in all my life." Another sister said of her stay in Seattle, "To me, it was one of the greatest things that the Lord did for the Seattle Carmel. Mother Aloysius was extraordinary in her unassuming way. So prudent! Consequently much was accomplished."

Shortly after her return, she was elected Prioress and the community that had missed her so greatly during her absence, again experienced the peace and strength of her guidance. Her concern for the nuns extended to every detail that touched their lives and particularly to their spiritual growth. As Prioress, she did much to provide her community with books that would help the nuns live their vocation more fully. Even when there was little money she saw the need to buy books for the monastery library.

In the works of St. Teresa of Avila, St. John of the Cross, St. Thérèse of Lisieux, and Elizabeth of the Trinity, she found abundant sustenance and insight into her Carmelite vocation; and in the classics of French spirituality, specifically the writings of Jean-Pierre de Caussade, S.J., Msgr. Charles Gay, and Archbishop François Fénelon, she found the inspiration for the surrender of self that is at the heart of her approach to the sacred; but above all her life was nourished by the Scriptures, especially the New Testament. She recognized the needs of others who sought works that were more speculative in nature than those she chose for herself; and if she were convinced that these would help one of the nuns, they would be provided. Pietistic literature was offensive to her.

Although her view of life was marked by its simplicity, it was far from narrow. A nun who was under her direction for many years said, "In spite of her own age and the climate of thought in which she grew up, she was phenomenally expansive." Her study of psychological works is illustrative of this openness.

M. Aloysius listened to the young women coming into the monastery, and she recognized the uniqueness of each soul entrusted to her care. As a young nun said some years ago of her personal experience under M. Aloysius' direction, "Mother listened to the Holy Spirit in each one. She waited for you to express yourself. For her, direction was always one of attentiveness to what God was doing in each soul." It is obvious why she was such an enlightened guide to many within her community and to those priests, brothers, sisters, seminarians as well as the laity who sought her help. When she recognized that a soul could profit from an introduction to Carmelite spirituality, she presented the basic ideas, then she would develop these as much as possible. St. Thérèse's teaching served well in M. Aloysius' own guidance of others.

Over the years her devotion to the Eucharist, her increasing awareness of the Indwelling of the Blessed Trinity, and her devotion to the priesthood of Christ developed in her the consciousness of Jesus living His life in her. She strove to see life through His eyes and offer, united with Him, all to the glory of the Father. Even those events that were frightening to others failed to disturb her peace. There were some who misjudged her; she was aware of this. She made them the special objects of her love, and she did all she could in showing them respect. In all situations she fostered harmony but was faithful at the same time to principles. To those who had trouble in relating to others she counseled, "Make yourself loved so that Christ may be more loved."

The ancient teaching of the priesthood of the faithful was illustrated in her daily life. When she would meet a person or even hear someone at a distance, she would offer up that person's day to the Lord. Often she would hear the milkman bringing milk to the monastery, and she would offer up his day to the Father just as she did her own. On one occasion a nun spoke lightly of what at the time seemed to be the approaching death of Nikita Khrushchev; M. Aloysius looked at her intently and said, "He was born in love and for love." Her zeal for the salvation of every soul reveals her consciousness of the sacredness of each human being and the awareness of God's saving grace.

Whether it was a lonely black boy needing a mother's love and longing for a daily meal, or an alcoholic priest struggling to remain sober and hoping to be accepted back in his diocese, or a jobless father trying to care for his family and fighting a sense of hopelessness, M. Aloysius found a way of helping. She recognized the suffering Christ in all who came seeking her aid. With the help of the other nuns, she was able to do much especially for the poor. Often the nuns used to joke about "Rev. Mother's Room," a place set aside in the monastery for clothing and toys for the poor. The once fashionable neighborhood of the monastery was changing dramatically and many who moved into the area turned to the nuns for help. In recalling M. Aloysius' helping him, a man said, "Were it not for her kindness, I would have taken my life."

In directing the novices, M. Aloysius revealed her own interior life. This is seen in her advice as to how to make a more meaningful thanksgiving after having received Holy Communion. On receiving the Sacrament, she adored Christ dwelling within her; and, united to Him, she went throughout the world "visiting" those in need. Among those visited were the prisoners, the forgotten in the slave labor camps, and others in dire need.

Sr. Christine of the Carmel of Cracow, Poland, wrote her this cryptic sentence, "We are going east for our health." The "east" meant the slave camps of Siberia. M. Aloysius responded by praying for these Polish Carmelites and "visiting" them at the time of her thanksgiving. Although their predicted deportation failed to take place, they suffered greatly under those who had but contempt for monastic life.

Throughout life, she looked to Mary as her model. In the mystery of the Annunciation, in particular, she delighted in Mary's surrender of self in assenting to Gabriel's tidings. As Mary carried the Lord within her very being, so did M. Aloysius realize that Jesus dwelled in her own life through grace, that he was united to her. The title "Virgin most faithful" was a favorite, for it spoke of Mary's continual surrender as revealed to us in the New Testament. Frequently she called attention to our Lady's faith and that of St. Joseph. Each day she said the rosary and also the beads of the "Seven Dolors" recalling Mary's sorrows. During her childhood years her Irish parents developed in her that love for the Mother of God that grew over the years and flowered in Carmel.

Prisoners were a great concern of M. Aloysius, and she did all she could to help them. When she learned of an approaching execution, so common during much of her life, she spent the entire night in prayer pleading with God for the salvation of the convict who was to be executed. On learning that the body of a Catholic went unclaimed following his execution in the electric chair, she begged her brother, Fr. Frank, to claim it and provide for its proper burial.

In 1945 Bishop Matthew F. Brady invited the nuns to make a foundation in Concord, New Hampshire, about seventy-five miles to the north of Boston. Sr. Margaret Mary's grandmother's home was available. Archbishop Cushing of Boston, later to be named cardinal, granted permission; and M. Aloysius with five nuns, established the foundation. On the following day, Bishop Brady offered the first Mass in the small chapel dedicated to the Blessed Trinity. It was June 20, 1946, the feast of Corpus Christi.

After their having lived at the large Boston monastery, the nuns found it difficult to adjust to their much smaller surroundings; but there was a good spirit. Every inconvenience had its humorous side. As they set about making the house more monastic, they hoped that before too long they would be able to build a monastery. Happily, the people of Concord and the surrounding cities and towns welcomed the nuns and gave generously toward the proposed new building.

Before long, they found land ideal for the monastery, and the architects began designing it. Recognizing the talents of two of the sisters for working with the architects, M. Aloysius appointed them to this; but she showed her interest in every detail both of design and construction. At times it was necessary to halt the construction because of lack of funds. Full of confidence she would say, "It is the Lord's work, and He will provide." On March 19, 1952, the feast of St. Joseph, they moved into the new monastery; the Lord had already blessed them with ten novices.

Three years later M. Aloysius made her retreat in preparation for celebrating her Golden Jubilee in May of 1955.

Because carpenters and masons were working in the still unfinished chapel, the chaplain moved the Blessed Sacrament to the infirmary Communion window on the second floor. The space before the little opening was large enough for only one person to kneel for the reception of Holy Communion. It was in this little space that M. Aloysius spent hours each day, delighted that the Lord had thus arranged for her retreat to be spent so close to the Eucharist.

This jubilee was a time for M. Aloysius to look back over her life. Only three of her sisters were still alive, Elizabeth, Annie, and Fannie. In 1896, typhoid fever claimed William as he was about to begin his studies at Harvard. In 1942, Fr. Frank died after many years of faithful service in the Boston Archdiocese. Only Mame and Bridget had married. Nell had already died, as had Catherine, the eldest child of the family. The Lord had taken to Himself many of her Sisters in Carmel, and M. Aloysius, ever a realist, knew that before long she too would pass from this life; yet there was no lessening in her activity. Her countenance radiated her peace and inner happiness and disguised the increasing suffering she endured, particularly from the curvature of her spine.

As Lent of 1961 drew to a close, her general condition deteriorated rapidly yet she did not want to accept the additional conveniences of the infirmary. On Holy Saturday she was unable to receive Holy Communion, but on Easter Sunday she was well enough to go to the little window. As Sr. Margaret Mary and Sr. Teresa, the infirmarian, were leading her from the Communion grille, they brought her to the infirmary rather than to her cell.

Even in her suffering she remained cheerful and interested in all that concerned the community and especially in a young sister about to receive the habit. M. Aloysius sent this message to that sister: "Give all — and ever." During this time, she spoke often on the spiritual life; and Sr. Teresa wrote many of her words on slips of paper.

Some of these have been printed in a collection entitled *Fragrance of Alabaster.*

On the following day, Fr. Albert Baillargeon, the chaplain, came to anoint her. She smiled at him and said, "Father, you have changed the face of the earth." As the hours passed, her suffering intensified, while those watching beside her could only marvel at the strength of the love that sustained her to endure the increasing pain. At nine o'clock in the evening she died. It was Sunday, April 16, 1961, the Third Sunday of Easter, but known in Carmel as "Good Shepherd Sunday." As the nuns knelt, Sr. Margaret Mary stood beside the bed, and then turned to the sorrowing nuns and said, "'Sisters, may we prove worthy of her."

In 1963 I was appointed to co-operate with Fr. John of Jesus and Mary, O.C.D., the Postulator General, in the investigation of the life of M. Aloysius. Bishop Ernest J. Primeau, at that time the Ordinary of Manchester, New Hampshire, approved the introduction of the cause. Since that time hundreds of pages of testimonies have been taken from many who knew M. Aloysius, some throughout their entire lives. Her sister, Fannie, was the sole survivor of the immediate family, but there were others alive who grew up with her in Billerica. Thousands of M. Aloysius' letters have been collected.

About a year before her death, a nun in a playful way asked, "What will you do in Heaven, Reverend Mother?" Smiling, she said in her gentle way, "I will do anything I can for anyone."

Rev. Adrian Cooney, O.C.D. is Vice Postulator of the cause for M. Aloysius. For further information, write Carmelite Monastery, Concord, New Hampshire, 03301.

PRAYER
(Private use only)

Most Blessed Trinity, Father, Son, and Holy Spirit, we praise You for Your gifts of grace to Mother Aloysius, and we pray that her example may help us to find happiness and holiness in loving surrender to Your Will of every moment. On earth she ever sought to lead souls to the realization that Your sanctifying action penetrates every circumstance, and all who had contact with her felt the warmth of her charity. If it be in Your divine designs to glorify her, may we experience now the power of her intercession in this our need. Amen.

FOR FURTHER READING

Fragrance from Alabaster: Thoughts of Reverend Mother Aloysius of the Blessed Sacrament, Discalced Carmelite (Concord, N.H.: Discalced Carmelite Nuns of Concord, 1961).

INDEX OF PERSONS

The names of the biographees in this volume and those who were associated with them.

373

INDEX OF PLACES

The places listed are associated with the biographees in this volume.